CONVERSATIO...

G...

PARENTS

Also by Neale Donald Walsch

Conversations with God, Book 1

Conversations with God, Book 1 Guidebook

Conversations with God, Book 2

Meditations from Conversations with God, Book 2

Conversations with God, Book 3

Questions and Answers from Conversations with God

Bringers of the Light

ReCreating Your Self

Conversations with God Re-MIND-er Cards

Moments of Grace

The Wedding Vows from Conversations with God

Neale Donald Walsch on Abundance and Right Livelihood

Neale Donald Walsch on Holistic Living

Neale Donald Walsch on Relationships

Conversations with God for Teens

Friendship with God

Communion with God

Tomorrow's God: Our Greatest Spiritual Challenge

The Little Soul and the Sun

The Little Soul and the Earth

The Complete Conversations with God

Home with God: In a Life that Never Ends

Happier Than God

When Everything Changes, Change Everything

The New Revelations: A Conversation with God

What God Wants: A Compelling Answer to Humanity's Biggest Question

*What God Said: The 25 Core Messages of Conversations with God
That Will Change Your Life and the World*

The Storm Before the Calm

The Only Thing That Matters

God's Message to the World: You've Got Me All Wrong

CONVERSATIONS WITH

GOD

for

PARENTS

Sharing the Messages with Children

Book 3 in the Conversations with Humanity Series

NEALE DONALD WALSCH

with Laurie Lankins Farley & Emily A. Filmore

RAINBOW RIDGE
BOOKS

Cover and interior design by Frame25 Productions
Cover photo © Christin Lola c/o Shutterstock.com

Published by:
Rainbow Ridge Books, LLC
140 Rainbow Ridge Road
Faber, Virginia 22938
www.rainbowridgebooks.com
434-361-1723

If you are unable to order this book from your local
bookseller, you may order directly from the distributor.

Square One Publishers, Inc.
115 Herricks Road
Garden City Park, NY 11040
Phone: (516) 535-2010
Fax: (516) 535-2014
Toll-free: 877-900-BOOK

Visit the author at:
www.nealedonaldwalsch.com
www.cwgforparents.com

Library of Congress Cataloging-in-Publication Data applied for.

ISBN 978-1-937907-36-5

10 9 8 7 6 5 4 3 2 1

Printed on acid-free recycled paper in Canada

To my Mom and Dad. I know that you can even now, from the Other Side, hear and know of my deep and eternal gratitude for your wonderful parenting. I owe you so much, and I will never stop praying my prayer of thanks to God for you both.
—Neale Donald Walsch

I dedicate this book to parents all over the world. To those of you who have decided to pick up this book and begin to read and share with your beloved children, what might be the most important messages, ideas, and understandings that I feel a parent could share with their children. And I dedicate this book to my parents, who allowed me to know myself with their divine brilliance. Ryan and Lane, you are my heart. Thank you for allowing me to be your mom.
—Laurie Lankins Farley

To Scott, Sage, Rickey, Lucas, and all my family and friends: Thank you for being the lights of my life. You make me want to leave the world happier than I found it. I hope this work will help ensure brighter tomorrows for all the world's children.
—Emily A. Filmore

CONTENTS

Foreword   ix

Preface   xi

1. We Are All One   1

2. God Talks to Everyone All the Time   19

3. There's Enough   35

4. There's Nothing You Must Do   63

5. There's No Such Thing as Right and Wrong   85

6. Love is All There Is   107

7. You Decide How Life Feels   125

8. You Affect Everyone   139

9. There Are Three Parts to You: Body, Mind, and Soul   153

10. Every Day You Can Start Over. Who Do
    You Dream Yourself to Be Today?   165

11. There is No Such Place as Hell   179

12. Death is the Same as Birth   195

13. There Are No Good Guys and No Bad Guys   211

14. There is No Such Thing as Failure   227

15. All Choices Can Serve the Highest Good   241

16. The Wonderful Ways to Be Are
    Truthful, Aware, and Responsible   255

17. God Needs Nothing From You   287

18. You Don't Have to Believe the Lies About Life 301

19. Conclusion 321

Addenda 323

About the Authors 343

FOREWORD

From the very first months after the first *Conversations with God* book was published in May 1995, the demand began to appear for tools that would assist parents in teaching the marvelous concepts of this extraordinary dialogue to children.

Readers wanted a way that they could share with their offspring what *CwG* had shared with them.

"If only I had been introduced to these ways of seeing God and myself when I was eight or nine, my whole life would have been different," were the words I heard in letter after letter, email after email, conversation after conversation.

My response to this so-often stated desire was the creation of the School of the New Spirituality, and the subsequent design of its *CwG* for Parents program. You may learn more about that wonderful resource by simply going to this address on the Internet: *www.cwgforparents.com*.

The book you are holding in your hands is an outgrowth of that program. In it, I have joined with Laurie Farley and Emily Filmore, the directors of the school, to put into one place all of the spiritual concepts of a home schooling curriculum.

We wanted to make available for parents not only the tools for *teaching CwG*'s concepts, but also a narrative summary of the concepts themselves, because we knew this special articulation for parents would form the backbone of the their home schooling efforts and help them to use the other tools created by our school with maximum effectiveness.

It was widely known that even though teachers in regular schools know their overall subject matter very well, they will very often (in fact, almost always) "read up" on the lesson they are about to teach their students, so that they are refreshed in each particular area of exploration and feel fully ready to answer the most case-specific or detailed questions.

Before parents can even begin to think of reducing highly nuanced, extremely sophisticated spiritual concepts for children in age-appropriate ways with age-understandable language, parents must feel confident that they, themselves, both comprehend the deeper meaning and grasp the day-to-day functional implications of those concepts.

Each chapter in this book is thus presented in two parts: (1) A narrative for parents that includes background information and interpretative commentary on the spiritual concept being explored; (2) Tools with which parents may effectively share these concepts with their children.

The text is intended to be a teacher's manual. The Preface, which follows, offers a complete list of the topics to be covered here, as well as an opening guide to how you might introduce the whole *idea* of "God" to your children to begin with.

Enjoy.

And do let us know if this book has been helpful, and how it might be improved in future editions. All of our contact information will be found in the Afterword.

PREFACE

The *CwG* dialogue covers over 3,000 pages, spread across nine books. Through the years many, many readers had asked if there might be a way for the wonderful messages on those pages to be reduced to something more manageable for the average person to absorb.

Not many people are going to sit down and read nine books in order to cover all the material, they told me, and if I really wanted to get the most important of the messages out, I may want to consider finding a way to make it easier for people to access them.

Thinking about this, I knew they were right. So in 2013, I gave the material in the nine *CwG* books another deep look, then picked out what I felt to be the most important of the many spiritual insights in those 3,000 pages. All of them were "important," of course. Still, I found it possible to rank the messages I had been given according to the impact that I thought each could have in daily life.

From this process emerged the book *What God Said,* condensing *CwG*'s thousands of pages across nine books into one text, carrying the subtitle: *The 25 Core Messages of Conversations with God that will change your life and the world.*

As I carefully selected these Core Messages, I found that they could each be powerfully stated in simple, direct articulations. The result is a summary trimmed to just 1,000 words. Those 1,000 words make up the entirety of Chapter Two of *What God Said.*

I've put it here in this Preface, so that you can know exactly what spiritual concepts and principles that the book you are now reading invites you to place before your children.

(Please note that these 25 Core Messages are framed for the adult mind. Following this listing I will share with you our re-articulation of *CwG*'s Core Concepts in language for young minds.)

The Core Messages of *Conversations with God*

Here, in 1,000 words, is all that the human race needs to know in order to live the life for which it has yearned and which, despite trying for thousands of years, it has yet to produce. Carry these messages to your world:

1. We are all One. All things are One Thing. There is only One Thing, and all things are part of the One Thing There Is. This means that you are Divine. You are not your body, you are not your mind, and you are not your soul. You are the unique combination of all three, which comprises the Totality Of You. You are an individuation of Divinity; an expression of God on Earth.

2. There's enough. It is not necessary to compete for, much less fight over, your resources. All you have to do is share.

3. There's nothing you have to do. There is much you *will* do, but nothing you are *required* to do. God wants nothing, needs nothing, demands nothing, commands nothing.

4. God talks to everyone, all the time. The question is not: To whom does God talk? The question is: Who listens?

5. There are Three Basic Principles of Life: *Functionality, Adaptability,* and *Sustainability.*

6. There is no such thing as Right and Wrong; there is only What Works and What Does Not Work, given what it is you are trying to do.

7. In the spiritual sense, there are no victims and no villains in the world, although in the human sense it appears that there surely are. Yet because you are Divine, nothing can happen against your will.

8. No one does anything inappropriate, given their model of the world.

9. There is no such place as hell, and eternal damnation does not exist.

10. Death does not exist. What you call "death" is merely a process of Re-Identification.

11. There is no such thing as Space and Time; there is only Here and Now.

12. Love is all there is.

13. You are the Creator of your own reality, using the Three Tools of Creation: *Thought, Word,* and *Action*.

14. Your life has nothing to do with you. It is about everyone whose life you touch, and how you touch it.

15. The purpose of your life is to recreate yourself anew in the next grandest version of the greatest vision ever you held about Who You Are.

16. The moment you declare anything, everything unlike it will come into the space. This is The Law of Opposites, producing a Contextual Field within which that which you wish to express may be experienced.

17. There is no such thing as Absolute Truth. All truth is subjective. Within this framework there are five levels of truth telling: *Tell your truth to yourself about yourself; Tell your truth to yourself about another; Tell your truth about yourself to another; Tell your truth about another to another; Tell your truth to everyone about everything.*

18. The human race lives within a precise set of illusions. The Ten Illusions of Humans are: *Need Exists, Failure Exists, Disunity Exists, Insufficiency Exists, Requirement Exists, Judgment Exists, Condemnation Exists, Conditionality Exists,*

Superiority Exists, Ignorance Exists. These illusions are meant to serve humanity, but it must learn how to use them.

19. The Three Core Concepts of Holistic Living are *Honesty, Awareness,* and *Responsibility.* Live according to these precepts and self-anger will disappear from your life.

20. Life functions within a Be-Do-Have paradigm. Most people have this backward, imagining that first one must "have" things in order to "do" things, thus to "be" what they wish to be. Reversing this process is the fastest way to experience mastery in living.

21. There are Three Levels of Awareness: *Hope, Faith,* and *Knowing.* Spiritual mastery is about living from the third level.

22. There are Five Fallacies about God that create crisis, violence, killing and war. First, the idea that God *needs* something. Second, the idea that God *can fail to get* what He needs. Third, the idea that God *has separated* you from Him because you have not given Him what He needs. Fourth, the idea that God still needs what He needs so badly that God now *requires* you, *from your separated position*, to give it to Him. Fifth, the idea that God *will destroy you* if you do not meet His requirements.

23. There are also Five Fallacies about life that likewise create crisis, violence, killing, and war. First, the idea that human beings are separate from each other. Second, the idea that there is not enough of what human beings need to be happy. Third, the idea that in order to get the stuff of which there is not enough, human beings must compete with each other. Fourth, the idea that some human beings are better than other human beings. Fifth, the idea that it is appropriate for human beings to resolve severe differences created by all the other fallacies by killing each other.

24. You think you are being terrorized by other people, but in truth you are being terrorized by your beliefs. Your experience of yourself and your world will shift dramatically if you adopt, collectively, the Five Steps to Peace:

   a) *Permit yourself to acknowledge that some of your old beliefs about God and about life are no longer working.*

   b) *Explore the possibility that there is something you do not fully understand about God and about life, the understanding of which would change everything.*

   c) *Announce that you are willing for new understandings of God and life to now be brought forth, understandings that could produce a new way of life on this planet.*

   d) *Courageously examine these new understandings and, if they align with your personal inner truth and knowing, enlarge your belief system to include them.*

   e) *Express your life as a demonstration of your highest beliefs, rather than as a denial of them.*

25. Let there be a New Gospel for all the people of Earth: "We are all one. Ours is not a better way; ours is merely another way."

The 1,000 words here, embraced and acted on, could change your world in a single generation.

Restating the Concepts for Children

The directors of the School of the New Spirituality and I looked at these Core Messages and created a re-articulation of them for young minds. We also re-ordered them just a bit, bringing them more in line with a sequence in which we felt these ideas might be best introduced to children.

Here's the list as it appears in our home schooling approach. (Some of the concepts are followed, in parentheses, by the "adult" principle that it echoes.):

1. We are all one.

2. God talks to everyone, all the time.

3. There's enough.

4. There's nothing you must do.

5. There is no such thing as Right and Wrong.

6. Love is all there is.

7. You decide how life feels. (You create your own reality.)

8. You affect everyone. (Your life is not about you. It's about everyone whose life you touch.)

9. There are three parts to you: Body, Mind, and Soul.

10. Every day you can start over. Who do you dream yourself to be today? (The purpose of your life is to recreate yourself anew in the next grandest version of the greatest vision ever you held about Who You Are.)

11. There is no such place as hell.

12. Death is the same as birth.

13. There are no good guys and no bad guys.

14. There is no such thing as failure.

15. The helpful way to make decisions is to ask: Will the decision work for me? Can I make it work? Can I keep doing it this way?

16. The wonderful ways to be are truthful, aware, and respon-
    sible. (The Three Core Concepts of Holistic Living are
    Honesty, Awareness, and *Responsibility.*)

17. God needs nothing from you.

18. You don't have to believe the wrong things that are often
    said about life.

Introducing your child to the concept and reality of God

Nothing will play a larger role in the reality experienced (and created) by
our children during their lifetime than the notions we give them about
what I call the Three Foundational Aspects of Physical Expression upon
the earth:

1. *life itself, and how it works*

2. *Themselves, and who and what they are*

3. *Life's Larger Realities, and what some people call "God"*

*The ideas that they carry forward about all of this will impact every area
of their day-to-day encounters from this moment until their final moments in
the body*—just as your thoughts and my thoughts about these things have
affected us in precisely the same way (though we may not have known it).

This cannot be overstated. What your children imagine to be true
about themselves and the environment in which they find themselves—
as well as who or what *controls* that environment—will not only impact,
but *create* . . .

- Their thoughts, their energies and moods

- Their willingness to attempt and to achieve

- Their decision to risk and to dare

- Their determination to reach and to strive

- Their choice to wonder and to solve, and . . .

- Their ability to step into and live the grandest concept of themselves, allowing them to fulfill their highest dreams

So what we are talking about here is pretty important. No. It is extremely important. No. It is of *ultimate* importance.

Let me share with you here what I imagine myself to know about how to introduce and discuss with your child the last and most important topic: God.

Before we begin, a question please . . .

The first thing you have to do is ask yourself a key question: Do you want your children to embrace an already established-in-your-own-mind and very particular set of beliefs? Or do you want your children to notice and be aware of your beliefs, and then be empowered to form their own beliefs, whatever they may be?

Always, in the issue of parenting, this becomes the key question. Not only as it relates to the subject of God, but as it relates to everything.

And yet, a conundrum

While we would imagine that most parents do not want their children to simply adopt the parents' point of view on everything—and particularly their point of view on something as important as God—the challenge becomes one of providing the child with a free mental space within which to come to their own conclusions while at the same time offering firm and sure modeling and guidance, which every child deserves.

Children don't want parents who are wishy-washy—and they don't deserve them. They want and deserve more.

If a child is afraid of the policeman on the corner, do we tell her, "Oh, sweetheart, the policeman is our *friend*. There's no need to be afraid of him. He's here to *protect* us and to *help* us."

Or . . . do we tell her, "Oh, sweetheart, I *think* the policeman is our friend. I *hope* there's no need to be afraid of him. I *wish that* he were here to protect us and to help us. Let's keep our fingers crossed."

If your son is afraid to go into his room at night because he imagines there's a monster under the bed, do you say, "Son, there's nothing to be afraid of. Come on, I'll go in there with you and show you."

Or . . . do you say, "Well, son, I sure hope there's nothing to be afraid of. Come on, I'll go in with you, and I'm going to wish with all my might that I'm right about this. But let's keep the door open in case we have to get out of there in a hurry."

Of course you offer the former, not the latter. You know that what your child looks to you for is *certainty*.

In all matters.

So the challenge becomes one of how to help your children feel certain about things, without robbing them of the opportunity (and the skill) of *becoming* certain *themselves* through the reaching of their own conclusions.

This is not an easy thing to do, and it can require us to sometimes walk a very thin line.

Self-discovery is the pathway to certainty

In nearly every situation in our children's lives it feels to me that we do our best job of parenting when we help them find things out for themselves. Yet how can children find out for themselves about something as hypothetical (and that sometimes seems even to *us* to be hypothetical) as God?

And the problem here is that many other people talk about God in *very definitive terms*. So what your child is hearing on the playground, or in the home of friends, can sound *very* certain. Then, when your child comes to you for clarity, what do you say? That you don't know? That you can't be sure? That you have your own ideas, but it's anybody's guess? That we should all keep our fingers crossed?

Suppose your child comes to you and says he is afraid of God. Do you say, "Oh, sweetheart, God is our *friend*. There's no need to be afraid of God. God's here to *protect* us and to *help* us."

Or . . . do you say, "Well, son, I *think* God is our friend. I don't *believe* there's a reason to be afraid of God. My own thought is that God is here to protect us. I *hope* there's no reason to be afraid of him. Let's hope I'm right."

Let's say that your daughter has heard at her friend's house that God punishes us if we don't do what He wants us to do. She's heard that if we are not careful, we could wind up going to "hell." Now what do you say? "Sweetheart, that's not true." *Or* . . . "I certainly *hope* that's not true. Let's cross our fingers."

Yes . . . these questions about how to proceed are not small questions.

Step One: Where to Begin

Recently I spoke with a forty-year-old woman on this subject, and she told me that while her family did not speak much about God and belonged to no religion, she, as a child, had friends whose families did. And her parents encouraged and allowed her to investigate the concept of God and decide for herself what it meant.

So, one week her friend's family invited her to join their own child and go to church with them. Here is this woman's own narrative, more than three decades later . . .

"I remember that I came home from my first church experience—I must have been six or seven—with the feeling that I had done something wrong, and that I had to bring Jesus into my heart or something really bad was going to happen to me, and so I lay in my bed night after night trying to bring Jesus into my heart, and feeling really stressed out about it."

The church folks had presented their newcomer with a child's Bible study reader, and in it this woman, when she was six or seven, read something about how God sent people to hell if they lived a gay lifestyle. And while she wasn't quite sure at that age what a "gay" lifestyle was, she was clear about what "hell" was (her one visit to church having made it abundantly clear that it was a very bad place of terrible suffering). So this little girl said to her mom, "I don't want to believe in a God who hurts people."

She remembers that her mom replied, without equivocation: "Well, sweetheart, we don't believe that God *does* hurt people, for any reason. Your father and I just don't believe that."

And that was the end of the fear for this little girl. Her parents' word was good enough for her.

This is an important lesson. Once more let me say that, particularly at the youngest ages, your children look to you for guidance, not uncertainty; for clarity, not confusion; for wisdom, not bewilderment.

You cannot be a clear, wise, and helpful guide, however, if you yourself have not come to clarity about God. So thank you for taking Step One, above. It is an important step in introducing your child to the concept and reality of God.

Step Two: The Central Question

Now that you have solidified your clarity around what *you* believe and think and know about God, you must ask yourself this question: *What do I want my children to believe and think and know about God?*

If you want them to know nothing at all about God until they are old enough to begin forming their own thoughts about who and what God is, then you may choose to say very little, if anything, about God in your home and around your children until they reach the so-called "age of reason"—generally around seven.

If you want them to come to know God as you have come to know God, but "get there" much faster than you did . . . or, if you want them to come to know God as you have come to know God rather than as many others have come to know God . . . then you may choose to speak of God, to refer to God, casually and affirmatively and cheerfully and lovingly in day-to-day conversation from your children's earliest days, so that by the age of seven they will have tons of Already Received Data about God against which to consider what they will soon be encountering (or what they have already encountered) in the outside world.

Sooner or later your children will hear about "God" from sources other than you as they move through childhood, and they will bring what they are hearing up with you.

If you have firm beliefs about God (and I hope you do), you will want to share them then, in an age-appropriate way. But if you had previously taken the Don't-Mention-It-Until-Asked route, do not be surprised if your children then say something like, "How come you never talked about God before?"—or words to that effect. You will need to be ready to answer such a question.

My suggestion would be that you might then say, "Well, sweetheart, lots of people have different thoughts and ideas about God, and we wanted you to be able to make up your own mind. But since you asked, here is what I feel in my heart is true . . . "

I must say, though, that I prefer the Casual-Mention-From-The-Beginning approach, in which you put God into your child's world without fanfare or huge initial explanation.

For instance, when your child asks a question about certain things, you can bring God into your answer. Example: "Mommy, how did the stars get into the sky?"

"God put them there, honey."

Or, "Daddy, why does it rain so hard that it makes noise?"

"Wow, that's a good question, Sweetie. I think that sometimes God just makes it happen that way."

Or, "Mommy, how can birds fly?"

"Well, honey, God gave birds a special gift, just as God gives everyone special gifts. Birds can fly, but they can't talk. They can sing, but they can't use words. You can talk, but you can't fly. But you can SING, just like a bird!"

By bringing "God" into regular conversation, it will be no time at all—perhaps on the very first mention—before your child asks, "Who is 'God'?" Now you are answering a question, rather than starting from a place of trying to *explain* something, or even bring up something that the child doesn't care about and hasn't even expressed an interest in.

So the idea here is to ignite in your child an *interest* in God.

Why not wait?

If you wait until someone in the child's outside world ignites her interest in God, by talking about God in *their* home when your child is there on a visit or is sharing a stay-over with a school friend, then your "starting place" in this exploration will be what your child has heard elsewhere. That may or may not be a good place to begin, as your child may be filled with images or ideas about God that could prove bewildering . . . or even scary.

My suggestion is that you allow yourself to be the first person to introduce your child to the concept and the reality of God. We know that first impressions are lasting impressions, and I'm sure you want your child's first impression of God to be different from the one to which many of us were subjected in our generation.

There are many ways, as I have alluded to already, to introduce your child to the concept and the reality of God without sitting your child down to have a "session" in which you say something like, "Let's talk about God."

Sex and God: Our two yearnings

Allowing your child to know that God is a part of your life is one of the most powerful things you can do to fuel your child's Greater World experience. I liken it to how we introduce our children to sex. They either never hear about it from us, and we talk to them about it only when, finally, they ask about it somewhere along the way, or they are introduced to it in an easy, casual way as a natural and normal, happy and fun part of life.

Sex and God are both dynamite subjects. That's why I'm using them as companion examples here. They are probably the two most critical topics that one could explore with children. (And—dare I say?—the most *taboo* in our current Cultural Story.) How you approach these subjects will form and shape important inner experiences for your children for the rest of their lives—even (and perhaps especially) if they create later experiences that counter or contradict what they picked up from you.

Yet children will not create experiences, nor place themselves in circumstances, that counter or contradict what they understood by being with you if what they understood was joyous, fun-filled, happy and wonderful, uplifting their spirits every single time, and filling them with glorious and exciting anticipation of what wonders their next moment in life can hold.

Sadly, the teachings and doctrines about God of many of our societies and cultures and belief systems too often do not fill children with glorious and exciting anticipation of what wonders their next moment in life can hold. In fact, if my own childhood is any example, they more often fill children with fear and dread that they might do something terribly inappropriate or downright wrong, producing worried and tentative steps into life. Sadly, the same can be said about our culture's teachings and doctrines about sex.

Yet the yearning for God as well as the yearning for sex will not and cannot be denied—and so off our children will go, seeking to satisfy these yearnings with wildly misguided instructions.

The impulse lives within all of us

Every human being has a yearning for God. That is the most important thing I could tell you here. Every sentient being understands, at a cellular level, that something larger exists, something grander forms Ultimate Reality. We may not know what It is, but we feel certain that there is more going on here than meets the eye, and that life in the universe is more than a series of chemical reactions and energy fusions and biological processes. The design is too perfect, the process is too engaging and exciting, and the outcome is too magnificent for the whole operation to have been created by happenstance.

We know, too, at a very deep level, that *we are part of all this*. We are not separate from it, simply bystanders, watching a parade going by. We sense that we are, at some level, the parade *organizers*. Or, if we don't believe that, we sense that at the very least, we are *in* the parade, part *of* it, not merely observers, not simply a fascinated but having-nothing-to-do-with-it audience.

Because we hold this deep inner knowing, we notice an unmistakable urge to *join in* when the parade is passing by. Our whole being is filled with what I have called an Impulse Towards the Divine. We feel a natural, inbred desire to unite, to become one again, with life itself at every level. We stick our nose in a flower, we bury our hands in the dirt, we spread our arms to the sunrise, we shed quiet tears of reverent awe at the utter magnificence of the night sky, we exult at the deep breathing in of the fresh morning, dew-filled air—we reach with humble joy for *Life!* And we desire *Oneness* with It in every way we can create.

Thus, the yearning for God. And for sex.

Neither is incidental, or coincidental.

I believe we are attracted to each other inherently, out of a deep knowing that in each other we will find our Selves. I believe we know at the highest level that We Are All One and that we are seeking daily on this planet to end, at last and forever, our sense of Separation. We know, we intuitively understand, that Separation is *not* the natural order of things; it is *not* the truth of our being, and so we seek to never again suffer the illusion of being alone.

Every child feels this yearning for Oneness as much as every adult, for Oneness is not an intellectual formulation; it is a cellular and spiritual awareness. And children are by no means less able to connect with deep spiritual awareness than adults. If anything, they're more able.

This inbred, inborn, innate ability of children to connect with or experience deep spiritual awareness is something that many parents seldom think about, but that all parents have an opportunity to tap into, when considering how to introduce their children to the concept and the reality of God.

For the idea is to pull *out* of the child, not put *into* the child, the truth and the awareness of humanity's connection with the Divine. We are not trying to *teach* our children something, but to help them *remember* something; we are not trying to *give* them something (knowledge, wisdom, understanding, a sense of Oneness with God), but to let them know that they already have it.

There is a world of difference.

Step Three: How to Do It

The question is, of course, how to do it. The answer begins with a willingness to assume and accept that your child may be far more attuned to Larger Realities than you might think. Therefore, talking about God in matter-of-fact ways will feed right into your child's already-present inner knowing.

True, your offspring may not know the *words* to describe that which they sense must exist and must be true, but they will readily and easily accept the notion that Something Larger is "out there" if they see their *parents* readily and easily accepting it—just as, in the area of sexuality, they will readily and easily accept the differences and the wonders of their bodies if they observe that their parents readily and easily accept these differences and the wonders.

We have touched on this matter-of-factness about God before, encouraging casual and off-handed mention of "God" in everyday conversation around the children. One easy and natural way to do this might be through the age-old tradition of "saying grace" before meals. If this happens from the time a child is old enough to hear, the child will have encountered the notion of "God" long before they ask for a fuller explanation, making that fuller explanation much easier for the child to absorb.

Is it okay to personify God?

One of the questions I am most often asked by parents is: "Is it okay to allow our children in the early stages of understanding God to think of God as a 'person' even if we, ourselves, don't really think that this is what God is?"

My answer is always yes. A small child may find it difficult to grasp oblique or inexplicit concepts such as "Essence" or "Energy." If offering thanks at meals to The Essence seems challenging for your three-year-old, allowing the child to personify God is perfectly okay. Indeed, as an adult *I personify God all the time.*

The dialogue in *Conversations with God* taught me that "God" is The Essence and The Prime Energy of life itself; the Source of all Love, all Wisdom, all Power, all Intelligence, and, indeed, *everything* in the universe. This Essence can form and shape Itself into any appearance or embodiment It desires, *and has done so*—including the form and shape of a wonderful, kind, gentle, caring, compassionate, understanding, unconditionally loving and incomparably wise woman or man.

I encourage people, in fact, to use the terms Mother/Father God and Father/Mother God interchangeably and as often as possible when referring to The Divine. This helps to remove the traditional male gender identification that so many children often attach to the idea of God in the early stages of their lives.

Here is a possible Grace that might work in your home:

> *Dear Mother/Father God . . . We thank you for the food we*
> *are about to eat, for the love that we feel at this table, and*
> *for all the wonderful gifts of life that we share. And thank*
> *you, too, for the good days and wonderful times that are still*
> *to come for the rest of our lives. We promise to share all good*
> *things with all those whose lives we touch. Amen.*

I love this little prayer because it introduces the concept of Sharing as well as the idea of God to the mind of the child.

Nightly prayers and morning prayers are another sweet way to place the concept and the reality of God before your little ones. Here is a wonderful, short nightly prayer for children . . .

> *Dear Father/Mother God . . . Thank you for this day, and everything that happened. Even the "bad stuff." Because I know that all of it helps me to be a nice person, and that's what I love to be! See you tomorrow . . . your friend . . . Neale.*

And here is a morning prayer I've been saying myself for many years.

> *Dear Mother/Father God . . . Thank you for another day, and another chance to be the very best Me I can be!*

Invite children's own *CwG*

If the "prayer" idea doesn't feel that it would work for you, you can encourage your children to have their own *conversations* with God, and to develop a positive attitude about life in the process, by inviting them to talk to God for one minute every night about The Things I Liked Best About Today.

Here's one way that could look . . .

> PARENT: (just before bedtime): Let's play the One Minute Game!

> CHILD: Yea!

> PARENT: Okay, we have one minute to think of what we liked best of all the things that happened today, and tell God about it. If we can think of at least two things between us, I think God will be very happy. I'll go first . . . "Hey, Mother/Father God . . . the thing I liked best about today was . . . the really neat time I had with all my kids

and with Mommy, playing that game after we had dinner! I just wanted to say 'thanks' for all the good stuff! You're neat, God!" (*Or* . . . "that I didn't have to put away all the groceries by myself, because my little sweetie helped me!") (*Or* . . . "How nice my little sweetheart Madelyn was when she didn't make a fuss at Daddy when nap time came . . .") (*Or* . . . "Making a super dinner for everybody that they really *liked*, because they told me so. It feels so good to do stuff that makes other people happy! Thanks, God!")

You can't even begin to imagine the many messages you can send to a three-, four-, or five-year-old with a nightly tradition such as this—without seeming to "preach" to the child at all. They're just listening to Mommy or Daddy talk to God!

In addition to setting up a positive attitude, this creates the habit of your children having their own conversations with God on a regular basis. That habit will extend into adulthood, I promise you. Especially if, later, when your child grows older . . . of if the child has had an especially rough day . . . you can model for her or him how to talk to God about that, too . . .

> *Well, God, things didn't go so well today, as I'm sure you know. So thanks for giving me the help to get through it—and thanks for making everything better . . . which I know is what is going to happen! I'm glad you're here, Father/Mother God. I'm really glad you're here!*

I think nothing could be more important than the time you spend with your child in this way. (Something could be equally important, but nothing could be more important.) And why? Because, if you will suffer me making the same point repeatedly, what your children come to understand about God and how they experience God *through you* will stick with them all the days of their life.

Childhood imagination and childlike faith

Do not discourage childhood imaginings. That is one of the biggest pieces of advice I offer to parents. Most parents would not discourage this anyway, but I try to make the point with them that they are on the right track in not doing so.

I have been told by a number of people that I have a child-like faith in God. (An important note here: child-*like* and child-*ish* are not the same thing.) I suppose I do. And I am glad of it. I have a childlike faith in all of life, in fact, not just in God. I have faith that life is on my side. I have faith that I can do anything I set my mind to. I have faith that things will always be okay with me, and that all things work out for my highest good in the end. I have faith that God loves me completely, without condition, reservation, or limitation, and that I am never alone, or outside the embrace of God. I have faith that I will be Home with God when this physical life ends.

Maybe I am imagining all of these things. Maybe I need to (as some of those who have observed me have said since I was a child) "grow up" and "face facts" and get my "head out of the clouds and feet on the ground." But I believe that my childlike faith has served me. It has given me strength when things did not seem to be going my way. It has brought me comfort in times of loss, optimism when I might have been tempted to feel hopeless, and enthusiasm for tomorrow even if my "today" made it look as if my future might not ever be bright again. In short, it has kept me in a positive frame of mind the majority of the time.

More often than not I look for the solution when others see problems. More often than not I see molehills where others make mountains. More often than not I go for the gold when others are willing to settle for the bronze—or no medal at all in the Olympics of life—not because I need or want to be a "winner," but because I hold quite naturally the idea that we are all *intended* to be winners, that life was made for us to be happy, and that all we have to do to get to that place is understand who we are and why we are here . . . and, of course, that God and life are on our side.

For more on this I strongly urge you to read—or if you have already done so, to *re*-read—*Happier Than God.*

I could, in *fact*, be imagining all these things. But if I am, I must say that my imagination seems to be a very effective mechanism, a wonderful tool used in the fashioning of life. And here is my point; here is the reason I am bringing this all up now:

My parents encouraged me to use *my imagination as a child.* And they did not *discourage* me when my imagination ran wild. Rather, they simply coached me to notice when my imagination served me (that is, made me happier or gave me confidence) and when it disserved me (that is, made me scared or tentative or sad or took my confidence away).

If they saw that I was imagining something that made me scared or tentative ("There's a monster under the bed!") ("I'll never get the part in the school play, so why bother even trying out!"), they would gently demonstrate to me that what I was imagining was (A) not helping matters any, and (B) probably not true anyway, if I just explored it.

If they saw that I was imagining something that made me happy or confident ("I'm Superman!") ("I'm going to try out for the play and I bet I get the part!"), they would gently smile and demonstrate that they loved all ideas that made me feel better about myself—whether I was imagining all the good stuff, or talking about actual reality.

In this way, the line between Good Imagining and Good Reality began to blur, and as I reached 10 or 11, I began *making a connection between the two.* By the time I'd hit 16, I had a reputation in our family: "Neale has all the luck! He always seems to get what he wants."

What I am saying here is that I think there *is* a direct connection between positive thinking and positive outcomes. And I am very clear that the way my parents worked with my imagination, and the way they encouraged it when my imaginings were positive, even if unrealistic, made that connection real for me. ("You know, son," my father once said to me, smiling, "in a lot of ways you *are* Superman.")

If you don't take away a child's dreams, you guarantee that he'll keep dreaming. And what does all this have to do with introducing your child to the concept and the reality of God? Well, *imagination is the tool of God.* Dreams are the stuff of God. Great visions for tomorrow create excitement today—and nothing makes a dream more exciting than knowing that God is on our side to help make them come true. And this is what my mother always encouraged me to feel.

"If that's what's best for you, God will help you make it happen. And if it's not what's best for you, God will bring you something better," is what I would say to children from the time they are old enough to understand that idea (which might be a lot younger than you think).

"Thank you, God, for this or something better" is, by the way, another wonderful prayer to share with children (and adults, for that matter).

Stories and books are terrific tools, too, of course

I know this is obvious, but just as a reminder . . . Story Time provides another wonderful opportunity to introduce your children to God. Some parents merge Story Time with Bed Time, so that children will look forward to, rather than revolt against, bedtime. Others like to create Story Time in the afternoon, or after dinner in the evening.

It used to be difficult to find children's books in which, if God is mentioned, the story and "the moral of the story" didn't emerge from a Traditional Idea About God. This is perfectly okay, of course, if what you hold, and what you wish to share with your children, are those traditional ideas. If, on the other hand, your ideas about God lean more towards what might be termed New Thought concepts (such as the concepts in the *Conversations with God* texts), it was not always easy to find children's books that reflected those values.

I am happy to say that these days it has become a bit easier. The *CwG* for Parents program has been gathering resources now for quite a while, and I think you'll be impressed with the number of children's stories that are out there—as well as short audio programs on CD, and even some animations on DVD.

For instance, there is a wonderful animation that a professional film company made of the *CwG* children's book, *The Little Soul and the Sun*, as well as an audio enactment of the story with original songs that kids love. The second book in the Little Soul series, titled *The Little Soul and the Earth*, offers another resource straight out of the *Conversations with God* cosmology, as does the very special Christmas story *Santa's God*, in which a little girl asks Santa the most important question of all time: Who is the real God? Who does *Santa* pray to?

The answer that Santa gives is exactly what you would want your children to hear if you, yourself, have embraced the message in *CwG*, yet it is placed before children in a way that is neither "preach-y" nor "teach-y," but is presented in language and through an example that all children can easily understand.

And there are other wonderful children's books and resources out there as well—and that's what the *CwG* for Parents program is all about. It is about helping parents to introduce their children to the concept and the reality of God in a way that aligns with how they would like their children to start out on their own search for inner truth.

Step Four: The Whole Curriculum

I said before that sex and God are both dynamite subjects. Pairing the two may have raised some eyebrows, but I did so because I know that they are two of the four most important and power-laden elements of life that you are going to be asked to tell your children about. I say "power-laden," because these topics are the Four Cornerstones of the Human Experience. They are:

Money

Love

Sex

God

Many years ago I created a program called The Truth Seminar. It focused on these topics, moving from least important to most important (as they are listed above), and acknowledging that of all the areas and activities within the human encounter, these are the Top 4 in terms of impact.

And I say that "sex" is more important than "love" in the above listing, because *CwG* does not talk about sex as merely a physical experience, but rather, it refers to the **S**ynergistic **E**nergy e**X**change that is *all of life*. For more on this angle, please go back and read *Conversations with God* again.

So now when you combine the Four Cornerstones of the Human Experience with the Three Foundational Aspects of Physical Expression that I introduced earlier, you have what is essentially a curriculum for mastering life.

I am saying that you don't have to look far, or read a hundred books, to find out what to share with your children if you want them to have a good life. At least, not in my opinion. Simply remind them about . . .

1. *life itself, and how it works*

2. *Themselves, and who and what they are*

3. *Life's Larger Realities, and what some people call "God"*

. . . then give them the True Story about the tools that life has given them:

A. *Money*

B. *Love*

C. *Sex*

D. *God*

You have no doubt noticed that "God" shows up on both lists. Both lists are presented, as I said earlier, in reverse order of importance. In every situation where you are invited to expand or enhance the remembrance of another, always approach the most important subject last. "Save the best for last." If you start with the most important information first, you run the risk of blowing people (especially children) away.

For instance, in sharing on the subject of God I never begin by saying, "You are God." It is true that you *are* God, but it is not the first thing I say. I have found it better to lead up to that. This wonderful truth is too radical, it runs too counter to the Current Cultural Story, for many people to find it acceptable at first blush. Indeed, for the vast majority of people, and for a wide variety of reasons, it might be rejected outright.

Certainly the idea that we are God is not the idea I would share with children in their first encounter with the notion of God. (Although, ultimately, I would teach them that We and God are One, just as a drop of the ocean is one with the ocean . . . an illustration that I would not fail to offer, by the way, if we were on or near a beach.)

So, the ideas that you share with your children (or demonstrate to them through your behaviors) about Money, Love, Sex, and God are among the most important impressions they will receive from you about life itself. They may be *the* most important—at least for the first twenty to thirty years of their life.

Somewhere within that decade, as their experience of life enlarges and their exposure to the world expands, they will begin to form their own opinions on these things, your ideas and demonstrations notwithstanding. Yet even then, and for the rest of their lives, their First Impressions about these topics will indeed be the basis, the cornerstones, and the foundation upon which all their own ideas—even their contradictory ones—are overlaid.

If you wish your children to begin their lives within the framework of a whole new Cultural Story about all these things, I want to end here by suggesting the obvious. Make sure that *you* understand and embrace that New Story fully.

First, read and re-read every book in the *Conversations with God* cosmology. There are nine of them in the dialogue series, and at least three other follow-up books that I believe are also extremely helpful. These are: *Happier Than God, When Everything Changes, Change Everything*, and *The Storm Before the Calm*.

Having read these books not once but several times (they never get old for me, and I find something newly inspiring and invigorating in them every time), you will find yourself "coming from" this story every day as you move through your life—and every time you engage your children in discussions *about* life.

Why do I encourage staying close to the *CwG* material? Well, it is as a friend of mine, Bill Fischofer, likes to say . . .

"In fairness, no religion claims they 'understand' God, for all believe that He is infinite and thus beyond understanding. The problem, always, is that our concepts of God are too small. Since God is infinite in all 'directions,' wherever one turns one finds an inexhaustible terrain.

"Religion A and Religion B both find themselves in infinite fields of wonder and thus assume that they have 'found God.' Indeed, they have, but God is so unfathomably vast that what they fail to notice is that God is 'big enough' to contain the entirety of their (seemingly different) infinite vistas (and more). This is why it is in the *mystical* traditions of religions that one finds spiritual unity (and, of course, in *Conversations with God),* for only here is this larger realization glimpsed."

It is precisely so that you may glimpse—and continue to glimpse—a larger realization about God that I encourage the reading and re-reading of the *CwG* books and their messages.

Having said all of that, I must say that I find it interesting to note that through all of my reading of the 3,000 pages of the *Conversations with God* dialogues I have found the messages that my father and my mother gave me from the time I was the littlest boy repeated in one form or another. And that is the point I am trying to make, that I am hoping to make, here. You will always be your child's First and Most Important Source of information about life. And life will seem to your child to confirm your own impressions of it, as given to your children. Put another way, your children will see in life what you have trained them to see.

So what did my parents train me to see about life? Well, here are the two most important messages that I got from my parents. To them I will be forever grateful.

> DAD: You can do anything you want to do, if you want to do it bad enough. There's no such thing as a "No Admittance" door. And remember, there's no "right" way to do anything; there is only the way you are doing it. You do it. Get it done. And suddenly everyone will call that "the right way." And always think of this: What's the worst that can happen? So try out for that play. Write that report. Go after that job. Ask the girl out. What's the worst that can happen?

MOM: God is always there, and always on your side. You don't have to go anywhere or do anything to find God. God's right here. God's with you always. You need help? Just ask. You'll get it.

I can't think of any better 128 words to share with anyone.

Okay, so now that you know what we're inviting you, in this book, to share with your children, let's get right to it. Here, one per chapter, are the narrative explorations, prepared for parents, of each *CwG* Core Message as it has been articulated for children, followed by Tools, Tips, and Strategies for sharing these messages with children.

Chapter One

WE ARE ALL ONE

I consider no message more important to the future of humanity—and therefore to the teaching of our children—than the four-word statement that the world was given in the first chapter of the first book in the 3,000+ page *Conversations with God* series . . .

WE ARE ALL ONE.

Most of us who have been taught about a God at all have been taught that God is the *All-in-All*, the *Unmoved Mover*, the *Alpha and the Omega*. God, we are told, is All Knowing, All Powerful, and Everywhere Present.

If we accept these teachings—that is, if we embrace the thought that what has been said above is true—then we are led to two immediate conclusions:

1. We are all a part of God, and cannot be separate from God.

2. We are all also a part of each other, and cannot be separate from each other.

Logical as they may be, both of these conclusions, it turns out, have become highly controversial—although they were not at all controversial among the earliest humans. It is an irony of humanity's "development" that we have stepped away from our earliest intuitive awareness of our Oneness.

How our Story of Separation began

This came about as a result of our first experiences of what we conceived of as "another"—and of our "separation" from that other.

That early story of separation had its origin in the first attempts of our species to understand the life we were experiencing.

What we now call "self-consciousness" arose when we began to see or know ourselves individually. Perhaps it was seeing our reflection in a cave-side pool that sparked this perception. We raised a hand to scratch our head and saw the "man in the pool" doing the same thing . . . and soon we began to conceive of "The Self."

The next step in producing the perception of separation came, perhaps, as we sat around the campfire of our clan and found ourselves startled by a sudden flash of lightning in the night sky, followed by a booming clap of thunder. We looked anxiously around the campfire and asked, with whatever facial and verbal expressions we'd developed, "Did *you* do that?" When everyone in the clan shook their head in a panicked "No!," we came to a startling awareness: *There is something Other Than Us.*

This Something Other also seemed, as subsequent events appeared to prove, far more *powerful* than us. It could cause wind and rain and violent storms; heat and dry spells that lasted, it seemed, forever; a frightening shaking and even an opening of the very ground on which we walked. It could even start fires in the woods all by Itself.

It became clear to us that we needed to find a way to *control* this Something Other, or our lives would forever be at Its mercy. Yet we could not conceive of or imagine a way that we could do this. We tried everything. We knew we had to find a way to appease the gods.

We didn't call the elements of life "gods," of course. That word came along at a much later time. But we did think of this Something Other as an aspect of our existence that was both powerful and uncontrollable.

We knew some members of our own clan in exactly the same way. The biggest and the strongest and most brutish among us ran rampant through the collective life of the clan, and efforts were continually made to appease them. They were brought offerings of every kind, from nubile virgins to plentiful food to beautiful things from the richness of the earth.

Once, when the most brutish among us became more sullen and angry than usual because of an unending drought and the sacrifices it imposed on them and the whole clan, we joined others in our small group to do whatever we could think of to calm them, lest they take out their anger on us—which they had done before.

We threw a camp-side "party" for them, sang and did dances for them. Someone in the group tore a dying branch from a nearby tree and shook it as part of his dance, its dry leaves making a rhythmic sound matching his gyrations as he twirled around the fire.

As it happens, at that exact moment the skies opened up, and a sudden hard rain drenched the site. Everyone was shocked! And, given the limited intellectual development of the clan at that time, the Dance With The Branch was credited with having produced the water from the sky.

A way had been found to please and appease Something Other! A way had been found to get that Something Other to do what we had been hoping for! All of us were so excited! The "rain man" was elevated to a position of highest status. Ritual, and a class within the clan of Those Who Performed It, was created.

The clan believed that the Dance of the Branch by the Rain Man created rain, and so it *did* in the future more often than not. And this was not by coincidence. Metaphysics being what it is, the formula worked! For the metaphysical process—whether modern or ancient—produces in physicality whatever it is fervently believed it will produce.

In that first instance, it was no doubt the ongoing, fervent hope, the deeply earnest wish, of the clan that the drought would end that generated the result. But the coincidence of the rain falling at the exact moment the noisy dance was performed could not be ignored.

The narrative above is, of course, all of my imagining. It was a vision of "what might have been," a fanciful insight, perhaps—maybe even an inspiration of the possible—that I received at the time that I was having my conversations with God. The entire story could be unreal . . . but I believe that either this, or something very similar to this, is what occurred in the early life of human beings and what produced our sense of separation, our sense of Something Other, and our sense that there might be, after all, a way of controlling—or at least *influencing*—that Something Other.

To me it seems clear that the earliest humans were dealing with the alchemy of the universe without knowing it. Thus was born what later came to be called "religion."

As our species grew more sophisticated in its understandings, we sought a more sophisticated way of seeking to "appease the gods" . . . and, later, the single God that the vast majority of us ultimately decided must surely exist.

The vast majority of us believe that to this day. We were, and we are, right about that. There *is* this thing that we now call Adonai, Akshar, Allah, Brahma, Deus, Divinity, Divine Mother, Eckankar, Elohim, God, Hari, Indra, Jehovah, Krishna, Lord, Mahesh, Manitou, Ormuzd, Parameshwar, Purush, Purushottam, Radha Soami, Ram, Rama, Theos, Thor, Varuna, Vishnu, Yahweh—and by a hundred other names known only to those who use them.

Yet our *idea* of God—that it is Something *Other*—is what has been inaccurate. That idea is a carryover from the earliest story we told ourselves about this Power Greater Than Us. That first conceptualization of our not-yet-fully-developed minds is what created what I have called Separation Theology.

What our earliest theology has produced

Separation Theology is a way of looking at God that insists that we are "over here" and God is "over there."

The problem with a Separation Theology is that it produces a Separation Cosmology. That is, a way of looking at all of life that says that everything is separate from everything else.

And a Separation Cosmology produces a Separation Psychology. That is, a psychological viewpoint that says that I am over here and you are over there.

And a Separation Psychology produces a Separation Sociology. That is, a way of socializing with each other that encourages the entire human society to act as separate entities serving their own separate interests.

And a Separation Sociology produces a Separation Pathology. That is, *pathological behaviors of self-destruction*, engaged in individually and collectively, and producing suffering, conflict, violence, and death by our own hands—as evidenced everywhere on our planet throughout human history.

Our minds are still not fully developed, of course. Those who know about these things tell us that even today, thousands and thousands of years after our beginnings, we are still using only about 10 percent of our brain's capacity. It is therefore not terribly surprising that most of humanity has not seen, has not recognized, the damage that our Separation Theology has done.

It has stopped us from embracing the one thought that could alter life on Earth irrevocably for the better forever: the idea that We Are All One. One with each other, one with all of life, and one with God.

Everything that we proclaim to believe about God (those of us who proclaim a belief in God at all) would seem to render the notion of our Unity with Deity in no way controversial.

If God is Everywhere Present (which we say we believe), that would mean that God is present in every human being. If God is present in every human being, that would mean that conversely, we are present in God.

If God is the All-in-All, then human beings would have to *not* be part of the All in order for humans to not be part of God. Yet humans *are* a part, obviously, of all that exists. We are, therefore, One with God.

It is our ancient beliefs that block us from accepting this otherwise obvious and irrefutable logic. Oh, and also, our fear. It is the fear of somehow losing ourselves.

The same "stuff" is not the same thing as The Same Thing

Many people make the mistake of assuming that because *Conversations with God* declares that "God and we are One," it is saying that God and we are *the same thing*. Of course, no one could agree with such a statement, any more than anyone could agree that because the ocean and a drop of ocean water are the same "stuff," the drop and the ocean are the same thing.

We are the "stuff" that God is, and God is the "stuff" that we are—that much is true—but God is the sum total of all the "stuff" that exists, while we are a single *individuation*, a particular *expression*, of it.

Teaching our unity with God to a child is, therefore, a very delicate matter, because we don't want to give them a false and potentially dangerous idea. We want our children to know that their essence is Divine, and we want them to know all that this means. Yet we also want them to know what it does *not* mean.

It does not mean, for instance, that we can jump off a building and fly. It does not mean that we can never be hurt or injured in any way. It does not mean that we are like Superman.

It does mean that God is always present within us, to offer us help and guidance along the way as we live each day. It does mean that we have been given the same Tools of Creation that God uses, and that if we learn to use them, too, we can produce wonderful outcomes in our own lives. It does mean that even if we are hurt or injured in some way, or find ourselves in some kind of trouble or difficulty, that if we ask God's help we can find our way out of it.

Essentially, it means that we are not "alone" in life. Even when it feels as if we are alone—perhaps especially when it feels this way—God's presence can heal us of our loneliness and provide us with the gentle companionship and the quiet courage to go on.

My interpretation is that the Christian tradition teaches this truth about Jesus when it quotes Jesus as saying: *I and the Father are one.* And, elsewhere, *Have I not said, Ye are Gods?* The official doctrine of the Christian Church, however, would not be in agreement with my interpretation. It would declare that Jesus and the Father *are* One—but that the rest of us and the Father are *not* One.

What, then, does "We Are All One" mean?

To me the *CwG* message that We Are All One means exactly what it says. The conversation elaborates, telling us that, "All Things are One Thing. There is only One Thing, and all things are part of the One Thing there is."

This means that we are One with each other, One with all of life, and One with God. There is no other way to interpret it, as I see it.

CwG is telling us that you are me and I am you; that we are part and parcel of Everything. We are intermingled as differing energy forms in a Larger Form that includes All That Is. And so, we are not only One with each other, but One with the Earth and every living thing upon it. One, as well, with the universe. And, as I've already said, One with that Divine Essence that we call God.

The implications of this for the human race are staggering. If we believed this was true, everything in our lives would change. Everything in our religions, in our politics, in our economics, in our education, and in our social constructions. And everything in our personal lives as well.

In our religions we would see the end of their seemingly endless competitions for human souls. Religions would stop insisting on portraying themselves as the One and Only Path to God. They would assist us on our own personal path, but they would not claim to *be* The Path. And they would cease using Fear as the chief tool in their arsenal.

They would stop teaching that unless we follow their doctrines, we are going to spend eternity in the everlasting fires of hell. They would be a source of comfort and guidance, of ever-present help, and of strength in times of need. Thus, religion would serve its highest purpose and its grandest function.

In our politics we would see the end of hidden agendas, and of power plays, and of the demonization of those with opposing points of view. Political parties would stop claiming that their way was the only way. And they would work together to find solutions to the most pressing problems, and to move society forward by seeking common ground.

They would seek to blend the most workable of their ideas with the most workable of the ideas of their opponents. Thus, politics would serve its highest purpose and its grandest function.

In our economics we would see the end of Bigger-Better-More as the international yardstick of Success. We would create a New Bottom Line, in which "maximum productivity" was redefined, and in which our endless drive for profits-profits-*profits* was replaced with a sense of awe and wonder in the universe, a reverence for all of life, and a dedication to creating a world in which each person can live in dignity, with basic needs being met. Thus, economics would serve its highest purpose and its grandest function.

In our education we would see the end of propaganda substituting for history, and of subject-driven curricula, where emphasis is placed on memorization of facts, rather than on the fundamental concepts of life which we want our children to understand: awareness, honesty, responsibility.

We would see a democratic school in which children have as much to say about what they are to learn and how they will learn it as teachers, and in which we do not use the environment to *pour knowledge into* children, but to *draw wisdom out* of them. Thus, education would serve its highest purpose and its grandest function.

What "We Are All One" does not mean

We Are All One does *not* mean that what's mine is yours and what's yours is mine. Not in the ordinarily understood human sense of those words. The concept of *Oneness* does not eliminate the possibility of personal possessions or individual expressions.

We may find ourselves experiencing a higher level of desire than ever before to *share* our personal possessions with others when we realize that there really *are* no "others," only and merely Additional Versions of the Self—yet we are not *required* to give our possessions away, nor are we authorized to take another's possessions from them.

Each human expression of the Divine may experience itself exactly the way it chooses—and what we gather and what we share becomes a striking aspect of that individual expression.

We Are All One also does not mean that we are all the *same*, or that we do not have a personal and singular and very specific identity. The Parable of the Snowflake, which first appeared in the book *The Only Thing That Matters* (Emnin Books, 2012, distributed by Hay House), explains this for children in a wonderful way.

I offer it for your reading here . . .

> Once upon a time there was a snowflake. Its name was Sara. Sara the Snowflake had a brother named Sam. Sam the Snowflake.
>
> Sara and Sam both lived a good life—but they feared for the day that they would die, melting away into the nothingness. Then one day the Snow Angel appeared

to both of them. "A snowflake is eternal. Did you know that?" the Angel said, and then the Angel explained:

"The very first snowflakes in the history of the world are the snowflakes that are falling today. They fall from the sky as highly individualized physicalizations. There are no two snowflakes alike. There never have been, in all the history of snowflakes.

"The flakes are awesomely beautiful in their individual design. No one who watches them falling from the heavens can fail to see their exquisite splendor. People run outside when snowflakes fall, beholding their breathtaking magnificence.

"As they land, they merge with one another. People call a huge collection of them on the ground simply 'snow.' They don't say, 'Look at that big pile of snowflakes.' They say, 'Look at that mountain of snow.' They see all the individual snowflakes as One. And indeed, the snowflakes *are* One with One Another."

The Angel went on . . .

"Soon the sun comes out and the snow melts, each flake disappearing, one by one. They don't, of course, disappear at all. They simply change form. Now they are water, rippling together in a sparkling puddle or flowing together in a little stream.

"The sun continues to work its magic, and soon the water itself disappears. Or *seems* to. Actually, it, too, simply changes form. It evaporates, rising into the air as invisible vapors and gathering there in such concentration that they are visible again—as clouds.

"As more and more vapors gather, the clouds become heavy with their moisture. Soon, once again, the moisture falls, raining down upon the earth. And if the temperature is just right, the falling rain turns into snowflakes again—no two snowflakes alike. Ever. In the history of snowflakes."

Sara and Sam were never so happy in their entire lives. Suddenly, everything was what you might call . . . *crystal clear.*

And so, in the snow we see the Cycle of Life and the Story of You.

Some ideas for sharing this concept with children

We Are All One is an amazing idea. It could end war forever, redefine how we resolve all conflict and disagreement, recreate how we share all resources, and reinvent ourselves as a society.

It will change the choices you make in your own home, the words you use at your own dinner table, the way you act in your own bed, the ideas that you hold in your own mind.

It will change the world.

For this reason, I believe that teaching the concept of Oneness to children is of prime importance—both to our offspring and to the world at large. Our opportunity as parents is to help our children produce a future of happiness rather than haplessness for the human race.

Here, then, are some strategies for sharing with the young ones in your life what I consider to be the single most important principle from *CwG*:

WE ARE ALL ONE.

The objective of the following teaching approach is to introduce the above concept to children by helping them to embrace their Oneness with all of life, starting with understanding how people and things are connected.

Lesson 1

IN TEACHING CHILDREN THIS CONCEPT, YOU MAY WISH TO BEGIN BY . . .

. . . exploring your child's understanding of others and of his or her own place in the world. Ask if the child knows what the words "separate" and "connected" mean.

Even with small children you can start by sharing with them the actual *definitions* of the words *separate, connected,* and *interconnected.*

With older children, simply reading the following would be helpful. For the younger ones you may wish to *start* by reading these definitions . . . but then *Explain & Explore* the definitions even further.

First, let's look at the definitions . . .

"SEPARATE" . . . means . . . 1a: set or kept apart: detached; b: solitary, secluded . . . 2a: not shared with another: individual b: estranged from a parent body . . . 3a: existing by itself: autonomous. [Excerpts taken from *www.merriam-webster.com/dictionary/separate.*]

"CONNECTED" . . . means . . . 1: joined or linked together; 2: having the parts or elements logically linked together; 3: related by blood or marriage; 4: having social, professional, or commercial relationships; 5: of a set; having the property that any two of its points can be joined by a line completely contained in the set; also: incapable of being separated into two or more closed disjoint subsets. [Excerpts taken from *www.merriam-webster.com/ dictionary/connected.*]

"INTERCONNECTED" . . . means . . . 1: mutually joined or related; 2: having internal connections between the parts or elements. [Excerpts taken from *www.mer-riam-webster.com/dictionary/connected.*]

※ Discuss the meanings with your child in more depth.

※ For the very young, break the meaning down to a few words. For instance: "separate" can be described simply as feeling that you are alone. "Connected" can be described simply as feeling that you matter to other people and to the world. "Interconnected" can be described as the idea that everything and every person affects many people—especially (but not only) every person who is nearby.

Lesson 2

OFFER YOUR CHILD CONCRETE EXAMPLES OF THE ABSTRACT CONCEPT OF "ONENESS" SUCH AS . . .

. . . discussing how the parts of her or his body are still part of the whole, even though they appear to be separate.

* You might use the parts of an egg (shell, yolk, egg white) to illustrate that it takes many parts to make a whole.

* You might use a tree and its various parts (leaves, trunk, branches, bark, roots) which all make up the whole to explain how things that appear separate can actually be part of the same whole.

* You could use a crayon box to illustrate parts of a whole (x number of crayons of different colors, a cardboard box and a built-in sharpener all come together to make the whole "crayon box."

Lesson 3

ENGAGE THE CHILD IN ACTIVITIES THAT YOU KNOW WILL CAPTURE INTEREST AND FEEL LIKE FUN. REMEMBER THAT . . .

. . . "we are all one" is a concept that might take some time for the child to understand and internalize. To make things easier, create fun-time activities, sometimes using items or experiences from your child's own life to which you think he or she will immediately relate.

❀ Invite your child to draw a picture of his or her idea of how we are all connected. Some children might draw lines, rainbows, rays of light, etc. If your child is having trouble drawing, you can draw your own idea of the concept and share it with the child. With the smaller children the point is really to get them thinking about the concept for later understanding. Older children will begin to "see" the connections between people as your discussion progresses.

❀ Draw a family tree to illustrate connectedness. Start with your child's family and then branch outward, showing the beginnings of connection.

❀ Use a ball of yarn to turn a room or your back yard into a web, wrapping around objects, weaving the yarn up and down through the previous runs of yarn. Seeing the web itself will help the child see that the chair is connected to the couch, etc. (or outside trees to bushes, etc.). Then have your child pick a beginning point on a string and follow it, counting how many other "strings" crossed it, touched it, and *connected* to it. Take a photo of the web before you deconstruct it, so that you can use the photo later for discussion.

❀ With older children you can create a game called "How many degrees of connection?" (a play on the old game of Six Degrees of Separation). Ask your older child to pick a person that he might have heard of (for ease, you may want to start locally) but never met. Then begin brainstorming together to trace back from that person to himself. It might actually take naming quite a few people (maybe more than six), but this game will nevertheless assist your older child in beginning to see the interconnectedness of people on a concrete level.

It is also possible with older offspring to use social media (Facebook, Twitter, etc.) as a perfect illustration of connection.

Show your child the nifty little "people you may know" function on Facebook. This function will pop up lots of people with whom you have no shared friends . . . but every once in a while it will actually be someone you know! Invite your child to ponder, "How does Facebook know this? How does it 'match up' people like that?" Tell them that the giant computer at Facebook sees all the connections between all the people on Facebook and lets you know about ones you may not even have been aware of!

You can also use Facebook to show your child that their friends might even know each other, even when it doesn't seem natural that your friend in California (when you are in Missouri) would know a person that you met in New York. Picking out a few unlikely, yet interesting, connections like this and showing this to your older child will help them see the concept of connectedness—which lays a great foundation for understanding of We Are All One!

Lesson 4

USE THE WORLD AROUND YOU, AND GIVE YOUR CHILD EXAMPLES OF HOW EVERYTHING IN IT IS CONNECTED. ONE WAY TO SHOW THIS IS BY . . .

. . . demonstrating the effect that one thing in the world has on another. "Cause and Effect" is a wonderful way to illustrate for children how *interactive* the world is. It is then a short leap from *Interaction* to *Interconnection*. Interaction can be shown to children in many ways that they can easily understand.

 * Have your child blow out a candle, then ask, "What do you think made the candle go out?" Explain that the force of the air *moving* extinguished the candle. Then hold up a thin piece of paper or a facial tissue. Have the child blow as if blowing out a candle. Invite the child to watch the movement that breath creates. Show in this way that everything affects everything else.

❊ Tell the "Wings of a Butterfly" story, explaining how if a butterfly flaps its wings in Singapore, it has an effect in San Francisco. If the child is not old enough to know about the names of these cities, just use words such as "way, way far away" and "over here" to make the same point. Explain that weather patterns change because of, among other things, wind currents, and that a butterfly's wings create wing currents—just as blowing out a candle does.

❊ Fill a very large kettle, or even the bathtub, with water, then illustrate the "pebble in the pond" effect, dropping something small, but heavy, into the water, and point out how the ripples extend outward, getting bigger and bigger. Use this to show how what starts out as a seemingly small event can grow as it moves along the atmosphere (or water) until it becomes something much larger than itself.

❊ You might be able to use this much simplified take on the idea to illustrate connectedness to your older child. You can take the idea at face value and just discuss how a ripple (or wing flap) travels distance because the atmosphere is interconnected. In other words, wind doesn't ever really just die out; it is transformed and continues.

If your child is older, you can ask your child to research the butterfly effect and go deeper. Either way, you can use the concept to assist your child in understanding connectedness, which again leads to later understanding of the notion that We Are All One.

Discuss the concept of "energy" with your older child, and talk about how it is energy that ultimately connects everything. Explain how an object at rest tends to stay at rest and an object in motion tends to stay in motion. Explore how this relates to "we are all one." Explain that it is about the connectedness and the continuity of life. Much like the gust created when a butterfly flaps its wings, energy also moves through the world along our connections. Energy can be physical or emotional. Use an illustration that most children will understand. For instance, it is easy to understand the hitting of a baseball. The pitcher winds up and throws, putting physical energy into the ball. The batter swings the bat, which transfers more energy to the ball, sending it farther than any arm could throw it. Then a person (or the ground) is impacted by the energy when it is caught or hits the grass. This is a small example to show the transfer of energy through the connections of a baseball game.

Now share with your child about how emotional energy is the same as physical energy. To illustrate emotional energy "transfers," try the following example: If I am mean to a person at school, and he goes home and is crabby to his mom, and she goes to work the next day and is rude to her assistant, then she goes home and is short with her partner, who goes to work the next day and is rude to a customer . . . the "effect" goes on and on. We can easily see how the negative attitude with which I created that energy can have a ripple effect that could go on indefinitely. So a person miles and miles away could be affected by my negative attitude today. It is also just as true that I can have a *positive* effect on the world through the energy that I create by being *nice* to just one person.

Lesson 5

INTRODUCE YOUR CHILD NOT ONLY TO THE CONCEPT OF 'ONENESS,' BUT TO THE EXPERIENCE OF IT, USING . . .

. . . the tools of meditation, visualization, and even yoga. Explain that these can be a wonderful help in many situations—especially if your child is feeling stress or sadness or "bad" in any way—to experience being connected to the inner self, nature, and God. Of course, if your children know that *you* meditate, if you tell them that *you* use visualizations, if they see *you* doing yoga, they will automatically want to do some of these things, because all children emulate and imitate their parents.

Meditation

Relaxation meditation

Practice a relaxation meditation. Ask your child to breathe deeply, guiding the breath with slow, deep inhales and slow, full exhales. At a young age, just this act of breathing deeply—with eyes open or closed—is often enough to begin teaching children meditation. You might explain that the warm, safe feeling they sometimes get when they are breathing deeply is their inner connection to life and to God making Itself known. Later, the child can begin to practice a more questioning type of meditation (where they ask a question, then move to the special place inside and see if the answer comes—sometimes it does and sometimes it doesn't just then), but at this point, just finding peace and quiet in meditation is perfect.

Guided meditation

Practice guided meditation by inviting your child to close her eyes and breathe deeply, allowing herself to relax and melt into herself, finding her spirit. Through chant (using the sound of *om*), deep breathing, and guided imagery (one idea: picture yourself rubbing soft plush black velvet against your face), many children can find a new, wonderful state of relaxation.

Connection

To illustrate connection you can ask your child to imagine himself hovering out above the Earth with strings on his hands. Ask her to picture where those strings connect, whether it is to the mountains, the trees, flowers, oceans, etc., or to the people she knows. Tell him that in this way he can begin to *feel* his connections on a soul level instead of just *hearing* about them from concrete examples.

Invite her to now imagine a much longer string, from her forehead, that goes out into the universe; ask her to imagine feeling love and light pouring into her from that string (from her God-Self), and then out through her hands back to Earth. Reverse the process to bring him back out of the guided meditation, bringing him back to his body gently and reminding him to keep the feeling of love and comfort he might have felt there, and take it into life.

Yoga

Do yoga together. This provides physical and mental stimulation at the same time, allowing your child to more fully understand her oneness with her own body, and then to maintain relaxation during meditation. It can also increase your own family bonds.

Chapter Two

GOD TALKS TO EVERYONE
ALL THE TIME

Of all the messages of *Conversations with God,* there is one that is the most difficult for most adults to believe—and the easiest for children to accept.

It's pretty clear why this is true. Children are not yet faced with the task of suspending *dis*belief. Yet for many adults, it seems almost *too good to be true* that . . .

GOD TALKS TO EVERYONE ALL THE TIME.

There is a great irony here. The irony is that most people who believe in God (nearly 90 percent of adults on the planet) believe that God revealed himself to humanity through *direct communication with a human being.*

So there seems to be little question among the members of our species that God talks directly to humans. The only questions seem to be, when did He stop? And precisely which humans did He talk to? But "Divine Revelation" itself is a "given" among the religions of the world.

Recent Divine Revelation, however, is labeled blasphemy. Most people look askance at anyone who says *today* that God spoke directly to him or her. Yet these doubters are the same people who swear that God spoke directly to the founder of their faith on some long ago *yesterday*. So the issue, it would seem, has to do with *timing.*

If Divine Revelation is said to have happened centuries or millennia ago, the event is presumed to be true. If it's said to have occurred months ago, it's denounced as delusion or blasphemy.

Yet this point of view opens up a whole other line of questioning. Why would God talk to humanity once, to only one person, and then never again across the long span of human history? And to which person did God speak directly? To whom and through whom did God reveal Himself. Lao Tzu? Buddha? Moses? Jesus? Muhammad? Bahá'u'lláh? Joseph Smith?

And why are there no women on this list? Is it true that God spoke only to men, and only to one of them, and only years ago? Or is it *possible* that God speaks to *all of us, all the time?*

Children—if they've been told that there even *is* a "God"—have no problem at all believing that God talks to people. "Why would God not?," they might ask innocently.

Many adults as well might embrace this point of view *if they had not been told not to.* They might embrace it because it has been their *experience.* They might feel they have to reject their experience, however, if it is not in accordance with the dogma or doctrine that has been taught them *since they were children.* This is, in fact, exactly what has happened. As a result . . .

Most people call their communications from the Divine something else: serendipity, coincidence, women's intuition, a "psychic hit," a marvelous insight, a brilliant idea, a sudden awareness, a bolt out of the blue, a moment of pure creation, or being "in the flow." They'll call it *anything* but a direct communication from the Divine, because in calling it *that* they risk being marginalized, criticized, or even ostracized.

Because children easily believe that God talks to them, adults have to literally *talk them out of it.* Yet what if we did not have to? What if we did not want to? What if we did not choose to? What if we told our children that God talks to everyone, all the time? What if they heard from us that Divine Inspiration is available to everyone, in every moment? How would our children grow up then?

They would grow up not only believing in God, but believing in a *personal* God, a God who cares about them, who knows and loves them specifically and individually, who is with them always, who never leaves their side, and who *of course* talks to them. Constantly. Continually. Consistently.

The question would be not "whether" but "how?"

Where the real teaching comes in

This is where the real lessons in life may be taught and learned. This is where some of life's most important information may be transferred to your child or grandchild. Exactly how does God talk to us? Well, it turns out that God's ways are unlimited.

One way is through words themselves, spoken to us directly by God and "heard" as "thoughts" in our mind.

Another way is through words spoken by persons sent to us as "messengers" from God. These could be friends, relatives, total strangers with whom we have a chance encounter on the street, at an airport, or in a train station, clergy or counselors with whom we consult, workshop presenters—or even authors whose works we read.

Four authors, in particular, have been widely read, and their writings are presumed to have been inspired by God. Their names are Matthew, Mark, Luke, and John.

Matthew was a former tax collector who was called by Jesus to be one of the twelve Apostles. Mark was a follower of Peter. Luke was a doctor who wrote what is now the book of Luke to a friend Theophilus. He is also believed to have written the book of Acts (or Acts of the Apostles) and was a close friend of Paul of Tarsus. John was a disciple of Jesus and possibly the youngest of the Apostles.

There are other ways, too

Another way that God communicates with us is through feelings. *Conversations with God* tells us that "feelings are the language of the soul." Indeed, we would be well to *prefer* this as a method of receiving God's communications, because—again as God said in *CwG*: "Words are the least reliable form of communication."

For instance, what does the word "cold" mean? Well, that depends on whether you are talking to someone from Alaska or someone from Texas. When we are looking at the sun, are we looking "up" at the sun, or "down" at the sun? When is "fast" actually "slow," and when does "slow" become "fast"? At what point, exactly?

(You can use these examples with your children in middle school or the upper grades of elementary school. It will really give them something to think about!)

So . . . *feelings* can be a powerful way that our soul communicates with us, using the fundamental energy that *is* the soul to cause us to "feel" a certain way.

As well, pictures and images can also communicate what "God in us" (that is, our soul) is sending our Mind to remember.

A book of teaching strategies

Many parents agree that God talks to all of us, all the time. They agree, as well, with all of the major messages from *Conversations with God*. They are, however, not sure about the most effective way to teach such huge ideas to their children.

As I said in the Preface, long ago I asked two of the most wonderful parents I know—Emily Filmore and Laurie Farley—to consider how this might be done . . . and to reflect on how they have done it with their own children.

Emily and Laurie are now the administrators of The School of the New Spirituality, the children's education platform of the *CwG* global outreach. Working together, they have created the *CwG* for Parents Program, which offers resources for sharing the messages of *Conversations with God* with the next generation.

Emily—working in collaboration with Laurie—has written specific lesson plans for all of the core concepts of the *CwG* cosmology, and both ladies have graciously agreed to work with me in co-creating this present book, of which I consider them the co-authors.

We've looked at their teaching ideas together, and I am so very happy to tell you that I wholeheartedly endorse their approach, seeing these strategies as wonderful tools for opening young minds to the excitement of exploring, with parents or grandparents, wonderful ways of looking at life, supported by the breathtaking ideas from *Conversations with God* about how things really are in our world—and how they could be experienced by everyone, if we all simply embraced these extraordinary principles.

Just to remind you now, as you move forward here, each chapter of this book, then, will open with my own explanation, written for parents, of the Core Concept, and conclude with some strategies that will equip parents to share the Core Concept with the young ones in their life.

Let's look now at some strategies for Core Concept #2 . . .

GOD TALKS TO EVERYONE, ALL THE TIME.

The objective of the following teaching approach is to introduce the above concept to children by helping them to begin *Hearing* God's messages through their feelings, intuition, and interactions with the people around them and to help them view God as an approachable, loving energy/being who needn't be feared.

Lesson 1

IN TEACHING CHILDREN THIS CONCEPT, YOU MAY WISH TO BEGIN BY . . .

. . . asking your children if they know what God is and if they believe God has ever spoken to them. Ask how God has done this in the past. The child may respond by saying, "a little voice in my head" or the answer may be something more dramatic. Encourage thinking outside the box! The answers will be as varied as the number of stars in the sky. This is because we all experience Oneness, the All, God or the universe in different ways. Acknowledge, support, and celebrate the child's responses.

Lesson 2

GIVE CONCRETE EXAMPLES OF YOUR OWN UNDERSTANDING OF GOD . . .

Many families use words such as the All, the universe and God, interchangeably. Emily started by telling her daughter that God is love, that we are all God, and that God is the love she feels inside. Once this introduction has been made, you can follow with concrete examples of your daily experiences of your own conversations with God as children express interest in learning more. Some early examples that can be used are the warmth of the sun as God touching your face; a beautiful flower as God painting a picture for you; a butterfly's flight as the power of God; and a hug as the perfect example of pure love/God. Explain that God speaks to everyone in different ways. Some of the ways that God speaks to us are:

* Emotions / Intuition / Gut Feelings

* Appropriate physical touch from loved ones

* Dreams

* Nature

* Prayer / Meditation / Consciousness

* Other people

* Through Music, Books, Pictures, Events and other creative means

Introduce Intuition as a concept

Read and *explore* the definition with your child. Again, with older children, simply reading the following would be helpful. For the younger ones you may wish to start by reading the definition . . . but then Explain & Explore the definition even further.

INTUITION means . . . 1: quick and ready insight; 2a: immediate apprehension or cognition; 2b: knowledge or conviction gained by intuition; 2c: the power or faculty of attaining to direct knowledge or cognition without evident rational thought and inference. (Downloaded from *http://www.merriam-webster.com/dictionary/intuition* on December 13, 2010.)

* Talk about a time your child showed intuition, even if they were too young to remember it now. For instance, talk about a time that your child picked up on some-one else's emotion without being told directly, or a time that your child trusted his or her own thoughts or feelings.

* Encourage trusting yourself; make this as simplistic as possible, laying the groundwork for later understanding.

* Talk about his or her own emotions as part of intuition.

Lesson 3

EXPLORE THESE QUESTIONS WITH YOUR CHILD

1. How does oneness (from the concept "We Are All One") help you understand that God is always there to talk to?

2. How do you feel when you think about starting to talk to God? It is a good idea to allow your child to answer freely here. The goal here is to find out if your child is nervous or shy about talking to God while being cau-tious that you do not plant or suggest apprehension in the child's mind if he is not already feeling that way. If your child expresses nervousness, you can reassure him or her that it is natural to feel nervous when beginning any new conversation, but also that it is unnecessary and that your child is safe.

3. How do we know if a message is from God or not? God speaks to us through our feelings primarily, but also through our thoughts. If the message makes you feel good and loved, this is a good indication that you should listen to it.

4. How does it feel when your parents, grandparents, or siblings give you hugs, hold your hand, or give you kisses? We convey many things through touch: love, acceptance, comfort, healing, etc. Sometimes God sends us these messages through the gentle touch of a trusted loved one.

5. Can you hear God's "voice"? Sometimes God speaks to us through thoughts. Usually these are thoughts that we have never had before or seem as if they are coming from outside of us.

6. Has God ever spoken to you through nature? Sometimes God talks to us through the beauty of the world around us. Once, one of the authors and her family experienced a sunset in the desert that was breathtaking and awe-inspiring; the child was able to experience that sunset as God's love and it added a measure of comfort that they would be safe on their tripg. We can look everywhere for these messages.

7. What happens when you pray? Do you feel anything? Answers will vary.

8. How come God doesn't speak to us the way we speak to one another? God does not speak to us through words as often as the other ways because words can be misunderstood.

9. Do you ever ask a friend or family member a question because you just KNOW that person will know how to help you? This is both your intuition (of which person to ask) and God's answer through another person's answer.

10. If you want to start a conversation with another person at school, at the library, or at a game, how do you start? Do you think this is the same basic way with God?

Lesson 4

SOME TOOLS AND ACTIVITIES WE THINK WILL BE REALLY FUN AND INFORMATIVE . . .

You might wonder why we re-use some of the same techniques repetitively throughout the book; this is not to be redundant, but to show you how these *Spiritual Skills* can be applied, *beneficially*, in multiple methods and circumstances.

Explore Dreams

Begin a dream journal. The challenge here is to remember dreams. The way we remember our dreams is by setting an intention. Committing to record your dreams is a powerful way to set an intention. Even if you only remember small portions of the dream, recording them will send a message to yourself that dreams are important, and your mind will begin to remember them. Encourage the child to draw pictures of his or her dreams. Each morning begin the habit of asking your child if she remembers her dreams. Discuss the dream and how it could be a message. Explain that dreams are made up of symbols and that monsters are usually a symbol representing something that may be bothering us. (Privately, use the Internet or dream books to look up the symbolic meaning of the dreams your child has relayed to you. If you feel the meanings you find are age-appropriate and helpful, share the insights about the symbols in those dreams with your child.)

Meditation

Use meditation as a way to be connected to God and seek answers to life's questions.

☀ Using breathing and relaxation techniques, you can help your child reach this helpful contemplative state. Explain that the warm, safe feeling you get when you are breathing deeply is God's way of telling you that you are okay. Later the child can begin to practice a more questioning type of meditation, but at this point, finding peace and quiet in meditation is perfect!

❋ With older children you can move into questioning meditation. Ask your child about something that has been concerning or bothersome. Ask your child to hold the thought in his or her mind with as few distractions as possible for about thirty seconds. After they have had the thought clearly in their mind for a few moments, release the thought and try to keep the mind as silent as possible. See what answers arise from the silent moment. This is the voice of God speaking to you. Ask the child to notice anything unusual about the voice that arises. Try to practice meditation a total of 5 minutes per day. This can be broken down into smaller chunks. For instance, 1-2 minutes before breakfast; 1-2 minutes after school; and 2-3 minutes at bedtime, reflecting on the day.

Yoga

Do yoga together and set an intention to use the session to connect with the Divine.

Talk *to* God

Expressing gratitude is a great way for a small child to begin talking to and listening for God. Find very concrete ways to help your child to think about and express being thankful. Once a child begins a conversation in this way, it will open his or her eyes to receiving God's love and messages as well.

❋ Make an "I am thankful" paper and ask your child about what he or she feels thankful. Help your child to draw or write things on the paper and hang it in your home as both a reminder and as a reward for his or her hard work.

✦ Show your child how you feel and express gratitude through your own actions.

✦ Have quiet prayer time where you and your child tell God about your day. Again, even though initially this is a one-way conversation, it will eventually leave your child more open to feeling and hearing God's answers.

Role-play

1. Pretend you are another student or child your child's age. Briefly role-play how your child initiates conversation with another person. Reflect on it and ask questions about how your child felt to be talking to someone with whom he or she was not familiar. If appropriate, and if your child has expressed any nervousness about talking to God, use this to explore those feelings about shyness or nervousness.

2. Using guided imagery, have your child close his or her eyes and picture his/her own idea of God. Encourage creative thinking; it doesn't have to be a person. God could be Light, a flower, a rainbow, or the family dog. Have him/her tell that image about the day silently in his/her head.

3. Ask your child to sit in a quiet private space with you and have the same sort of one-way dialogue with God aloud, with you there to support and encourage.

4. Explain that by having this one-way dialogue, the child can begin to feel more comfortable with talking TO God and eventually start looking for answers in his or her feelings, signs, etc. (as mentioned in other portions of this lesson) as the second half of a two-way Conversation with God.

5. Ask your child why he or she thinks God wants to talk to everyone. Talk about how God wants the best for us, wanting to guide us, help us fulfill our potential, etc.

6. Encourage your child to do this 1-2 (or more as your child desires) times per day, initially with your prompting, but hopefully, eventually the child will take ownership and begin having an all-day, open-ended conversation with God.

7. Ask your child to keep a journal of how it feels to talk AT God, and how it feels when he or she feels she receives a message/inspiration FROM God. (Parent note: this can be used to move into meditation.)

Explore Nature

Go for a walk in nature. Collect leaves and flowers from your walk. Look at pictures of things from nature that move you. Spend time tumbling and playing with a pet. Listen to music with nature sounds. Help your child understand that since ALL comes from God and ALL is God, interacting with nature is a way of communicating with and hearing God.

Active Listening

When we listen with the thought in mind that God is speaking to us through another, a sign or through music, we are active listening. When conversations go in one ear and out the other, we are being passive listeners. This doesn't mean that what is said is not heard, but that it is not registering with us on a conscious level. One of the most profound experiences that I had with God speaking to me occurred with music. During the song I had a sense that God was speaking to me through the music. I felt a strong sense of love, and I listened to the lyrics as if they were meant for me, from God. Ask your child to pay attention to their feelings when others are speaking to them or they are listening to music, a film, etc. When strong feelings come up, tell your child to pay attention to their feelings. Tell the children to ask themselves if a message is being delivered.

* Play the game "telephone" with four or more people. Point out the differences in the first message and the final message. Use this to explain that words are not always understood.

* Show how hard it is to understand words through song. Look up the lyrics of a song your child knows and likes. Play the song once and have the child tell you the words as they are sung; write down a few lines at a time. Then read the lyrics aloud. Find the missed words or the misunderstood words. Even as adults we don't always hear the right words in songs. This exercise will help your child understand the difficulty in understanding what others might be saying.

* Use both of these examples to explain why it is difficult for God to communicate with words since they are so easy to misinterpret.

* Hear God's message from others. Talk to your child about the important people in your life. Talk about who the child feels most comfortable asking questions about different things. Acknowledge that sometimes Dad is who you are most comfortable asking about how to do one thing, while Mom or Grandma is who you are comfortable asking about other things. Encourage your child to feel safe asking questions and let them know that through these questions and these trusted people we enable God to speak to us.

Creative expression

Encourage your child to draw pictures of God, sing songs, hum, do an interpretive dance, take photos in nature, write a story, make up a play, etc. Anything that allows them to open their creative doors and allow expression to manifest will enable them to feel and experience God.

Talk about and read about God

Read a favorite book about God with some good snuggle time. The more comfortable your child is with the concept of God, the more comfortable he or she will be in trying to initiate communication.

Synchronicity

Has something ever happened that seemed to fit with what you were thinking about that day? Help your child to find ways that synchronicity has shown in his or her life. For instance, your child decides to learn to read, and he or she really likes a specific character from books or TV. Then suddenly, and seemingly randomly, your child finds books about the character everywhere that would help him or her to learn to read. This is an instance of synchronicity.

Share the following information with older children as a great example of synchronicity. Swiss psychologist Carl Jung is the father of synchronicity (meaningful coincidence). We have all had moments when a phone call comes at just the right time, or a symbol lands in front of us during a pivotal moment of a conversation. This is one of the more obvious ways the Spirit communicates with us. Synchronicity can't really be practiced on demand. Divine timing happens on its own schedule. But we can learn to interpret moments of synchronicity. Learning to see symbolically goes a long way towards interpreting synchronous moments. In the now-famous example of the scarab beetle, Carl Jung was treating a woman who was describing a dream in which she was given a golden scarab (beetle). At that moment, a real live beetle made a noise on the window directly outside Dr. Jung's office. The beetle is a symbol of rebirth and symbolized the transformation the woman would need to undertake to complete her therapy. When synchronous moments occur, it would be a good idea to Google the symbolism behind the event as a means to understanding God's communication with us.

Exploring Feelings

God speaks to us through our feelings. When we feel something strongly, it can be described as a "knowing." A feeling "rings true" to us. This is sometimes referred to as intuition. Often the problem is that we tend to think our way out of trusting this knowing. Building confidence in our feelings is tricky for some and second nature to others. We learn to trust in our intuition through experience, letting it guide us through life's obstacles. Telling your child to trust in their feelings is the first stepg. Emily had an experience with her daughter where she couldn't decide which of an object to buy. She thought about the price of each quite a bit. Finally, Emily told her to close her eyes and "ask her heart" which was the best choice. Have your student "ask their heart" and not their head when important decisions are to be reached. Have the child write down their feelings into a journal. Have them underline thoughts and circle feelings. Learning to distinguish thoughts from feelings will help the child get in touch with messages from God.

Free-flowing ideas and expression

Invite your child to draw or write his or her own impression of his or her conversation with God. Some children, while verbally able to describe the interaction at this age, will enjoy and derive benefit by incorporating creativity into this exercise. Discuss that opening your mind and inviting inspiration in is a type of conversation with God! Explore and ask about how it feels to make a beautiful drawing or write a nice poem. Give your child license to describe feelings and support this expression.

Acceptance

Express to your child that acceptance of themselves, exactly the way they are, is the gift of being human. In *CwG* it says, "If you saw yourself the way God sees you, you would never have a bad feeling about yourself ever again." Accepting yourself as a perfect being, who was created in the eyes of God and the essence of the universe, is an important part of communicating (talking) with God.

Chapter Three

THERE'S ENOUGH

Few things affect a child with more impact than the thought that *something is going to "run out."*

If a child is having a good time, she will hate it when "time runs out" and it's "time to go to bed."

If a child is enjoying a piece of chocolate cake or a bowl of strawberry ice cream, you may see him eating it slowly to prolong the time before it "runs out."

And, of course, we all know that children cannot get "enough" of their parents' attention. (Or *anybody's* attention, for that matter!)

This having been said, parents should be told that nothing can be more empowering to a child than being taught, and coming to an interior knowing, that . . .

THERE'S ENOUGH.

The Law of Infinite Supply is one of the most joyous understandings that I have absorbed as an adult. Unfortunately, I didn't acquire this information until I was in my late 40s. By then I had spent countless moments over dozens of years worrying and fretting, agonizing, and *anxieting.* (That's a new word I just made upg. I like it.) I had been concerned over what seemed like in-the-moment or anticipated insufficiencies all my life.

It just didn't occur to me that God can't possibly "run out" of *any-thing*, since God is *The Creator of Everything* and The Source of All.

The only way that God could exhaust the supply of anything would be if God only made a finite quantity of something. Yet the word "finite" and "God" are oxymorons. They contradict each other. For God is The Infinite, and That Which Is Infinite is infinitely incapable of producing that which is finite. Therefore, all things in life are infinite—including life itself, which is everlasting and eternal.

The trick is to *know how to tap into* God's Infinity Supply—and also to understand the difference between *experiences* and *things*. God supplies experiences. We create "things" because we imagine them to be required in order for us to have certain experiences. This is not true, but we very much think that it is.

What all people truly want

Let us be clear. In the end, human beings don't care about "things." What human beings crave is experiences. This is true of all humans, but it is especially "present" and at the forefront in the desires of children.

As noted, physical objects are merely tools with which to create experiences.

The highest and grandest experience we can have is the experience of God. Or, if you please, of what we would call "divinity."

Children wouldn't frame it this way, as a rule, but they know intuitively that what they want to experience is their most magnificent Self.

It is, of course, this experience for which we all yearn. And, in fact, it is this experience for which life itself was created. Children simply have not forgotten this. Most adults have.

God created what we know as physical life as a means by which God could experience Itself in all its wonder and glory.

There are two ways that a human being can realize (that is, make real) this experience. One way is through *impression*; another is through *expression*.

The first is created by incoming energy, the second by outgoing energy.

What we are talking about here is love

An immutably beautiful sunrise offers us a wonderful example. There is probably no one who has not experienced at least one beautiful sunrise in her or his life. In that moment we are awestruck with the wonder and the glory of the universe; of Divinity Itself; of "God" flowing through us.

There is also probably no one who has not experienced at least once during a lifetime a "sunrise of the heart." This is a moment when all the warmth, all the beauty, all the glory that we are *by nature* rises from deep within, to be expressed through us, as us, towards some other person, place, or thing.

We have found a word for all of this. It is called Love. And yes, we can even contextualize this as a *thing*. The sun, and its rising, becomes a thing we call "love." And so, standing in the presence of that awesome sunrise, we send out innermost love, our innermost essence, right back out to the sun! We might even sing out, "Sun! I love you!"

In that moment we can even be awestruck by our own wonder and glory. We all know how expansively good it feels to not only receive life's most glorious incoming energy, but also to be the source of life's most glorious *outgoing* energy—both energies expressed and experienced at once! Here, then, is an experience of Divinity. Both the glorious sunrise, and our joyful response *to* it.

The first is an *im*pression, and the second an *ex*pression.

This is the experience which we all crave. We crave it because it is the experience of our very Self—and we know it. We know ourselves to be nothing more than a physicalization of Love. And we know that love is the grandest experience of the Self of which we are capable of receiving and sending. And when we receive and send it *at the same time*, the Circle of Life is complete. We have known God.

We call this making love.

Making love has to do with far, far more than sex. In fact, human sexual activity is the least of it. We are talking here about S.E.X.—Synergistic Energy eXchange. This is when two elements of life exchange the Essential Essence of which all life is composed.

That essence is called God. In my world, that essence is called God. So we might say that Synergistic Energy eXchange is when two elements of life exchange Godliness—of which all life is composed.

This is the part of life, the aspect of existence, that can never run out. This is not an object; this is not a physical *thing*. This is the circle of expression-impression-expression that is life itself, fully realized.

And out of this circulating energy, virtually anything can be created, for it creates *life itself* as we know ourselves in physical form, and so many of the other physical forms that surround us in the life that we live.

The magic of more

When I was a child, I was walking through Mitchell Part in Milwaukee, Wisconsin with my older brother and my father one day, enjoying some cotton candy that Dad had gotten for us.

I dropped mine, and I started to cry. I knew that I couldn't eat anymore because it picked up grit and dirt and stones from the pathway. So I wept at my loss. But my father healed my sadness on the spot. "No reason to cry," he said. "There's more where that came from."

He then turned around, took me by the hand, and led me back to the stand where the cotton candy was being sold. I had another one in my hands within minutes. This demonstration told me more about life and all of the little "sermons" or "lessons" that I might have been subjected to had my father not been so clear about what he wanted to teach me.

My dad sent me this same message over and over again throughout my childhood. The result is that when I became an adult, I carried that notion with me as an idea about "how life is." From that time on, and right up until this present day, I have moved through my days actually *expecting* that there'll be "more where that came from."

And do you know what? *There always has been.*

I have been put in touch with the law of infinite supply, and that law has never failed me from that moment on. Even during the time that I was living as a street person in a homeless park (most of you who know my story are aware that I was homeless for an entire year of my life), I had everything I needed to survive. The proof, of course, is that I'm still here.

The question during those times was not whether I was going to survive, but how I would experience my survival. Would it be an experience of joyfulness or joylessness? Everything depended, of course, on how I looked at my condition and circumstance. And we will talk more about that later in this book as we continue to focus on parenting according to the messages of *Conversations with God.*

For now I want to impress on you the incredible "magic of more." I want to suggest that you do whatever you can as you move through daily life with your children to help them to understand the nature of sufficiency through the *experiencing* of it.

A wonderful way to show this

One of the most wonderful ways we can show our offspring that there is more than enough of everything we need to be happy is by sharing with others in the presence of our children.

Let them see you tithing at church. Let them see you sharing the money that you are carrying around in your pocket with the street people that you both will pass from time to time. Let them watch you give things away, sharing all that is yours free with all those whose lives you touch.

Teach them, as well, to share with others. Teach them to share with their siblings and with their friends, with their schoolmates, and yes, even with strangers.

If you give your children an allowance, or some spending money from time to time, give them an opportunity to share a little bit of it with others. Maybe at Christmas time by dropping a few coins in the Salvation Army kettles at the corner. Or by putting a dime or two into the collection boxes we occasionally see in the checkout line at supermarkets that collect money to provide food for the hungry.

Many parents teach their children how to save, but some parents fail to teach their children how to share their money with others. My father taught me how to save, and got me into the habit of doing so, but he never got me into the habit of giving a portion of my money away.

That would've been a good thing to learn. I formed the habit on my own, much later in life than I probably would have, had I learned from my father.

I learned it when I was living on the street and realized that the only way that I was surviving was through the generosity of others. This was a powerful, *powerful* teaching. It's one of many wonderful things that I learned during the time that I was homeless.

I have since come to experience that the more I give away, the more I receive. It turns out that it is true that "what goes around comes around." I now understand the deeper wisdom in the admonition to "do unto others as you would have them do unto you."

So that your children see you giving your money away freely, let them see you giving your time to worthy causes as well. Let them see you giving your love, openly and freely, to all those lives you touch. Let them see you sharing, sharing, *sharing* everything that is yours. In this they will learn that you are clearly not afraid of ever "running out." They will see that you do not hold any thought that there is "not enough."

Of anything.

This will be a grand teaching, indeed.

The biggest lesson of all

God has told us to rely on God as the source of everything that we wish to experience in our lifetime. Not everything we wish to *have*. Everything we wish to *experience*. I have already made the point here that the two are not the same.

The sharing of all that is ours to share is merely a means of experiencing the truth of who we are. We are love, personified. We are divinity, expressed. We are sufficiency, experienced.

Nothing creates experience more than experience itself. Life is a process that informs life about life through the process of life itself.

The things that we do in life are avenues through which we experience the many and endless aspects of divinity. And this is the biggest lesson of all that we could teach our children. The things that we *have* in life are among the outcomes of that experience, but not the reason for it. When they become the reason for it, we have lost our way.

For example, when the reason that we work hard, and maybe even work overtime, is so that we can have that new car we've been dreaming of, or that new computer we've been eyeing, or any other version of

Bigger-Better-More, we've missed the whole point of what we are doing in the world.

The point of what we are doing in the world is to express and to experience our true identity as an aspect of the Divine. In this case, the personification and the epitome of sufficiency. The purpose of what we call "work" is not to "earn a living," but to demonstrate that we have a sufficient amount of our gifts to give them away, offering them to others who need them. We know we are in "right livelihood" when we are enjoying what we are doing so much that we would do it for free, and when the fact that someone is paying us feels like icing on the cake—more good than life could reasonably be expected to be offering us.

When we choose to make a life, rather than a living, we demonstrate that in giving to the world abundantly of the gifts that we have to share, we receive abundantly the gifts that life has to offer.

The trick is to know that we can do this even if we find ourselves in a job we don't like. The person who is spiritually attuned to life can "like" any job, because it is not what that person is doing that provides his soul with the experience for which it yearns, but what that person is *being*, no matter what the person is doing.

The basis of "enoughness"

We will never experience that there's enough of anything so long as we imagine that we are separate from one another. Only when we fully embrace the notion of our oneness will we be clear that there's enough for everyone.

The example that I like to use when illustrating this understanding is the story of the holiday dinner guest.

The host and hostess have prepared dinner for a certain number of people who have been invited; but then, moments before dinner is to be served, the doorbell rings, and a long-lost relative who has just returned to town and has heard about the gathering asks if he might come in.

Of course he is welcomed with open arms; and even though just moments before, the party's host was a bit worried that there might not be enough to go around, the newly arrived family member is invited to join in the festivities.

Suddenly there is no question as to whether there's enough to go around. Those at the table make *sure* that there's enough by dividing the food in such a way that everyone has a good and fair portion.

This is the way it would be on the entire planet if we considered every member of our species to be a member of our family. And this is the biggest lesson we can teach our children: that all human beings are members of our family—the Only Family There Is.

God's family.

We are all a part of God and God is a part of all of us. There is really only one of us. Each of us is a part of the body of God. When we understand this and apply this as functioning truth in our daily lives, we will find that by simply dividing the abundance that this planet provides, there will be more than enough for everyone.

It comes down to this simple formula: when we have enough love for everyone, we will have enough of what is required to survive for everyone. And, indeed, enough for everyone to live peacefully and happily together. This is not an unattainable goal. This is an achievable outcome.

All we have to do is wish to create it. And what we teach our children about this will determine whether our future as a species includes that experience.

Now here, from Laurie and Emily, are some strategies and ideas about how we might get some of these ideas across to the young ones who fill our home. The concept, again, is . . .

THERE'S ENOUGH.

The objective of the following teaching approach is to introduce the above concept to children by helping them to embrace their Oneness with all of life, starting with understanding how people and things are connected.

Lesson 1

IN TEACHING CHILDREN THIS CONCEPT, YOU MAY WISH TO BEGIN BY . . .

. . . remembering that this topic is difficult to understand and even more difficult to apply in real life. Indeed, even very spiritual people have difficulty with applying this concept as it is so contrary to the way our society functions and motivates. As such we want you to keep in mind that with very young children we are not necessarily trying to have them fully understand the whole concept. Instead, we are merely trying to lay groundwork for later understanding. We think it is very important to start children off thinking in terms of internal completeness so that they will learn to look inside instead of out for their identity. We begin with minute, concrete ideas and items to aid in laying this groundwork. We can begin to see older children making connections between literal and abstract interpretation of ideas so this lesson incorporates some more abstract ideas along with the concrete examples to aid in laying this groundwork; and while they may not fully grasp everything you are sharing with them, they will still benefit from the conversation.

Lesson 2

ONE OF THE MOST BENEFICIAL AND LOVING IDEAS WE CAN TEACH OUR CHILDREN ABOUT THE WORLD IS . . .

. . . that "There's enough." In a society which focuses on competition, winning and acquiring things, children would be well served to learn that while these things might be fun and even (at times) desirable, they are not necessary. Children can learn to "fill themselves up" with spirituality and experience their internal connection to God instead of looking to the external. External things such as other people's approval, material objects, and activities, when kept in perspective, can have a positive place in our lives, but they do not make up Who We Really Are. The concept "There's Enough" means that we don't have to *experience fear* of scarcity. When we look inside to find the unconditional love and acceptance of ourselves, for ourselves, we will not need external things or validation to be complete.

God is All and All is God. Since each of us are God we cannot truly experience a lack of what we need or want . . . except if we choose to experience that part (the experience of lacking) of who we Are. Helping children learn to distinguish between internal connection to God (which gives them everything they need) and the external motivations (for which society has taught us to strive) will enable them to remember that who they really are is perfect—perfectly connected to God, perfectly complete, perfectly whole—and that only by forgetting this true nature of themselves can they experience a life of less than perfect abundance.

As you can see, we have varied the complexity of information for application across all ages. That is because we feel families can re-explore the materials as their children grow, enabling them to gain more understanding of abundance, sharing, personal power and love as they grow. This concept can be very difficult for adults to understand so we know that children may have trouble with it. Our hope is that through these strategies you will be able to open your child's mind to begin to embrace the concept that as spiritual beings in human bodies who are infinitely connected to the Source, we have access to everything that we can ever need or want. While these initial ideas may be difficult to understand, starting children with those words in their minds can help to overcome the human tendency to feel (and fear) scarcity.

Lesson 3

WHY IS "THERE'S ENOUGH" HARD TO SEE IN OUR WORLD?

One of the hard realities to reconcile with the concept "There's Enough" is that spiritual people say there's enough; yet we know there are people starving, people are struggling financially, and otherwise experiencing stressful times. Scarcity only exists as we (collectively) allow it to persist. We have the tools to end scarcity and end suffering. We just haven't done it yet. (*CwG, Book 1*, pg. 49-52). There's enough for all. By teaching children to share, to only take what they can use, and to pool resources—we can help them to finally end poverty, hunger, etc.

Another aspect of this discussion is that we would be well-served, for ourselves and our children, to not experience any judgment from or towards ourselves regarding this discussion and also to avoid feeling guilt. It is natural for children and adults to like fine things . . . the goal is not to define (de-fine!) ourselves by those things. To feel guilt or judgment about this natural state is to deny Who We Really Are. Having things, people's approval, money, etc. can be positive experiences and expressions of ourselves as long as we keep them in perspective and only use them in love. *CwG, Book 2* explains that there is nothing "wrong" (by our own construct of wrong—God doesn't have opinions of right and wrong) with wanting money, power or even fame as long as we do not use the money, power or fame to cause others harm.

As long as we are only allowing those "things" to be EXPRESSIONS of who we are, not allowing them to DEFINE us, and not using them to put down or harm others, but instead using them to HELP those around us, we have not done anything "wrong" (again our own construct). (*CwG, Book 2*, pg. 74-77).

Lesson 4

A FRAMEWORK FOR UNDERSTANDING CONSISTS OF THREE PARTS . . .

. . . We begin with the concrete, seeable, physical aspects of "There's Enough," then take your child through the more abstract ideas of love and connection, and then try to tie them together to show that when you allow yourself to feel the completeness of oneness with God, you will not experience scarcity. Since the discussion is divided into three sections (concrete/physical, spiritual, and putting them together) we highly recommend that you, the parent, read through the rest of the chapter prior to approaching it with your child. Then we suggest that you do at least one activity from each section with your child so that he or she can begin to see the whole picture. We hope that you will revisit this topic often over the child-rearing years so that you can continue to reinforce and build understanding.

Remember, these are only suggestions, so be creative! You know your child best, so follow your intuition if additional material/physical and spiritual examples come to mind. We hope that you will use our examples for opening the conversation and also as fodder for your own imagination to design specific examples that apply to your life.

Lesson 5

SOME QUESTIONS TO GET YOUR CHILD THINKING ABOUT THE TOPIC ARE . . .

How much food do you *need* to nourish your body? What tells you your stomach is full? How many toys do you need to have to be happy? What is happy (fulfilled is probably too big of a word for this group, but this is the type of "happy" of which we speak)?

How much love do your parents feel for you? How much do you love your parents (or caregivers, grandparents, etc.)? What makes you special? If there are siblings, do you know that each child is equally special and loved?

What can you do to feel your connection to God? What is your favorite part of you?

What things are necessary to lead a happy life?

* Children may say things such as food, toys, school, clothes, good grades, water, shelter and people are required to live. The point, at this time, is to just help them begin thinking about needs and for older kids to start assessing the difference between needs vs. wants.

* Give your child concrete examples of times that you feel happy and "filled upg." For instance: When I meditate and experience my connection to God, I feel I can do and be anything!

* Discuss family moments of bonding which have helped you feel closer to God.

Lesson 6

CONCRETE AND PHYSICAL EXAMPLES TO EXHIBIT "THERE'S ENOUGH" IN YOUR HOME . . .

On Food

Eating consciously

Discuss actual food needs versus food desires. Consult the information and guidelines for food consumption here: http://www.mypyramid.gov/ and here: *http://www.letsmove.gov/eat-healthy*. Speak with your child about listening to your body's cues about fullness as a beginning to eating only what is needed and not just mindlessly finishing what is in front of you.

Animal vs. Human eating behavior

Discuss how animals find and store their food. Even the animals that store food for future use do not stockpile multiple years' worth of food or an overabundance of food that they cannot reasonably eat. Animals, instinctively, store what they need for one winter and place no value judgment (obviously, right?) on how much they stored. It is all about ensuring survival through the harsh months where food availability is limited. Compare this to human storage and consumption. Humans eat more than we need; and as a result, we are, as a species, unhealthy. We place value judgments on the sizes of our pantries, our stockpiles of food—this may not be overt or even overly conscious; however, we do not buy the amount of food we *need* for a day or even a week. We purchase large freezers to stockpile food, we buy in bulk, and we waste and throw away tons of uneaten food daily. Then in other parts of the world, or even within our own neighborhoods, others are starving. We have made distribution of food a wealth-based activity instead of need-based. If we purchased and consumed only what was actually needed to nourish and fuel our bodies, there would be enough food to feed everyone. But instead, we hoard it, we CREATE scarcity for others, we judge our own worth on how much we have of it, and then we jeopardize our own health by consuming too much of it.

Create

One way to create "enough" in your own life is to "create" healthful, nutritious food. Help your child plant a garden of herbs, fruits or veggies and then enjoy eating the fruits of your labor as a family! This will help your child see that there is always a way to create abundance, giving them the power to understand themselves as Creator.

On Material Things

Consumerism

It seems our children are receiving marketing information earlier and earlier in their lives (some might even argue from within the womb!?). Oftentimes it seems that before we even get home and get a new item, toy, or video game out of the package, there is a commercial for the "newer and better" version. The "newer and better" version phenomenon has worked against us in that, if we listen to the advertising messages, the one we have isn't good enough and we need more, more, more! The problem is, by the time you get home and get that newer item out and going, there could be a "newer-er and better-er" one out already!

* This obsession with consumerism is causing our children to be in a constant state of reaching for more, thereby experiencing a feeling of lacking or that there is NOT enough. In order to break this cycle we need to stop reaching for more and become content with what we have.

* Of course, we can try to limit our children's exposure to media and advertising, but it is unrealistic that we can shelter them from all of the messages. What would be more effective is to teach your child to not internalize the message that their toy isn't enough; to discuss that the new toy is only different in XYZ ways, and to encourage your child to use her own imagination to use the toy she has to its fullest.

Assess—Using our things consciously

Most modern families have more "stuff" and "things" than we can reasonably use. Our houses are filled with unused toys. In many families, based on our own experience, we would guess there are a few favored toys which get most of the play time, then some peripheral toys which get some play time, and then there are others which collect dust. Going back to questions you asked your child in the introduction, discuss the number of toys your child thinks are necessary to be happy. Talk about how many toys he has. Ask your child how many of his toys he actually uses on a daily basis and make a list (or pile) of a few (3-4?) toys which he never uses.

Share or Toy Swap

Many extended families have multiple children near the same age, and many neighborhoods have multiple families with children around the same age. Think about how many toys your child has that other children in your life also have. One thing we can do to encourage children to make conscious decisions about their belongings is to form a toy "co-op" with some trusted family members or friends. When we share our toys and others share with us, we have access to more toys than we could ever have on our own. If your child has toys A, B and C and another child has toys D, E and F, each child can benefit from the enjoyment of more toys (all six of the different toys A-F) through sharing and swapping. In this way, they learn that through sharing we get more, or in other words, "There's Enough."

Contemplate making a Donation

There are places such as children's hospitals and group homes which supply care to many children on temporary bases. These institutions operate on skeleton budgets and have high needs for things with which their residents/patients can play. Check with your local facilities to see if they accept donations of gently used toys and discuss the possibility of donating a couple of toys to such facilities. This will help your child learn that we can all impact scarcity and help another child experience "There's Enough."

Pooling Resources

Help create "more" for your family and others by pooling resources. Many of us have wasted food we discard every day, and many people, for various reasons, do not like to eat reheated leftover food. A way to eliminate this waste and conserve resources is to share meals with family or friends. If you usually make a big pot of chili for a family of four and know 2-3 bowls' worth will likely go to waste, invite friends over for that meal and enjoy great company while eating all of the prepared food. Sitting down to meals together builds community, and taking turns preparing meals to share will end up saving money (due to the non-wasted food since most people cook a set amount each meal whether it will be eaten or not). Spending less wasted money is a way to create financial abundance; building community is a way to create emotional abundance.

* Pooling resources can also go further than the sharing of toys discussed above. Older kids can actually organize to purchase their toys together and take turns using them. This could be especially helpful with things that are expensive and become outdated rapidly, especially if they are things that kids typically like to play together (e.g., video game systems, expensive sporting equipment, etc.). Many of us overextend ourselves and live closely to (or above) our means. In our society, there is a tendency to measure our identities by the type, year and model of car we drive (or other belongings); yet, while we complain loudly about the price of gas, we continue to purchase inefficient vehicles that use excessive amounts of gas.

* Environmentally, our dependence on oil is detrimental; politically, it is the cause of much unrest and fighting across the globe. One way to cut costs, preserve financial and environmental resources, and demonstrate to our children that "There's Enough" is to carpool, use public transportation, and ride share. In addition to saving resources, these activities can help your children build a sense of responsibility, build a feeling of community with others, and learn to feel more gratitude for what they have. Whichever of these three (or other)

ways of sharing your "things" with others your family chooses, it is a great lesson for your child to learn that sharing is deeper than just being polite—it is about creating abundance . . . for yourself and for another.

Solve Waste: Reduce—Reuse—Recycle

Waste is a hard concept for young children to graspg. We live in a society in which grocery shelves are always full. They see packaging on their toys which is 3-4 times more material than the toy itself. They see us throw away unused foods, computers, paper, clothes and other objects long before their useful lives have been exhausted.

At the same time that we live in fear of scarcity, we seem to be in denial (or arrogant defiance) of that fear as we waste the resources that are available to us. Our dependence on gas and electricity is enormous, yet our removal from their production can serve to have us forget that these are finite resources that are very expensive (and sometimes dangerous) to produce. Teaching our children about conscious living can lead them to be more respectful of resources and less likely to waste resources. Using fewer resources is a way to ensure abundance for all. With this new conceptualization and understanding, using fewer resources will not cause a feeling of deprivation. Instead it will instill a feeling of power as your child realizes that he can make a difference in the creation of abundance or the widespread understanding that "There's Enough."

* One way you can instill the desire to minimize waste is to start using the three R's in your own home and making it a part of your child's awareness and daily life. Explain to your child the process of making a specific type of good he uses, for example paper. Then discuss ways he can save paper. Draw on both sides of the paper, turn drawings into wall hangings, paper airplanes, or wrapping paper for an upcoming birthday party.

✳ Search the Internet or the library for information about environmental awareness. Great keywords to start with are "Reduce Reuse Recycle," which yielded this site: *http://kids.niehs.nih.gov/recycle.htm* for some hints and tips.

On competition, winning, and fairness

Modern society places premium value on winning and out-competing others. In nature, competition is about getting what is needed for survival. It is not so in society. While competition is fun when it revolves around a soccer game, an ice skating competition or a rousing game of chess, these same activities might help to produce overly-competitive adults. Even spiritually-conscious adults can fall into traps of comparing: Is your house bigger than mine? Do you seem more well-liked than I am? Is your car newer? Is your spiritual path more rewarding?

✳ Parents wish the "best" for their children, which sometimes manifests in pushing them to rise to the top, to be noticed, and to achieve great "things;" but we might want to be careful in how we relay this message as it can distort the understanding of true success and happiness by confusing "more" with always wanting or, in the negative, lacking something we perceive we do not have.

✳ Children who live in these environments where comparisons are taken to the level of judgment and status can begin to think that the acquiring of things and status is the goal in life. Speak with your child about these topics.

✳ Encourage them to love themselves and the playing of a soccer game, the experience of skating, and the puzzle of moving a chess piece. Try to deemphasize the competitive outcome and encourage them to feel great for trying! Emphasize gratitude and excitement at their own accomplishments, not in the lens of being OVER or BETTER than someone else, but in improving themselves and enjoying the ride. Also look to your own life and find where your own actions and words are encouraging competitiveness. Remind yourself to be grateful, excited, and content with where you are; not in relation to others, but in relation to Who You Really Are, where you have been, and Where You Want to Be!

"It's not fair!"

Anecdotal story from Laurie: A child sees another child with five action figures in his hand, while he only has four. He begins fretting that he doesn't have enough because he should have at least as many as the other child. He asks his mother to get him more. He throws a tantrum because she will not. He wails at the sky, *"It's not fair!* I should have five like him!" The mom calmly explains that "not fair" is really a very strong reaction to only having four action figure toys. "Not fair" is not having enough food, "not fair" is dealing with illness or loss of your parents, "not fair" is being homeless. "Not fair" is a very strong phrase that is reserved for much bigger things than the number of action figures you have. She then asks her child if he still thinks the action figure dilemma, while disappointing, actually rises to the level of "not fair." Laurie says that boy never used the words "not fair" again.

Lesson 7

ABSTRACT/SPIRITUAL EXAMPLES TO EXHIBIT "THERE'S ENOUGH" IN YOUR HOME . . .

Exploring "There's Enough" in the spiritual

Choosing experiences

In *The Little Soul and the Sun: A Children's Parable*, a soul living in the perfection of heaven makes a choice to leave paradise and become human to have a new experience—the art of being forgiving. The soul must leave heaven because there is nothing imperfect in heaven that one needs to forgive. In order to assist the first soul in achieving her goal of being forgiving, another soul volunteers to come to Earth as a human as well to do something to the first soul that could be forgiven. This perfect relationship, agreed to in heaven, probably causes each soul (in their human states) distress and pain once entered into on Earth. But neither soul would be harmed in the long run because the goal was to experience their agreement (one to do something that needs forgiving, and the other to forgive).

In this same way, we can choose to see our lives as things happening to us, or things that arise out of our choices. Once we see our lives as having arisen out of our choices, we can begin to feel the Creator within us that allows us to produce the life we want. By choosing abundance, we do not necessarily choose to have the most money, the most things, the biggest houses . . . abundance is more a fundamental choice that says we will be satisfied, contented, and FULFILLED with what we have. No matter how much we have, we can choose to feel the experience of having enough when we go inside ourselves to the place where God dwells.

※ Discuss with your child Who She (or He) Really is Today. A young child is probably not going to be able to articulate his reason for coming to Earth, but she will be able to tell you who she is TODAY. This is a great start, a great inquiry and internal conversation to have throughout her life. Who Am I? What Am I Doing? What (or who) do I want to be today? Are my actions and thoughts in line with the ME inside?

Other people's approval

As children enter the school-aged years, they begin being exposed to an almost constant assessment. Even in kindergarten, children are subjected to testing, comparison, and being pushed to "succeed" or "exceed." Labels are used by the school systems early on in an attempt to assist students in succeeding, but even if the labels are not intended to be negative, they can sometimes be internalized as such. It is very easy for us, as humans, to begin to define ourselves by the ways in which others assess and judge us.

Our children soon learn that they need to meet certain expectations and criteria to be accepted. The emphasis on achievement leaves little room for personal expression and creativity.

We can assist our children in minimizing the effect of those labels, grades, and assessments by discussing them with our children. We can explain that these things do not define us and Who We Really Are inside. We can help our children to understand that when we look inward to find God's light and love, we will cease to allow outside categories to define us. We can also, as parents, deemphasize the importance of grades and early achievement, taking the focus off the outcomes and placing it more on the process. For example, speak with your child about the enjoyment he gets out of writing his name, not the outcome of if he writes it perfectly.

Discuss the joy of the LEARNING to read, not the final outcome of READING. Emphasize strengths that may accompany labels (or diagnoses) instead of the limitations. If a child has attention "problems," speak with the child about the strengths of having that attribute; for instance, thinking outside the box, creativity, being able to enjoy things on a different level than others. Giving your child a way to like things about themselves will help them to not define them by the things with which they struggle. When a child takes an emotional "hit" from a "poor" review or a "bad" grade, remind them that they are not their grades or reviews. They are the light and love of God, and they are special. No grade or review can take that away.

Love is Infinite

Another type of abundance is the feeling of love for and from the people around you. The best example of the infinite amount of love available is a parent's love. When a parent has one child, he or she may think, *I have never loved another being the way I love this child, and I could never love this deeply again!* However, as soon as a parent has additional children, he or she soon finds that the parental love has multiplied—the parent loves each child equally (even if differently), and no additional child detracts from how much the parent loves the first. This is the clearest instance, on Earth, of there being enough.

Likewise, there's enough of God's spirituality and love for all to experience on an infinite level.

Meditation

Practice relaxation and guided meditations with your child.

* *CwG, Book 1* shares that the laws of the universe show that inward reflection is the answer to all of your needs, wants, and desires. (*CwG, Book 1*, pg. 43.) Most of abundance comes from within: "If I do not go within, I *go without*. You have been going without all your life. Yet you do not have to, and never did. There is nothing you cannot be, there is nothing you cannot do. There is nothing you cannot have . . . [B]elief in God produces belief in God's greatest gift—unconditional love—and God's greatest promise—unlimited potential." (pg. 44). Using meditation to find that internal unconditional love is a wonderful way to tap into your potential as well.

* Do yoga together. This provides physical and mental stimulation, at the same time that it can allow them to more fully understand and maintain meditation. It helps children to feel true appreciation and security, which will help the child experience the abundance of life and the fact that they have everything they need . . . right inside themselves.

Lesson 8

PUTTING THE CONCRETE (PHYSICAL) AND ABSTRACT (SPIRITUAL) TOGETHER FOR DEEPER UNDERSTANDING . . .

. . . will help show that there is no reason to fear. The reason we fear there is not enough is because we, as humans, hoard and exceed in our wants and needs, causing another to go without. If a child understands that they have no need to have more than they actually need and share what they do have, God will always provide. It is even more amazing for a child to understand that, as each of us IS the light of God, we each have the power to manifest abundance for ourselves.

Expectations

Teaching children less is more is a wonderful tool for helping your family experience abundance and not scarcity. Laurie believes, *To teach our children there's enough, don't give them more, but rather give them less so they can be happy with and expect less . . . thereby having more appreciation for what they have.*

Gratitude leads to respect and responsibility

Help your child to express gratitude for life, for health, for Who he or she Really is, etc. Make an *I am thankful* list. *Conversations with God* teaches that living a life with great gratitude helps us to get along better in the world. It helps us to look within to feel complete, instead of always looking out.

Who You Really Are!

Encourage your child to think about this daily. This can be inside the meditations discussed above or at other times. The part of Who You (or your child) Really Are that applies in this lesson is the manifestation of God within. That is the part that can experience abundance—physically, emotionally, materially, and spiritually. That part of Who You Really Are (the manifestation of God within) is also the part of you that can allow you to feel you have enough, even when you don't have as much as you'd like. It is the part of you that will not allow your "being" to be defined by what you do or do not own, but by your connection to God. It is also the part that can learn from feedback you get from others at school or work, but it does not define your soul. Your soul remains untouched by the outside world, as long as you remember that your soul IS GOD so it can be nothing less than perfect.

An amazing gift!

Once we have embraced this part of ourselves fully, once we understand that there is nothing we need that we cannot achieve, once we internalize the idea that we are a soul living in a human body within a human, fallible experience, then we can begin to experience the fullness of God within and the creative power that entails as being "Enough."

Coming home

Being at home inside our soul diminishes our dependence on outside things. We may choose to live more simply, choose to eat more consciously, share, not compete, and help others instead of hoarding. On the other hand, we may still choose all of those same things. We may just choose them for other reasons—we will be less likely to choose them out of desperation to define ourselves and more as means to the end of comfort and enjoyment.

Drawing on the Creator within

Older children can begin to see themselves as Creator and begin to understand themselves as part of the collective and a member of the larger human family. This can help the child to feel the fullness inside, and also feel more desire to care for the earth and other members of her "Earth family." This melding of the physical and spiritual can lead a child to desire a more centered life, using and taking less and sharing more.

Going Forward

With older children you can begin to ask deeper, more intense, and more difficult questions of your child. You can also explain things more abstractly than in the younger ages. We believe that each age level can delve deeper into the same material than the one before. We hope that you will encourage your child to see his or her place in the world from the perspective of "There's Enough." Through this perspective, you can teach your children that they each have the ability to eradicate physical and spiritual scarcity.

We live in human bodies in a physical world and we often neglect our spirit. (*CwG, Book 2*, pg. 100). Abundance is something that can be experienced no matter how many physical things, friends, etc. (or lack thereof) we possess. Above, we talked about different physical things our society mistakenly looks to for fulfillment. Unfortunately, these physical things leave us hungry for more because while they can provide creature comforts, they do not fill the soul. In the spiritual section, we discussed ways in which children can explore their connection to God, the true, loving connection to others and the choices that brought them here (or Who They Really Are) so that they can understand themselves as complete and perfect. By putting the physical and spiritual together, we can feel our connection to God. In looking inward to find completeness and abundance, we are less likely to experience scarcity because we do not NEED those things to feel filled upg. By teaching our children to expect less, they actually experience more feelings of abundance because they do not experience a feeling of LACK-ing something.

It is very easy to unconsciously convey our own thoughts, fears, and reactions about scarcity to our children. Even when we are saying the "right" words to them about abundance, there being enough, and feeling your power and identity from within, if our own actions and reactions do not measure up, we can undermine our own words. Practicing the above suggestions as a family can help all members of the family to keep their material wants and insecurities in check with the concept of Who You Really Are. Finding and keeping your individual and family's collective, spiritual connection to God will assist you in teaching your child this very beautiful lesson. We all want the best for our children. We want them to experience as much joy and as little unneeded pain as possible on this Earth journey. We want them to have a positive place in, and a positive impact on, the world around them. Equipping your child with the inner strength and belief that *They Are Enough* is the best way to teach them *There's Enough!*

Chapter Four

THERE'S NOTHING YOU MUST DO

From the earliest days of their experience, many children feel that they have been surrounded by "stoppages"—what we would call "rules and regulations," "do's and don'ts," and "no-no's" at every turn.

So many, in fact, that after about 24 months of this, some children may enter into a rebellious stage during which they start imitating what they have heard from their parents.

Namely: *"No!"*

And so, many parents experience what are called the "Terrible Two's."

This does not happen with every child, but it happens enough to make it into a cultural myth. And it certainly is true that all parents feel the need to watch over their children and make sure that these beloved young ones don't get themselves into trouble. Or worse yet, cause themselves harm.

Now along comes *Conversations with God* with a startling message for the whole human race: There's nothing you have to do.

How do we teach such an idea to our children? Many parents don't even understand the concept themselves. *What does this mean?*, they ask. Are we to believe that nothing is required of us in this life?

If there is a God, are we to understand that this deity wants and needs nothing from us?

Only a brand new kind of spirituality could teach such a thing

How can it be possible that there's nothing we have to do, when all we have learned only too well all of our lives is that there are thousands of things we have to do? Nay, hundreds of thousands of things that we have to do!

There are commandments to follow, laws to follow, rules to follow, regulations to follow, and guidelines to follow! What kind of theology, what kind of spiritual teaching, brings us a message that tells us exactly the opposite?

Well, it would be a *New Spirituality* for sure. It would be a spirituality based on an understanding that God needs nothing, that Deity is sufficient unto Itself; and that since God is whole, complete, and perfect just the way It is, It requires and demands nothing at all from anything that It has created.

It would be a spirituality that understands, further, that the *reason* that God requires nothing from anything it has created is not only that God is whole, complete, and perfect, but also that God is *separate from nothing that it has created.* Therefore, for God to need or require anything from something it has created would mean that God would have to need or require something from Itself. Yet there is nothing that God *could* require from Itself or need from Itself, because there is nothing that God is not. God lacks nothing and is, by definition, the totality of everything.

We see, then, that there is nothing that we have to do in order to please God or meet some imagined requirement that God has presumably placed before us. God has done no such thing.

This is, it must be acknowledged, an advanced theological understanding. How, then, do we teach it to our children?

Use the words literally

A good place to begin may be to make certain that we have a deep understanding of the words themselves. What is actually being said when we announce the truth that "there is nothing you have to do"?

In considering the question we are advised to take the words quite literally. "There's nothing you have to do" means exactly that. There is nothing that you *have* to do.

That is, there is nothing you are required to do, nothing that it is demanded that you do. This does not mean that there is nothing that you *will* do, but simply that there is nothing that you are *commanded* to do.

All of us are doing something all of the time. Each of us have our reasons for doing what we do. Most of us do what we do in order to feel a certain way, in order to experience a particular aspect of ourselves. Most of the things we do, we do because we want to, not because we are required to. This is true of 95 percent of everything we think, say, and do all day.

The trick in understanding human behavior, then, is understanding what makes us want to do one thing rather than another; what makes us choose to do *this* rather than *that*.

This is the same process we are invited to engage with our offspring. We are invited to learn to understand what makes them want to do one thing rather than another, what makes them choose *this* rather than *that*. Then we are invited to use this understanding as a tool that joyfully motivates them to exhibit a particular behavior and to make a particular choice.

Our follow-up opportunity is to help them see that they're not making certain choices because they *have* to, but because they choose to.

As good parents, we place ourselves in the position of allowing our children to become clear that there is nothing they *must* do, but some things they may *choose* to do for reasons of their own.

Our job is to help our children understand that they are very much "at choice" in the matter of how any moment is experienced, how any hour of the day is encountered, and how any day itself proceeds.

And we best do this by laying out, far in advance of any choices having to be made, the full array of outcomes that are possible. This allows the child to become self-reliant and self-determining. But it is important to discuss all possible outcomes of their choices with children at a time when those choices are not confronting them directly—and to *engage them in the process* of helping you both devise and invent outcomes.

In other words, it is not wise to impose negative outcomes on children *after* they have made decisions or exhibited behaviors with which we disagree. If you do this, children will have the direct experience of an outcome having been *imposed upon them*, rather than an outcome *they helped to choose* having been brought upon themselves by their own decisions and behaviors.

So it is very wise to discuss with your children—at a time when they are calm and happy and just enjoying quietly being with you—the many outcomes and the varied results that can proceed from certain choices that they will find themselves in a position to make during a normal day. Then, *solicit their input and join together in agreeing on what outcomes should occur.*

What this looks like

Describe frequently arising situations in the home and in their lives. Then describe the outcomes that will quite naturally occur as a result of certain choices they are being allowed to make as they experience their own autonomy.

Of course, we will not use the word "autonomy" with our children. We will simply tell them that there is nothing that they must do, but that everything they *choose* to do produces an outcome. Let them know that, therefore, they may wish to make their choices carefully, because when they are making their choices, they are making their outcomes.

As noted already, invite them to discuss with you the various outcomes that could occur (place several options before the child)—and then choose together the option you can both agree on.

Again: the information about outcomes is far better received and more completely "processed" by the child prior to behaviors having been exhibited, rather than afterward.

Sweetly demonstrate control

One final note: when the results of a child's behavior are put into place by a parent, it is important not to do so from a place of upset or anger, if at all possible. Of course, all parents understand this, and I do not wish to be patronizing or seem to be "talking down" when I say this. I understand perfectly well that it is very often impossible to stay out of our negative emotions when children behave in particular ways— particularly if it is a repeated behavior.

Nevertheless, as parents continue to make a repeated effort to contain their emotions and demonstrate to their children that, as adults, they are in control of their feelings, they teach their children an extraordinarily valuable lesson that goes far beyond simple in-the-moment behavior modification.

All parents have come to understand that if children know you are emotionally discombobulated, they will use their behaviors as a device to create this outcome in the future—often as a means of getting your attention, and frequently as a means of showing that it is they who are in control, not you.

It is quite natural for children to want to do this. Their entire experience of life at this stage is about testing their boundaries, and seeing how much they can control. Indeed, you should *desire* that they demonstrate these proclivities, for it will serve your children well when they reach adulthood themselves and need to reach within themselves to find the ability to take control of a situation.

Yet when they are still children, the best way to teach them how to control their situation is to show them how *controlling their own behaviors,* rather than trying to manipulate the behavior of others, is what produces exactly that result.

Therefore, when putting outcomes that you know your child will consider to be undesirable into the space of your child's experience, it is very wise to do so in a soft and gentle way.

You may even want to let the child know that you feel sorry that the child has made that choice, but that the outcome was announced way in advance, and that what is now happening is not a *punishment*, but simply a *naturally occurring result.*

In this way, children will attach the experience of the outcome to their own behaviors, rather than to yours. They will see what is now occurring as the result of something they have done, rather than something you are doing.

To assist in this process, keep gently reminding the child that he or she is the one making the decisions, and that you are merely responding to them in the way that the child knows that you will—because you both have already *agreed upon the outcome in advance.*

But what if . . . ?

But what if your child demonstrated behaviors that far exceeds anything that either one of you have talked about in any previous discussion?

Well, that, too, should be talked about in advance. Say to your child quite directly, "And if something should happen that we haven't talked about here, I may have to decide in the very moment that this happens what the outcome will be. This is part of what mommies and daddies do, honey, and if that should ever happen, I will try to create an outcome that you and I can both agree is fair. But if we don't agree, I want you to know that as your parent, it's probably going to go my way. So it's important for you to know that. Are we clear?"

You will find that children feel more secure when they know that their parents are more secure in their authority; when they know that their parents have set boundaries and created a safe space within which they can be and experience themselves.

Again, the trick is to move through all of this—or as much as is humanly possible—with a quiet, gentle authority, always demonstrating that the expression of love is your highest priority.

Show your children that it is because you love them that you want them to be clear there is nothing that they *must* do, but only things that they may *choose* to do because they wish to control the outcomes that they experience in their lives. This is a marvelous teaching, and they will thank you for it until their final day on the Earth.

Let's now see what other tools we might share with you here about Concept #4 . . .

THERE'S NOTHING YOU MUST DO.

The objective of this strategy is to help children see that while there is nothing you *have* to do to please God, there are many things that we choose to do to make our lives enjoyable and run more smoothly. Using concrete examples, children are able to see that they really are in control of many of their own decisions, and they are also able to see the natural consequences which follow. Parents will also remember that in becoming a parent, we *chose* to take on a certain role. Some of the more obvious decisions inherent in that choice are an implicit agreement to feed, clothe, and give shelter to our children, and very few people doubt those vows; however, you can also include in your commitment that you will listen, be empathetic, communicate expectations clearly and freely, and allow your child to have the autonomy to remember Who They Really Are.

Lesson 1

IN TEACHING CHILDREN THIS CONCEPT, IT MAY BE HELPFUL TO REMEMBER THAT . . .

. . . much of living a *Conversations with God*-inspired life includes being fully present in the moment and making choices rather than blindly following rules. In the abstract, of course, this concept means there is nothing you have to do to "please" God or stay in God's "good graces"; but we find that it is beneficial to teach children first from the concrete formulation of everyday life. Many times words such as *should, have to, rules,* and *must* are replaced with words such as *highest goal, benefit,* and *best choice.* In these strategies children will learn that having a conversation with God means feeling connection to the All and living an ethical, positive life. It means having every action you make be an expression of Who You Really Are! You can help your child see that there are reasons for acting responsibly beyond fear of negative responses, begin being able to see the actual result of their actions, and be inspired to be more aware of their impact on those around them and the world at large.

> *Enlightenment is understanding that there is nowhere to go, nothing to do, and nobody you have to be except exactly who you're being right now. (CwG, Book 1, pg. 98.)*

Lesson 2

WHAT ARE "RULES" ANYWAY?

Our use of the word *rules,* in spite of its negative connotation, in this strategy is a device to help children understand things we strongly desire to keep them safe and explain expectations. Please feel free to substitute other words in your own conversations according to your understanding and comfort. Give your child concrete examples of "rules" by which you, yourself, live. For instance: I speak kindly to other people, or I wash the dishes immediately after we finish eating a meal. Use your own experiences to illustrate that while you don't *have* to do these things, you *choose* to do them in order to live a harmonious, respectful, clean life. Explain two or three of your expectations for your child in the same way. Include examples of emotionally non-threatening, easy to understand things. A possible example could be: We do not touch the stove because it may be hot, and the natural consequence of touching a hot stove is that we would hurt our hands. Explain there are many reasons that you might have made different types of rules, such as:

* Safety

* Taking care of our things

* Taking care of ourselves

* Treatment of others

* Having a peaceful environment

Lesson 3

LOOK AT YOUR PARENT-CHILD RELATIONSHIP AS A PARTNERSHIP BY ENGAGING IN A CONSTANT CONVERSATION WITH YOUR CHILD . . .

. . . to create a type of easy flow in your parenting. Through daily conversations, the parent-child relationship forms bonds that naturally create a partnershipg. All relationships have some sort of partnering, and every interaction has "give and take." The parent-child partnership can be the largest, most cooperative and most rewarding partnership as you see your child grow into the adult they are meant to be! When a parent approaches a child with the understanding that they are working together to build a beautiful, happy life, the child is empowered to treat the parent in a more loving and respectful way, without force or fear. Then instead of having to discipline actions, we are free to discuss our choices together and how they affect the family climate. We can show them that just as we are responsible to them for basic needs and emotional health, they are also responsible for our feelings, whether they know it or not. Being in a family means that we all affect each other and can choose for that to be positive or negative.

As parents we can sometimes forget that children are not mindless robots who should follow our direction. We all have things we want to get done, places to be, and people to see. It can be frustrating when your child doesn't cooperate or comply with requests. When we stop that *running around in circles* cycle for a moment and remember to view our children as individuals with ideas, wants, needs and opinions, it is much easier to understand why they sometimes resist the things we ask them to do. By teaching our children how to make positive choices about cleaning their rooms, treating others with kindness, etc., we teach them invaluable life skills of how to act in the world. By acting with humility in the face of your own mistakes, you show them how to behave with humility. By acting with love when they make mistakes, you show them how to love more fully. By showing them unconditional love, we show them the unconditional love God has for them; it reminds them that since "there is nothing you have to do" God will not judge you for getting "it" wrong.

Lesson 4

SOME QUESTIONS YOU CAN EXPLORE TOGETHER . . .

. . . which will help children to form ideas about themselves that can be used in making choices and determining behavior are:

* Do you know "Who You Really Are?" Decisions become much easier and less scary when the questions are tested against an internal knowing of yourself.

* Do you know why our family rules—keeping your room clean, not talking to strangers, calling if you will be later than expected (for older children)—have been put into place? Explore if there are any such rules that your child doesn't understand or agree are necessary. Make note of all of your child's responses for later.

* Discuss your child's place in the world. Ask your child to begin considering the ripple effect his or her actions have on the world/people around them.

Once you have explored the above questions, you can go even deeper into *why* we have guidelines and expectations:

* How do you feel when your room is clean? Can you find toys easier? Do you enjoy your toys more?

🌺 How do you feel when a parent asks you to do something? How do you feel when we ask you to stop doing something?

🌺 How does it feel when you say something nice to another person? How does it feel when you say something that's not-so-nice to another person? How does it feel when someone says something nice to you? How does it feel when someone says something not-so-nice to you?

🌺 How do you feel when you make a big accomplishment?

🌺 What is the difference between positive and negative? This will be explored later in terms of positive vs. negative expectations and outcomes. This question is to help you gauge whether (or how much) your child knows the difference between positive and negative in general.

🌺 What is something you know needs to be done but you don't like to do? Is schoolwork important? Why?

🌺 Do you know the definition of altruism?

Lesson 5

DEFINE, EXPLAIN, AND EXPLORE . . .

Altruism is defined as . . .

" . . . unselfish regard for or devotion to the welfare of others . . . " as defined at *http://www.merriam-webster.com/dictionary/altruism* (retrieved February 7, 2010). Discuss giving of yourself to others out of a sense of love (altruism) rather than in hopes of a reward. Children can begin understanding the difference and expanding their idea of "Who They Really Are" to include altruistic tendencies. Explain that it is not wrong or right to be giving (or not) to others, just another opportunity for people to express "Who They Really Are."

Positive vs. negative consequences

Discuss the difference between the consequences of your decisions. Use examples to show that positive action leads to positive consequences and negative action leads to negative consequences. A couple of examples to consider:

* When you say something nice to another person, they smile and that feels good (positive). When you say something that's not nice to another person, they cry and that feels yucky (negative).

* When you keep your toys picked up and put away, it is easier to find the one you want to play with later (positive). When you leave your toys out, they may get stepped on and broken, or you cannot find the ones you want when you want to play (negative).

* When you brush your teeth 2-3 times per day, you keep them healthy, clean and looking pretty (positive). If you did not brush your teeth daily, they would not look pretty; they might get cavities and become sick (negative).

* When you do your homework on time: you get positive feedback, you feel good about your accomplishment, you have more time to play, etc. (positive). When you do not get your homework done on time: you might feel stressed, you might feel sad, you have to spend more time to make it up, you do not get positive feedback, you may have to miss play time at school or home, you won't learn what it was intended to teach, etc. (negative).

Ask your child to describe his own example of a positive and negative outcome, or brainstorm together if he cannot come up with an idea on his own.

Help your child sort the categories above: safety, taking care of our things, taking care of ourselves, treatment of others, and having a peaceful environment into whether each one is intended to attain positive outcomes or to prevent negative outcomes. (i.e., safety is to prevent a negative outcome of an injury; having a peaceful environment is to attain a positive outcome of peace— although these could easily be interpreted in the opposite ways depending on how you look at each scenario).

Ask your child to broaden this inquiry to discuss how the categories fit into society at large. Together, discuss the ways in which the categories can actually blend together and be harder to distinguish. Ask your child how he will make decisions when the outcome is more murky or more gray instead of cut and dried. Brainstorm some questions your child can keep in the back of his mind to determine how the outcome will affect him or others. Encourage your child to consider his decisions carefully in order to attain his highest goal.

Explore positive and negative expectations

Using examples, explain the difference between an expectation you have for your child that is positive (a "please do") and an expectation that is negative (a "please don't do"). On a piece of paper, help your child make a list of some family expectations and sort them by "please do" and "please don't do."

The Reason Behind Expectations

Using the categories listed above (safety, taking care of our things, taking care of ourselves, treatment of others, and having a peaceful environment), help your child to decide the reason behind each of the listed expectations. This will help your child see that things you ask/expect of him or her are not arbitrary rules but actually have rational, reasonable goals. In turn, this will help your child to start being able to make choices based on desired outcomes (positive consequences), not fear of punishments (negative consequences).

Rules

Discuss any "rules" in your house that are inviolate or non-negotiable, such as: you do not get into cars with strangers, you do not run into the street, or you do not walk out of the house without telling a parent. *Conversations with God* discusses the negative effects of fear at length, so the goal here is to discuss the very important reasons for these rules without instilling fear. For instance, instead of saying, "You don't get into cars with strangers because the stranger might want to hurt you," explain it more lovingly—"You don't get into cars with strangers because you will be safer if you only get into cars with people you know and who have permission from your mom and dad." It may seem like a small, even trivial, distinction to you, as an adult. But to teach your child to choose safety is much more useful and non-threatening than to teach them to choose to avoid something out of fear.

Points of view

Ask your child to make up a rule he thinks would be a good one for safety (or another category). Have him help you go through the above process: finding the category (safety, taking care of our things, etc.), classify the rule as positive or negative in expectation (please do/please don't do), classify as positive or negative in desired outcome/consequence, list examples of opposite (or undesired behavior). Older children might start to have more solid ideas of their own; allow them to brainstorm. Encourage them to consider the ideas from their own point of view and the point of view of another person (a friend, another family member, even your standpoint); you may even broaden the question to how the decision might impact society. Keep the message and discussion non-threatening. Have fun! Allow your child to work through this with the aim of deeper understanding of the interplay of expectations, natural consequences and the way the proposed "rule" might affect other people.

Identify a goal

Ask your child to identify a goal or expectation she has today that she would like to accomplish. Walk her through the whole decision-making process, throwing in examples of roadblocks or tough choices she may encounter. Assist in thinking through the decisions based on the goal she set for the day. This process of working through a hypothetical situation will be good practice when your child is actually making a real decision. Assist your child in broadening this understanding to how this decision might have affected others or impacted the world around her.

Explanations and Responsibility

Earlier, you may have identified family rules your child does not understand or agree are necessary. Explain these now using what you did together in the last activity. Not only will this help your child to start making aware choices, but it will also help your child feel as if she is a participating member of the family instead of just being told what to do. Responsibility will add to a child's feeling respected and also will instill a desire to act even more responsibly (a positive consequence) rather than feeling that she should follow a rule to avoid being in trouble (a negative consequence). Children who feel they are part of the decision-making process are empowered to act and make positive choices! Ask your child to explain the same rule back to you in her own words. Give her a chance to understand better through teaching it to you!

Foster Mutual Respect

When parents lay down edicts of behavior with older children such as, "You must be home by a certain time," without giving rational reasons and explanations, you can set up the opposite effect in which the child feels that if they break the "rules" they can do so without rational reason. However, if you approach them with reason and respect, they will give it back to you.

Shared responsibility

Help your child to see their part of responsibility for the family climate. If you say, "I am worried when I do not know where you are or when you will be home. Please keep me informed," instead of bullying them into doing as you say, you empower them to make informed decisions.

Expectations

For instance, as children get more independence by having access to transportation, through friends or their own, you can lay out your expectations in a way that gives them the power to be your parenting partner. It is hard to not try to control your child's every minute; but in helping them to grow, it is beneficial to allow them to explore the world . . . even when we don't "approve" of their actions. The most important part of this is that your child understands that you will be there for them, no matter what got them into a situation. For instance, if your child Rick says, "I am going to Jimmy's," and you have an idea that Jimmy is "dangerous" (really meaning someone you don't trust to have your child's best interests at heart), you can voice your opinion about why you may be worried about that situation. But if you forbid him from going, Rick might lie about where he goes the next time and sneak there. In the end, we don't think this is a habit we really want to set upg. It seems it would be much more efficient for all involved to allow the child to make their own mistakes with the knowledge that we will catch them when they fall.

If there is a situation where your child wants to go, for instance, to a known Meth house, and life and limb is actually in danger, it is different. Hopefully you will have the type of relationship where they will listen to your gut—however, some children will find their way there anyway, and the most important part is that when they call and say, "I got myself into a mess, please come get me," you still show unconditional love and help them out of it to your best ability, and then talk about it in depth later. Screaming at them when you pick them up is probably not going to help them learn, and again, will just push them farther away. Showing that you stand by your word that you will always be there for them helps them want (and eventually learn how) to make healthier decisions for themselves in the future.

Meditation and Yoga

Revisit meditation, both guided and questioning (using some of the questions and ideas above) and yoga as described in previous chapters. Explain that when we are faced with a big decision, we can meditate to ask our inner selves and God or the universe for guidance.

Gratitude leads to respect and responsibility

Help your child to express gratitude for her belongings, for the people in her life, for health, etc. Make an *I am thankful* list. *Conversations with God* teaches that living a life with great gratitude helps us to get along better in the world. It helps us to feel responsibility, it helps us to feel respect for others, and it helps us to feel respect for the world around us. When we feel self-respect, we make positive choices. When we feel respect for others, we choose to treat them with love and respect.

Create an atmosphere of Fun!

When there are tasks that you feel need to be done, try to make them fun instead of dreadful, like dancing or singing as you clean a room. Children like fun and will forget they are working if you make it fun and challenging! It is even better if you give them the chance to create their own ways to make chores fun.

Dealing with unwanted tasks

Discuss ways your child can use her creative energy to make things easier to do. Encourage your child to find his own happy way to deal with unwanted tasks. Some people like to sing, others tell a story about what they are doing, others set goals for how they will reward themselves after completing an undesirable task. For instance, I do not like to do dishes, but I know that my kitchen will not smell nice if I neglect them. So I remind myself of the importance of doing them, and then I set a time goal for how long it will take me to (safely) rinse and then load the dishes into the dishwasher. By setting a goal, I challenge myself and feel happy with my accomplishment once my task is complete. You can even reward yourself for a "job well done" by doing something fun! The sky and your child's imagination are the limit on how to lighten the mood while doing tasks.

Hugs and Love

Everybody makes mistakes, and every person makes choices at some point that end up in negative consequences. A way to teach your child self-acceptance is to show him unconditional love and acceptance (through a big, comforting bear hug) even when he makes a mistake. Taking the time, even as you explain how he could have made a better choice in a particular situation, to hug and give your child love will reinforce his self-worth, self-love, and self-acceptance. He will learn that you love him unconditionally and that he should love himself in the same way. He will also gain confidence to make his own choices because he will realize that you are always there for him. He will also learn that he can learn from his mistakes and move on. Giving your child this gift of unconditional love and support is one of the best gifts you can give a child as he forms his choice-making abilities.

Mistakes

Give yourself room to make mistakes as well. None of the foregoing is to say that parents are exempt from making mistakes. Even with the best of intentions parents sometimes yell, get upset, and react in ways that they wish they hadn't. What a perfect learning opportunity for your child to learn! When a parent makes a mistake, admits it to his or her child, and apologizes to the child, it shows that child that mistakes are not the end of the world and that the parent is truly living what they are teaching. This is such a valuable lesson, an affirming action to show the child the true meaning of living an ethical, responsible, *Conversations with God*-inspired life!

Celebrate your child's successes

Part of learning how to make choices is celebrating and reinforcing the positive choices a child makes. Catch your child making choices that you like! Give lots of hugs, high-fives, special talks to reward them for choosing to clean their rooms without arguing, or for completing a task without whining, or for acting lovingly to a sibling or friend. You can even keep a chart of stickers on which you put a sticker each day the child completes homework (or does some other goal) without a fuss—then make sure to follow-up with a celebration (hugs, high-fives, a dance-around-the-room-together celebration) of your child's success when she has earned a sticker for a certain number of days in a row. These rewards will reinforce positive decision making and encourage the child to seek out opportunities to make more positive choices.

Who You Really Are!

Encourage your child to think about this daily. For young children, it might be that today "I am a ballet dancer!" and tomorrow "I am a soccer player!" or "I am an artist!" At this age, their ideas of themselves may be limited to their activities, and that is natural. Older children might also view themselves in small scale by their activities, but they will also probably be thinking abstractly about who they are. If your child says things like, "I am nice to people," or, "I show the world respect," encourage them to find ways to live that truth for today and explain to them that those truths may fluctuate from day to day. This is a hard concept! But wherever your child is today—encourage your child to live out that truth for today.

Avoid nagging!

We have all been there; a child just *won't do what you ask!* Some-times, reasoning gets you nowhere, asking is a moot point, and bribery (come on, we've all done it!) is futile because they just don't want to comply. Nagging, cajoling, and arguing may seem like they will elicit the result (the child actually doing the thing you asked), but we ask you to think before you "nag." If you are trying to build a mutually beneficial relationship and partnership, in which your child trusts and respects that you trust and respect them, badgering them into compliance will undermine every-thing you have worked for. Remind them of the consequence of their choice and allow them to experience it (for instance, living in a filthy bedroom) for a time before you step in. They will see your point more clearly when they arrive at it on their own than if you try to force it upon them.

Lesson 6

AS YOUR CHILD STARTS UNDERSTANDING THE CONCRETE, YOU CAN GO INTO THE ABSTRACT . . .

About heaven

Your child may not be asking about heaven yet, but if he or she is, here are some talking points:

* *CwG* discusses "getting into heaven" by saying that there is no such "getting." heaven is everywhere, because we are all God and God is everywhere, heaven is everywhere and yet nowhere or "Now Here." (*CwG, Book 1*, pg. 98.)

* God does not discipline or judge. There is no score sheet for your "sins," because there is nothing you have to do and nothing that is prohibited. God only asks you to do what is in your heart as the best result-pro-ducing decision.

❋ Discuss with your child that there is no need to please God because God *is* everything and everyone; and therefore, *God has everything.* God expects nothing except that you work to fulfill your highest self, whatever that may be for you: Who You Really Are.

❋ To describe more fully, compare and explain this to your own love for your child. Do you like when your child does something "wrong"? Maybe not. But does it make you disown them? Would you cast your child out of your house? NO! Most parents cannot even imagine a "sin" their child could do that would have such a cost as that parent's love.

❋ Use this unconditional love to explain to your child that God's love is the same. Since God expects nothing from us, there is nothing we can do wrong that would cause a separation from God. Ask your child for feedback. Keep in mind at young ages, this may not sink in yet, but it will lay a good foundation for later. Ask your child for examples of such acceptance. Give your child the chance to voice any fears and confusion resulting from the conflicting messages he or she may have received from friends (society) about this topic.

Lesson 7

UNDERSTAND THE LONG-TERM BENEFITS AND KEEP YOUR EYE ON THE PRIZE . . .

. . . believe us, we know this is a radically different way to approach rules than the mainstream way of parenting, which has been perpetuated by the Old Cultural Story of fear as mechanisms of control. We believe helping children to view their decisions in terms of the natural consequences of their actions rather than from a standpoint of fear of punishment is empowering. Empowering your children to make healthy, positive decisions from a young age is a huge step towards helping them be happy, healthy, responsible members of society. While in the immediate future it may also lead to a more peaceful home. Children who understand their expectations and the reasons behind them are more inclined to go with the flow and act responsibly instead of acting out. Punishment isn't fun for the child or the parent. By including your children in this dialogue and creating a working partnership in which all members work for the "greater good" of the family or society at large, you will minimize the times in which you have power struggles. Supplying your children with the ability to make positive choices is supplying a life-long tool which will serve them well all the way into adulthood.

Isn't that what being a parent is all about? Empowering your children to be their highest, most empowered self? By empowering our children to reach their full potentials, we empower ourselves to be the best parents we can be!

Chapter Five

THERE'S NO SUCH THING AS RIGHT AND WRONG

Of all the astonishing messages in *Conversations with God*, none have created more controversy than the eight words above. And I have to admit, I was, myself, fairly shocked by the statement when it first arose in the dialogue.

How could such a thing be possible? In the world—and for that matter, in the universe—where it would seem that there needs to be some kind of order for life to proceed, how is it possible for there to be no such thing as Right and Wrong?

The whole world depends on its understanding of right and wrong to move forward creating its collective experience in some way that makes sense to all of us. If we take "Right" and "Wrong" off the table, what measure will we use to determine if any choice or decision or action by any of us is acceptable? What deserves praise and what requires punishment?

These are not small questions, and so *Conversations with God* addresses them directly.

A foundational truth

First of all, *nothing* requires punishment. God punishes nothing and no one. This is the underlying spiritual principle that supports the truth that there is no such thing as Right and Wrong. Yet this is the principle that cannot be accepted or embraced for the largest number of people on this planet, for to do so disrupts the very foundation of humanity's value system.

In order for human beings to entertain the notion that God punishes no one and nothing, and that there is no such thing as Right and Wrong, a new measure, a new yardstick, must be found by which our species can determine what thoughts, choices, and actions are acceptable and beneficial.

Conversations with God has, of course, given us just such a yardstick. First, it tells us that God punishes no one and nothing because God has no reason to seek retribution regarding anything, since God cannot be hurt or injured or damaged in any way.

Nor does God need to punish in order to "balance the scales of justice," as some have insisted.

The need for "justice" does not exist in God's World. Indeed, the very concept is foreign to God, because the concept itself requires that some "wrong" has been committed and must be "righted." It requires that some damage has been inflicted and must be healed. Such a notion cannot exist in the Mind of God, for nothing—as we have just said — can hurt or injure God in any way.

Nor does God have to eliminate the possibility of certain souls entering into heaven because they are somehow too "imperfect" to enter into the Kingdom of God. There is no such thing as that which is imperfect, for all things are perfect just the way they are, given that everything that occurs moves all of life everywhere forward on the eternal path that is evolution itself.

This is another way of saying that everything that occurs is ultimately beneficial to life, even if in the present moment it does not appear to be so. Nothing can occur that does not benefit life. This is a fundamental law of the universe, as solid and foundational as the law of gravity or any other fundamental law by which the functioning of life itself—both what is called "physical" and "spiritual"—is governed.

The three basic life principles

Conversations with God tells us that there are three basic life principles. These are . . .

1. Functionality

2. Adaptability

3. Sustainability

These life principles replaced our primitive human notions of . . .

1. Morality

2. Justice

3. Ownership

Interestingly, what we call "morality" is simply what we have decided works to advance our best interests in any given situation. Thus, the notion of morality is, at best, a movable feast. What we say is moral and good in one situation, we say is immoral and bad in another.

We claim that something is "moral" if it works, given what it is we are trying to do. The most striking example of this is war. We say that if we are trying to win a just war, killing people is moral. But unless we have "moral justification" for our actions, killing people is immoral.

In other words, our values are situational. This is, of course, as it should be. No evolving species can live by a standard of Right and Wrong that is rigid, immovable, and set in concrete. Things change as conditions change. Morality shifts as circumstances shift.

There is nothing dysfunctional about such an arrangement. Indeed, it is ultimately functional. What *is* dysfunctional, however, is that we do not admit what we are doing. We do not acknowledge it. We try to pretend that Right and Wrong are Absolutes, announced and pronounced by God, even as our every action demonstrates that we don't believe this for a minute. Or, if we do believe it, that we are excused from its restrictions and definitions by situations and circumstances in which we find ourselves. God, we say, understands. And suddenly, our moral rigidity becomes very flexible indeed.

Our new measuring stick

The so-called new measure by which human beings can determine the appropriateness of their choices and actions is, therefore, not new at all. What may be new is simply our admission that we have been using it for a very long time.

In humanity's value system, the yardstick by which we determine what we call Right and Wrong is *what works* and what does *not* work, given what it is we are trying to do.

It is *functionality* that renders a choice or action appropriate in the human mind. Does what we are now doing accomplish what we have set out to accomplish? Does it achieve our purpose? Does it produce a desired result?

In truth, as *Conversations with God* tells us, "no one does anything inappropriate, given their model of the world."

What we want to change, then, is not a particular or specific choice or action, but the model of the world—the underlying belief—which creates it.

The adaptation of ultimate outcomes in any given series of events (that is, the altering or expanding of them to suit our emotional needs) is what we presently call "justice."

Since God has no emotional needs, God has no requirement for "justice." In human life, by contrast, when we don't like how something has turned out, we use all the forces at our command to generate a different final result or consequence of someone's preceding choice or action. And when we, through personal intervention, produce a conclusion to any sequence of events—a conclusion with which we are happy (or, at least, satisfied)—we say that "justice has been done" or "justice has been served."

This is an extension of the notion that for every action there is a reaction, and that for every "bad" action there must be a "good" reaction. Bad must be offset by good in every circumstance for life to be brought back into balance. This is how we have it constructed in our limited human understanding. This is not however, how it is in God's kingdom.

In God's kingdom, that which is "bad" simply does not exist. No judgment of good or bad is overlaid on any choice, decision, action, or circumstance. Everything is in perfect balance in every moment.

Imbalance is impossible in the Kingdom of God, because God Itself is the mechanism that brings balance to the universe.

This brings us to another core teaching of *Conversations with God*, which is that God is not a Big Person living high in the sky. God is a *process*. The process that we call life itself. And God is the supreme intelligence that informs this process. And God is the unending and unconditional love that characterizes this process, and permeates it throughout all eternity. And God is the Essential Essence that can take any form and adopt any personality or characteristic that suits the Mind of God as human beings seek to interact with this Single and Only Element of the universe.

Nothing stands outside of the Process that is God, and nothing within that process is or can be "ungodly," since the process of life itself = God Itself, expressing.

Only within the cosmic context of the continually-evolving Ultimate Reality, however, could everything be considered perfect, in that it all moves evolution itself forward (a point made earlier).

In strictly (and limited) human terms, the central question underlying our value system is this: Is the choice, decision, or action in question producing, or likely to produce, the outcome desired?

Of course, the important *underlying* question following that is: What is the outcome that is desired?

This is the key to everything. This must be humanity's focal point in this day and time if we seek to empower our children and our grandchildren to create a different world and better life in their future.

The key to speeding humanity's evolution is to *change the outcomes desired* in our individual and collective lives.

Changing what we want changes everything

The fact is that changing, as a global civilization, that which we desire, that which we seek, that for which we yearn, is the only way we are ever going to civilize civilization.

As well, *changing that which we say is okay with us*. And we must base "okayness" on *functionality*, not some sense of acceptability that varies from culture to culture, religion to religion, race to race, party to party, country to country, group to group, and person to person.

In other words, we must *set a new global standard.*

And when we don't meet that standard, we must point to logical outcomes and predictable consequences, rather than punishments, as the result.

Children (and adults, for that matter) don't respond positively to punishment as a behavior modification technique. They respond to their own noticing of *what happens* as a natural consequence, rather than an unnaturally overlaid reflexive response, to their actions.

In this way they begin to internally choose particular behaviors, rather than have them externally imposed. And this is what we want for all children, is it not? We want them to develop their own internal guidance system regarding "what works" and "what does not work" in life, given what it is they are trying to do, and their own internal values regarding what they are trying to do with and in their lives.

They can only do this when they know the difference between "punishment" and "consequences," "acceptability" and "functionality."

Here, below, are some ideas and strategies that you might find useful in sharing with your children the idea from *Conversations with God* that . . .

THERE'S NO SUCH THING AS RIGHT AND WRONG.

The objective of the following teaching approach is to remove fear of judgment from children's lives. By doing so, you can enable your children to embrace their own decision-making abilities to become the fullest versions of who they envision themselves to be.

Lesson 1

IN TEACHING CHILDREN THIS CONCEPT, YOU MAY WISH TO BEGIN BY . . .

. . . remembering that Right and Wrong are not concrete rules but are, instead, malleable guidelines you define for yourself based on the life you choose to live, and who you wish to be. While these guidelines can be effective for determining one's spiritual path and internal values, that only occurs when the

question is approached, without guilt, in the spirit of self-defini-
tion. Often, Right and Wrong are issued as edicts or commandments that cause guilt and can implant a fear of God's judgment.
We hope to help you reframe your family's conversation of "values" from one about Right and Wrong to "what works and what
does not work, given what it is that you are trying to do." We
have found that one of the ways to help remove fear of God from
your child's understanding is to remove the fear of YOU from
their understanding and replace it with love and respect.

The main point of this concept is for children to understand
that God does not judge our behavior; but instead, we guide our
own behavior based on what we think is in line with our highest
goals for ourselves. We might continually choose to assess our
own actions to see if they coincide with who we wish to be, but
no one outside of ourselves fills that judging role. As parents, we
can guide our children to make decisions that are positive for
their highest goals. Throughout this strategy, you might wish to
consider the topic from one of two possible points of view. The
first view is of healing the pain of separation that prior teachings
of sin may have caused your child, and the second view is if your
child has never been taught to fear God's judgment.

Viewpoint One

If you and/or your children are new to the *CwG* body of work
and New Spirituality, and are coming from a traditional religious
background in which sin and punishment by God were taught,
then you may wish to begin by telling your child that you are
going to learn a new perspective about how God views or doesn't
view our actions. You may wish to tell your child that while your
previous belief system included being judged (by God) for your
actions, the New Spirituality does not. Please keep in mind that,
even for an adult, it can be a huge transition to hear that sin does
not exist; so this may be difficult for a child to understand and
accept. You may meet resistance and fear of what will happen if
they embrace a new system of beliefs; how the God your child

has known until now will react. Please reassure the child that even in this, there are no Right or Wrong answers, so you will love and accept whatever he or she comes away from the experience believing. You may want to tell your child that the New Spirituality assists us in taking guilt and fear out of our decision-making, which allows us to fully embrace who we really are. You may also wish to tell your child that there are many paths to God, and that just because you have chosen to learn about a new path doesn't mean that the people you love on the old path will not "go to heaven." All paths lead to God; this is just the one that feels good to your family now. That way, your child will not feel any distress about loved ones.

Viewpoint Two

If you did not previously embrace a belief system that included sin, you will not necessarily have to "undo" the idea of sin. You may, instead, choose to discuss, from a theoretical perspective, the idea that some people believe that God judges and punishes, but that your understanding of God is different. You may wonder why you would even acknowledge that others believe God judges. We feel this is beneficial because your child will not live in a bubble. Other people's opinions are bound to invade your child's space. Society, movies, TV, politics, media, etc. often speak about, even assume, the traditional understanding of a judging God and the concept of sin. If children are not aware that the concept exists, they may be frightened when they hear about it from sources other than you. So if you wish for your child to grow up without internalizing the ideas presented by others, it might be helpful to address the concepts from an intellectual standpoint. For instance, you can say, "Some people believe this . . . ; but we believe this . . ."

Lesson 2

THINK ABOUT HOW YOUR CHILD MAKES DECISIONS . . .

. . . about his or her behaviors, as well as how you influence and facilitate those decisions. Children, naturally, have positive outlooks on life. They are born with confidence, optimism, love, zest for life, peace in their hearts, and trust! They look to the people around them for the social cues on how to interpret the world, and, unfortunately, the negativity, preconceived notions, and lessons adults learned from the Old Cultural Story can eventually erode the initial positive outlooks of children. If they haven't been taught early on that they create their own reality, then when they hear words like "good and bad/evil," "right and wrong," "success and failure," and "win and lose," their understanding of the world can be changed greatly. Explore these questions for yourself and with your child.

* When approaching a decision, does your child think about his personal goals, or does she think about avoiding punishment and guilt?

* Does your child view God as a being that loves and accepts unconditionally, or as a being that requires compliance to give love and favor?

* Do you tell your child how to act, or do you demonstrate your desired attributes?

* What would a life without Fear of God look like?

* What does *Who You Really Are* mean?

* How do you choose who it is that you wish to be (Who You Really Are)?

* What is the difference between being told what to do and choosing your own behavior?

Lesson 3

UNDERSTANDING HOW THE WORLD INFLUENCES A CHILD'S INNER DIALOGUE . . .

. . . is an important stepg. Children may hear that things are bad or wrong from other people and begin to question what is true. Luckily, through an open dialogue, you can help your child through anything!

How can nothing be "Wrong"?

The Little Soul and the Sun: A Children's Parable is a wonderful introduction to this principle.

When one looks at the pain that was caused on Earth . . . and *only* looks at that pain *within* the confines of the short time on Earth . . . it stands to reason that you could call the action "bad." The perspective changes, however, when you expand your definition to think of the soul's eternal purpose, to Be and Express Who It Really Is—*an indivisible part of Divinity*—*rather* than just the human's current purpose. It is through this exercise, and the understanding of the soul that you can begin to see nothing done on Earth can change the perfection of the soul. God only "wants" for us what we want for ourselves. God doesn't judge our actions, so if we are making choices that we feel are "right" for us, then God will be "happy" with the choices as well.

Does God ever get mad at me?

What happens when your children hear, from someone else, about God's supposed punishment, judgment or wrath and ask you, "Does God ever get mad at me?" For children being raised in the New Spirituality, this can be a life-shattering concept. They have probably only ever heard of a loving being who is full of non-judgment, and this fearful depiction of God will not feel the same. The most important thing to do when your child experiences this fear is to comfort him or her that some people do believe that God acts that way, but that it is not your understanding.

You can also explain Unconditional Love to your child as follows: "When you do something I wish you hadn't (insert something like acting meanly to a sibling or leaving toys out on the floor), do you think it makes me love you any less? Do you think anything could ever make me love you any less?" Hopefully they will know and understand your love enough to answer, "No, nothing could ever make Mom (or Dad) love me less!" Next, you can ask, "Do you think it is any different with God? Do you think that God could love you any less than I do?"

Of course, with children, questions can be never-ending, so they might proceed with, "Well Mom/Dad, you are sometimes upset when I do things I 'shouldn't' do . . . like paint the cat, or color on the wall, or scratch your hardwood floors, or . . . or . . . or . . . ! Does God get upset with me, too?"

Here is an optional answer filled with love, hope, and empowerment. "Well, honey, while there are times I wish you would choose different behaviors, I would never wish you were a different person than who you are. Similarly, this is what I think God would say if she were standing in front of you: 'Things didn't go as well as I would've wished for you in that situation and while I could never be mad at you, I hope you will choose differently in the future so you can have a happier ending.'"

Why does it matter how I act as a parent, in relation to this concept?

It would be easy to limit the discussion of Right and Wrong to sin and God's judgment; and that is, in fact, the very root of this concept. However, much of a child's early experience of God is vicarious, through interactions with other people, especially his or her parents. In fact, like it or not, parents are, and forever will be, God's first surrogates for children on Earth.

We also realize that, unless you have your children enrolled in a highly traditional religious school or program (which might be unlikely since you have sought out this book) your child's experience of "judgment" is likely to be more inadvertent and subtle. Therefore, the remainder of the strategy will be about the everyday occurrences of judgment and how they manifest subconsciously—referring back to the roots of those judgments where appropriate.

If you happen to have your child in a situation through which they are receiving instruction contrary to your beliefs, we wish to empower you right now . . . right here . . . to ask yourself—Why is that? Why have you placed yourself and your child in a position to receive contradictory messages? Is it to appease family members? Is it for financial, cultural, traditional, or other reasons? No judgment here, of course. We just feel it important to give you safe space to ask yourself, to give yourself license to explore how it is that you find yourself believing and living one thing and potentially allowing your child to be taught another. Is this something that you feel you wish to change? If so, are you in a position to be able to do so?

The truth is, we aren't likely to act consistent with our beliefs 100 percent of the time and neither are our children, no matter how hard we all may try. Our souls would never consciously choose to hurt another, but the soul is only one part of the triumvirate. The mind and body also get a say in how we act. When we chose to come to Earth we bought whole-*heart*-edly into the human existence, frailties and all. Sometimes we wear our emotions openly and speak before we think things through. Consequently: We all get tired. We all lash out. We all say things we wish we hadn't. And we all, at some point, have the opportunity to play both roles, the forgiver and the forgiven, from *The Little Soul and the Sun*. The goal is to remember that there is nothing that MUST be forgiven, for nothing is WRONG. Forgiving another is a gift to relieve them of the pain of knowing they did something they wish they hadn't. Forgiving is also a gift to ourselves so that we don't carry around the pain of having been hurt. It really is a gift to ALL!

What about when kids do things that make us, as parents, want to scream?

In the Old Cultural Story we spoke in terms of *punishment and reward, good and bad, behaved and misbehaved* children. In the New Spirituality, we find it is more beneficial to talk about whether behaviors and actions work or don't work. We can also be more mindful of how we react to the things our children do that we wish they hadn't done. The next time you are about to walk out the door and your child spills the proverbial glass of milk, you can respond with a smile and say, "Oh, sweetie, I know you must really feel sorry that you spilled it, and I am sorry that you did as well; but you know we don't get upset about spills in this house, we just clean them up, together! Now let's get to work so we can get on our way!" Not only will you illustrate compassion and respect; but sharing the clean-up responsibility helps your children know that you are always there for them, even when the day is rough. These types of gentle interactions can be applied in any situation, at any time, if only you take a moment and breathe before you speak. Think before you react.

Another way that you can assist your child in maintaining the understanding that there is no such thing as Right and Wrong is by differentiating between the child and the behaviors. A child is more likely to internalize redirection as judgmental, criticism if it feels like a personal attack, "You are so mean!" than if it is addressing the behavior, "I wish you would not *act* meanly to your brother." Or even less personal, "I wish you would try to act more nicely to your brother."

What do words have to do with it?

Actually they can mean a lot, unless they don't. Words carry energy with them. Positive words said with love can carry positive energy. Negative words said with negativity can carry negative energy. And words, with innocuous meanings but with ill-intent behind them can pack a wallop of negative energy. Within the concept of "There Is No Such Thing as Right and

Wrong," kids pick up their cues about their behavior, and your *perception and reception of it* through many ways, including your words. So if you are conveying love and peace in all other ways but using words like "wrong" or "that was bad," even with the sweetest voice, the incongruence might still convey judgment.

The truth is the words like Right, Wrong, Good, Bad, etc. are all around us, and it can be so hard to un-program the vernacular of our societal speech patterns. To some, it is natural to say "good girl" when your daughter jumps really high, so you may not want to beat yourself up every time you do that; while others may choose to eliminate those words entirely. Again, even in the word usage there are no right and wrong answers. It depends on your intent and how you wish to implement the lesson. Realistically it would probably be really difficult to eliminate the word "good" altogether as in good job, good try, that food was really good, etc. You can see that trying to eliminate the word could get out of control quickly.

However, if you are fully implementing the concept that there is no judgment, then when your child is acting outside of how you would prefer, you might choose words like, "Jake, I would like you to XYZ" instead of, "Jake, stop being bad!" Again, as long as there is consistency in the intent and the usage, as well as within all other aspects of your parenting, you should be fine. Keep in mind that when you make the decision for how you will, or will not use the words, you are realistic about it, though. You don't want to set yourself up for a situation where you will continually "slip" and use the word "good" like in the jumping example and then beat yourself up for it—because that will do you "no good!"

You can also help your child establish different words as his or her way of viewing the world. Instead of thinking in terms of "I am a good boy!", teach your child to look at how he treats others. "I was nice to that child!" "I treated that other kid with kindness!" "I shared my toys!" "I listened to my teacher and followed directions today." "I was respectful." By using these statements instead of "Was I a good or bad boy at school today?", you assist your child in taking the judgment out of actions and just allow your child to *Be* who he wishes to *Be*.

Lesson 4

YOU CAN APPLY THIS CONCEPT TO ACTIVITIES TO MAINTAIN CONSISTENCY . . .

. . . between what you believe and how you interact with your child.

Art relates to a Core Concept?

Have you ever sat down with your child to do an art project and immediately felt the need to direct every aspect of it? I'll admit it, I have! I plan out the project, gather the materials, and have a finished product in mind. When my daughter was about three years old, I realized I was crushing her spirit because I wasn't allowing her to do the project the way she wanted to . . . she wasn't doing it "right" in my mind, but as a result I was sucking the joy out of the activity and stifling her creativity. In the experience that led to my epiphany, what resulted was a horrible experience for both of us, and the art project turned out terribly anyway. I promised both of us that I would be aware, from then on, of my intentions and control issues whenever we sat down for projects. As a result, in spite of me, she has created some beautiful works of art.

Sports relate to a Core Concept?

Children should be encouraged to try whatever they are interested in without fear of failure, knowing that they can change their minds. It is more beneficial to teach them that it is better to try with the freedom to later change their minds, than never to try at all because they are afraid of failure (or is it actually our, the parent's, fear of failure that stops them?).

This may be a major shift in our consciousness. In the Old Cultural Story we hear the mantra, "Don't be a quitter." But what does that mean, really? How can you ever really learn about yourself if you don't try a new thing? If you have to stick with everything you ever try you could easily have 200 activities by the time you are 12. Ha, Ha, Ha. We are kidding. We know that "Don't be a quitter" means you have to finish out a season. But do you really? Why? Will you internally combust if you don't? No.

Oh, yeah, the reason is so that you don't "let the team down." That's right. *The team. The almighty team.* Is the team more important than the happiness and well-being of your child? Not to me. Is it better for the team to pull someone along *against their will* who doesn't want to be there, whose attention may be elsewhere, who is possibly taking a spot someone else might desire, who is probably resenting their time there and possibly directing negative energy at the experience? Makes perfect sense. Not really, it doesn't seem like that would be beneficial to *anyone!*

Oh, that's right, "Don't be a quitter" works because if you quit a sport, activity or the like, it means you will never be responsible, never be able to hold a job, never take things seriously. Seriously, this is the pressure we put on kids? Sounds harsh and pretty unrealistic to me . . .

What about "doing things we don't like builds character"? We'll let you answer that one for yourself . . . but wouldn't you rather see your child build her character through love rather than struggle?

Okay, now that we have debunked the reasons for "Don't be a quitter", let's discuss what can happen when you assist your child in making meaningful choices about activities. The New Spirituality allows us, as parents, to understand that life has many choices and that we can change our minds over and over again, without fear. Further, it helps us understand that no way of thinking is wrong, even the choices our children make, with which we may not, initially, agree.

Children and teens are learning about themselves, their minds, their spirits, and their bodies. They are testing limits mentally, emotionally, and physically. They are finding out what they can do with their mind and physical bodies; how high they can jump, how fast they can run, how far they can throw, how well they can draw, write, do math, write equations, etc. They are growing and they are constantly changing. It stands to reason that changing their minds about something, after attempting it, is not wrong, it's not failure; it is a way to build character and their understanding about Who They Really Are.

Since there is no Right and Wrong, then, how do we go about showing this to our children? The old way would be to say something like this: "If you start that sport, or that project, do not stop or give up and don't quit! When you make a commitment, it is wrong to abandon it. You *will see it through!*" This could give your child an understanding of your love and acceptance as conditional, as if you will be disappointed in him if he changes his mind because you see quitting as "wrong." Then, even if he sticks it out to "the end" of the season, he may not only be miserable, it might also lead him to feel distrustful of you, his parent, because he feels you didn't put his feelings first.

Also, if you start to program your child to look for the Right and Wrong of a situation, you take away the opportunity for her to make decisions for herself about how something comports with whom she wants to be. Instead you have just started to prescribe behavior rather than teach her to think. Her goal will then become to look to others for cues on how to act "right" instead of her own internal compass of how she thinks she wishes to act. By thinking for herself, she has the opportunity to build her own character instead of reacting to what others think about how she should act. By the way, this trait in children that needs the approval and guidance of others is what people charged with indoctrinating children into cults look for—not that we are trying to incite fear—but making the point that impressionability is not a trait that leads to strong independent thinking.

Back to sports and activities, if they really love something that they, themselves, decide to try, they will continue whole-heartedly. You will not need to remind, cajole, and force them to go to practice. It's important to know that some kids may need encouragement to get started, but you cannot push it after they have tried it out. Let them know that you noticed how hard they tried and how proud you are of them *for their effort*—not necessarily for results.

If they choose to change course (or quit) after starting the activity, it might be helpful to squelch your initial desire to say: "I told you so," "That could be the 'wrong' decision," "Make sure you're not doing it for the wrong reason," or "Are you doing it right or for the right reason?" The most beneficial way to show them is to use your words softly, to guide them to an under-standing of what works best for them within their own under-standing of Who They Are and then, within your own means, assist them in getting there. Words are very powerful when we use them in a way that reflects choices and changes. It is helpful when we as parents are mindful of our own fears and what we "think" is *Right and Wrong* . . . and start to believe and respond with answers like: "What choice did you make? (or are you mak-ing) and how do you feel about that?" Encouraging and com-mending them for a good try and for knowing that they are wise to decide to change their mind may not seem like much to you, but it will give them confidence so that they know in the future they are equipped to make their own decisions.

Lesson 5

INVITE YOUR CHILDREN TO EXPLORE AND DISCUSS THEIR OWN UNDERSTANDING OF THIS CONCEPT . . .

. . . on their own and with you.

Discussion Starters

Share these discussion starters, one at a time, at the dinner table, in the car, or wherever else your family is together with time to talk. Ask your children to think about and discuss one of the following for 10-15 minutes (have the whole family participate). Hopefully, the questions will inspire discussion beyond just the answer to the question.

* *CwG, Book 1*, pg. 48 quote: "A thing is only right or wrong because you say it is. A thing is not right or wrong intrinsically." What does this mean to each member of the family?

* Have you ever made your own choice about something without second-guessing it? How did you *know* it was the choice you wanted to make? Where did you feel it?

* Have you ever felt afraid of God? Why? What made you feel that way? How do you feel now?

* Have you ever felt afraid of us, your parents? Why? What made you feel that way? How do you feel now?

* Has anyone ever made you feel "wrong" for changing your mind?

* Did you ever avoid trying something new because you were afraid of "failing"?

* Did you ever avoid trying something new because you weren't sure if you would like it but you didn't want to be labeled a "quitter"?

Journal Activity

Older children can be encouraged to journal about their decision-making process (and their thoughts about life in general). It will help them as they encounter bigger and more difficult decisions to look back on how they made earlier ones, so they can see both process and thoughts. It also will help them to gain inner strength and confidence in themselves.

Lesson 6

ENJOY WATCHING YOUR CHILD EMBRACE THE FREEDOM TO BE WHO THEY REALLY ARE . . .

. . . because when you do that, you get to know them on a different level and are gifted with the opportunity to watch them blossom. *Conversations with God* says that God does not punish or judge us for anything including changing our minds, getting divorced, etc. God exists in ultimate perfection; therefore, It doesn't lack anything. If nothing is lacking, It therefore doesn't need anything to make up for a lack.

If God doesn't need anything from us, there is no way we can fail to live up to an expectation. If there is not expectation, then there is no failure, or, in other words, no Right and Wrong. Applying the ideas from this unit will assist your child in finding the path that is best for them, and perhaps the family as a whole, not out of fear of retribution, but out of freedom and love. The freedom and love that comes with the understanding of natural give and take, ebb and flow, cause and effect, natural action and consequence.

When we ask, "How does that relate to children? Do they make their own rules?" we, as parents, have some tough decisions on which lines we cannot allow them to cross yet (for safety reasons); and which lines we can, so that they can learn to make their own decisions. Because God does not judge perfection, there is no punishment for choosing, or not choosing, anything. We can start by inviting them to know God from a new perspective, as an all-loving, all-embracing type of being, who doesn't judge no matter our prior background. We can prepare our children for what they might hear from other people about God. We can take care that our own interactions with our children are not judgmental in nature, because we are the surrogates for God in our children's eyes. Most children wish to experience any and everything they can, but it is us, the fearful parents that begin the Right and Wrong theory. This is where we might fall into old patterns, where we might wish to re-direct our words and ideas about choices for our children. We can start by allowing them to be heard and allowing them to change their minds. We can allow and assist each soul to walk along their own paths.

The understanding that no one will ever sit in judgment of your actions, that the only person you answer to for your actions is yourself, is oddly liberating; and yet, it also carries with it a new level of accountability (to one's self) through which most often, the person chooses peace and love over power and harm to others. Some people wonder if this lack of fear of the afterlife would cause "anarchy" and people in the New Spirituality will feel "free" to go out doing "bad" things (of course, again the New Spirituality doesn't call anything bad, but we get the point). The opposite is often true because, as explained above, people who embrace oneness and interconnectedness find themselves unable or unwilling to cause intentional harm to others because they feel a pervasive and powerful love towards all beings. They begin to feel that their time here on Earth has a higher purpose, that they have an opportunity to reach their highest goals, to examine their connection to others, to experience divinity, to remember oneness, to embrace love.

Chapter Six

LOVE IS ALL THERE IS

I never really understood life until I understood the remarkable statement above. On the surface of it, life seems to call this statement a lie.
Only upon close examination can we see it to be true. Yet seeing it to be
true can be the most important thing we've ever done.

Understanding that *love is all there is* changes our central viewpoint
about life. It alters our entire *positioning*. And this change in our *positioning* produces a change in our *personality*. Often, a dramatic change.

So let's explore this idea to see how it could possibly be true, given
our life experience that just the opposite seems to be what is "what's so."

What this statement means

We'll begin by noticing that the statement "Love is all there is" is nothing more than a new and more human definition of The Fundamental
Energy of Life.

The entire cosmology of *Conversations with God* revolves around the
notion that all of life is simply energy, expressing in different and variable
forms. The *basic* form, the *core* form, the *original* form, if you please, is
what I have often described as the Stem Cell of the universe.

It is the Prime Force. It is the Essential Essence. It is the Foundational Formulation, from which has sprung every other manifestation of
physicality. It is First Cause.

It is difficult to describe, with a single word and in human terms, the
nature of this phenomenon. What we know about it is that it is nothing

but good, nothing but magnificent, nothing but wondrous and benevo-
lent, glorious and kind, self-sufficient and without need of any kind.

The closest we can come to capturing all of this in a definitive way
in human language is by using the word "love." In our language love is a
feeling, a force, an energy that moves between people and that feels like
all of these things.

If we substitute the words Prime Force or Essential Essence for the
word love, we come up with these statements:

> *Prime Force is all there is.*
> *Essential Essence is all there is.*

Very few people have any argument with that. We all understand it
perfectly. Therefore, as we begin to teach the idea that love is all there is
to our children, the first thing we will want to do is to help our children
understand that love is not just a concept; it's feeling, an energy, that can
be sent and felt by many people. It can be felt by people without their
even being touched. Even without their being in the same room as the
person who loves them. Or even the same country.

If this is the first thing that children learn about love, it is the first
thing they will remember when love is being discussed afterward.

The birth energy of every action

Once we get children to understand that love is an energy—the raw,
fundamental, basic energy of life itself—it will be much easier to teach
them that love is all there is, and that this means that everything is made
of love, emerges from love, and arises from this singular energy. Yes, even
that which does not look like love at all.

Every human action is birthed by love, and the sooner we teach this to
our children, the sooner they will understand what motivates all the actions
that they see around. This does not mean that they will be happy about or
approve of or agree with all of those actions, but it does mean that they will
begin to see why and how certain things are done by certain people.

As children get older, this will become a foundational and vitally
important understanding in their continuing encounters with the world.

The lesson below explores how it can be possible that every act is an act originating in love. For now, let's just assume that it's true and look at what an understanding of this can add to the conduct of human affairs.

If we know and comprehend that anything and everything a person or a group does, it emerges from a deep love of something, then all we have to do is show them how they can express their love in a way which does not hurt or damage themselves or others.

We can actually agree in many cases with their motivation, without agreeing with their actions. This ability to at least be able to see and comprehend their initial reason for doing things can very often be an acute first step in healing the divide that can be created by their choices and decisions.

The reason that I so like this particular message from *Conversations with God* is that it helps children to deal with the natural fears that arise during a normal childhood passage through life. If they know that love is all there is, they will move through their early years with a deep sense of trust in the experience they are undergoing on this planet. Even when things don't turn out the way they wanted them to, even when others have been cruel or unkind to them, parents will have a tool—an amazingly powerful tool—with which to help children understand, and therefore better cope with their youthful travails.

People just don't know how to *use* the Prime Force and the Essential Essence of life, we can tell them. They have not yet learned how to do so. But you know (we can tell our children), *you know* how to use that magnificent energy as if it were . . . well . . . *magic.* Because it can and does produce magical results.

All people are good at heart, we can tell them. Even the bully on the playground. Even the bad person in the TV show. They just want something that they love, and they don't know how to get it without hurting others. We might ask our young ones: "Can you tell me what you think it is that they love? Can you think of a way they might get that without hurting themselves or others?"—and just like that, you'll have started a wonderful conversation that even children can easily follow and clearly understand.

They will enjoy the mental exercise, the feeling that you are treating them like adults and having a back-and-forth discussion with them about something meaningful. Even more important, they will remember this exchange and its mind-stretching process the next time they find *themselves* wanting something badly that it looks like they can't have and trying to decide what to do about it.

Now here, below, are some ideas and strategies that you might find useful in sharing with your children the idea from *Conversations with God* that . . .

LOVE IS ALL THERE IS.

The objective of the following teaching approach is to show children that every emotion they have is valid because all emotions are rooted in love—since *God is Love*! This is a very big concept for all of us . . . but understanding and internalizing it is a huge step towards realizing Who We Really Are.

Lesson 1

IN TEACHING CHILDREN THIS CONCEPT, YOU MAY WISH TO BEGIN BY . . .

. . . acknowledging that all emotions are important. We do a great service to our children when we support and validate their feelings. It is empowering to a child to be told that they can, and "should" (would benefit from), allow themselves to feel what they are feeling, giving them the chance to process through their emotions. This helps them to not bury the emotions because shoving them down can cause problems later. In this lesson we will help children to understand that at the root of all other emotions are the two basics—love and fear—and that in the end both are rooted in LOVE! Love is all there is!

Lesson 2

SOME GREAT QUESTIONS TO GET THE CONVERSATION STARTED WILL . . .

. . . dive into your child's self-awareness.

* Start by asking your children where, in their bodies, they feel love.

* Ask them to list a few emotions they felt in the past.

  • What makes us feel love? How do we show love? How does love feel?

  • Have you ever felt scared/fear? What made you feel fear? What made you feel better?

  • Have you ever felt angry or mad? What made you mad? How long were you mad? What made you feel better?

  • Have you ever felt jealousy/envy? How did you deal with feeling like that?

  • Have you ever felt sad/grief? What kinds of things make you feel sad?

* Ask where, in their bodies, they feel the other emotions.

Most emotions have a physical reaction, which can vary with the person. In other words, while one child might feel fear in his gut, anger in his head and love in his chest, another will feel fear in her throat, anger in her hands and love as a fluttering all-over sensation. There is no wrong place to experience the physical sensation, but getting to know the specific ways in which we feel our emotions helps us to tune into them.

Lesson 3

RELAX! THIS CONCEPT ISN'T AS HARD AS IT SEEMS . . .

. . . Children are often more intuitive and understand more than we give them credit for, so discuss the topic in a way that you think your child will begin to understand, allow his questions to guide the depth of your explanation and use examples from your own life to help them "get" it. Sometimes just telling your child about a concept once or twice, and then making sure they see you living it by example, is a far more effective teaching tool than explaining, re-explaining, and drilling it into their heads. We think "Love is All There Is" is one of those concepts. Children need to FEEL love, feel your ACCEPT-ance of their emotions and SEE you living out your own expression of your natural emotions.

Lesson 4

LOVE IS ALL THERE IS; BUT WHAT IS LOVE?

. . . Love is energy brought over from the collective, from oneness with the All. Love is experienced in that heart-lift you feel when you see a family member, hope, wishing the highest goal for another. It is the Creator, the sun on your back, the bees buzzing, the leaves on the trees, the flowers blooming, and a bird singing . . . Love is the circle of life (God—You—Everything—God).

❋ Ask your child, "What is love to you?"

❋ *Find examples.* Read books about love and spirituality with your child to emphasize that LOVE is really the root of everything. We have listed a few books that we recommend in the *Addenda* section at the back of the book.

Show Love

Show LOVE, help your child FEEL the experience of your love!

* Find a special non-verbal way to convey love/comfort to your own child that you can use anywhere and at any time. Some parents use touch to help their child feel love (hand on heart, hugs, a head pat, shoulder squeeze, etc.). Others use symbolic things such as a gesture of the Peace sign (two fingers), thumbs up, Namaste (hands together at chest with a slight bow like in yoga), or simple eye contact to indicate love radiating from parent to child.

* Discuss—What if love was expressed to/with your child without the word "love"?

* How would that look or FEEL? How do families express/show their love to infants before the infant can understand the spoken word? How do families with a non-hearing member show their love without words? How would a family with a non-verbal child or a child with alternative communication styles express and show their love? All of these different situations would require creative ways of expression.

Play a Non-Verbal Love Game

Decide that for a few minutes, hours or for a full day you and your child will play a game where you only communicate non-verbally. Explain that for that time period you and your child will try not to speak using words but only using body language, touch, eye contact and gestures to express love or any other needs, desires, activities, etc. Then when your time is up (or you just decide to end it), talk to your child about how the experience felt.

* Ask her/him if it was hard to communicate this way; ask what he/she liked about this type of communication.

❋ Ask if your child FELT your love differently through the silence and if he or she felt the love that lived inside of them.

❋ Describe how the experience felt to you.

Discuss any other emotions that either of you experienced because of this different way of being. Perhaps one of you felt frustration, anger or grief for having difficulty making the other understand, or perhaps one of you felt fear of not being understood and consequently not getting what you wanted. This activity may open up some non-verbal communications between you that you can continue to use throughout your life. Hopefully, through this experience your child will get a better understanding of the FEELING, instead of the WORD, of love.

❋ *Explain the difference between "I love cake" and "I love you!"*—We use the word love in so many situations that it can be confusing to a child to distinguish between loving objects (preferring) and loving people (feeling connection). With the younger children, it is probably enough to start by pointing out that these ARE different concepts rather than trying to explain how. In older age groups, your conversations are likely to be more in depth. As always, allow your child to guide the depth of your discussion.

Let your child guide you—Ask your child, "What is your favorite way that you feel my love, aside from when I say the words 'I Love you'?" This can open up a fun, serious, humorous, or just sweet discussion!

Lesson 5

SO THEN WHAT DO ALL THE OTHER FEELINGS MEAN? BEGIN BY UNDERSTANDING THE ROOT OF EMOTIONS . . .

. . . *Conversations with God, Book 3* lists five natural emotions: grief, anger, envy, fear, and love. It then explains that all can be traced back to the dichotomy of fear and love and that at its base, fear is a part of love (pg. 24). Referring back to the questions above about your child's experiences with the different emotions, discuss those experiences further. Give your child your own experiences with feeling an emotion that seemed negative (fear, grief, anger, envy) and how it relates back to love.

For instance:

* A parent feels fear that his child might get hurt if she runs into the street. This fear is a manifestation/example of love and wanting to keep the child safe. (pg. 24).

* A grandparent feels grief (sadness) because her grandchild lives in another state. This feels negative because it hurts to be away from her family, but this is again a manifestation/example of love because if she didn't love her family, she wouldn't care where they were.

* Someone driving on the road gets cut off, slams on their brakes, swerves, and is safe but feels anger. In this case, the anger stems from the fear that arose when he was afraid he was going to have a car accident. He is angry that his safety was risked because someone else wasn't driving safely, arising out of his fear of getting hurt. That fear stems from his love of life, his family, his job, or something else that makes him not want to have an accident because he doesn't want to risk losing what he loves. So even though anger looks very different from love, we can see it stems from love.

Envy

Envy has a negative reputation, but it can actually have a positive use in our lives. *CwG, Book 3* talks about a child reaching for a doorknob and being unable to reach it. The child watches the parent reach the doorknob with ease and feels envy, which inspires the child to strive harder to reach it. In this way, envy can be a positive agent of change. We can use envy to propel us to new accomplishments, turning envy into action through words or work. However, if we allow that envy to fester and do not use it to encourage ourselves, it can turn into jealousy. Jealousy is sitting back, feeling anger at another's accomplishment (and our own lack of that accomplishment) without trying to achieve the same for ourselves. It is rooted in fear that another has something we want; but instead of striving to achieve it for ourselves, we resent the other's act of having it. Envy then can be a manifestation of love because it is creative and allows progress.

Love

Love can even have a negative side if not allowed to be expressed fully. Children who experience being told to reign their love in, are made to feel embarrassed about feeling love strongly, who are manipulated through love, etc., grow up with a warped sense of what love is, and it can lead them to have difficulties expressing and receiving love in their futures. Allowing children to experience themselves as pure love leads them to develop into strong, loving, healthy adults.

What happens when the five natural emotions are not expressed fully?

There is a wonderfully clear discussion in *CwG, Book 3* about the following on pages 23-28. We encourage you to look there for the full explanation, but we summarize it here for you to share the basic idea with your child. When natural emotions are not expressed, they turn to extreme and unhealthy negative emotions. The book points out that in each case, the negative result of squashing the natural emotion causes great damage.

* ❋ Repression of Fear—Leads to Panic

* ❋ Repression of Grief—Leads to Depression

* ❋ Repression of Envy—Leads to Jealousy

* ❋ Repression of Anger—Leads to Rage

* ❋ Repression of Love—Leads to Possessiveness

Having negative emotions or experiences

Even when we try to surround our children with loving people, and we do our best to protect them from harm, we cannot control every moment or interaction of their lives.

Positive Choices

One of Emily's least favorite things to hear is, "Well, kids will be kids—let them work it out." I think kids do what we expect of them; and by repeating this phrase over and over throughout the years, I think we reinforce an energy that says hurting others is a fact of life, and therefore something we shouldn't try to prevent. I think we can only change a mindset from the Old Cultural Story by changing our own minds about it first! So I start with my daughter. I try to help her understand that any hurt/harm she causes another hurts her and so encourage her to only kind/ loving interactions; but she sometimes chooses differently, and so then we deal with apologizing and discussing making more positive choices the next time.

Hurt Feelings

As in the case of my daughter, even with the best of intentions, people will at some point do something to cause another to get their feelings hurt. The most beneficial way we can protect our children when situations go awry is to equip them ahead of time with the tools to protect themselves and to keep from allowing others to penetrate their sense of being. Talking to your child(ren) about their self-worth, about their connection to God and giving them all the love and support you can to show that they are LOVED, truly loved, unconditionally loved, is a wonderful way to help them feel whole—even when another person is not so nice to them (or when they do not act in a way that is consistent with their sense of themselves—and are unkind to another child). Another way is to equip him with the tools of how to handle negative situations—things he can say when he doesn't like how someone is treating him, permission to find an adult or teacher for help, etc. Doing this often reinforces it. It also helps to override any negative self-talk he might be doing in his head based on things other children have said to/about him. And you can continue to help your child to maintain a positive sense of self by talking to him about treating others with kindness, always, even when others aren't kind to him. Knowing that he treats others kindly will help him to know who he really is on a more profound level and will help him to be more secure in himself when confronted with unkindness from others.

Understanding that buried emotions do not stay buried

Society tries to teach us that in order to be considered strong or grown up we have to "stuff" our negative feelings or "bury" them. We can often hear parents telling kids to "buck up" or "just stop crying" when they are upset. This is a dangerous practice because we do not have an internal, impenetrable lock box in which these buried emotions stay safely put away. These past negative emotions if not dealt with, fully experienced, and then released can (and likely, will!) resurface later, causing more harm the second time around, and become the harmful emotions listed above. This activity will help you to illustrate to your child how burying emotions doesn't get rid of them but only delays our having to deal with them. It will help you open a discussion with your child about dealing with and processing emotions when they occur so that they can be released and replaced with love.

1. Using an ample amount of play-clay (about the size of the palm of an adult hand) help your child bury a smaller object (small rock, a bean, or a penny) in the dough.

2. Smash it around so that the object is completely covered and encased in the dough. Now have the child play with the ball of dough rolling it between his hands, trying to flatten it out, pulling it like taffy, etc. What will probably start happening is that the smaller object will eventually work its way out of the dough, putting a hole in the dough.

3. Explain to your child that this is much like how emotions work when we bury them. Emotions, much like the object in the play-clay, do not go away when you shove them down into your heart, soul, or stomach. They will eventually be activated and pulled, pushed or shoved back out. And like the object coming out of the play-clay, they will cause a hole (damage to Who You Really Are) on their way out. Helping your child to understand that all of her feelings are valid and that she is allowed to feel hurt, sad, angry or mad is a very important step in your child's future growth and trust in herself. Replacing hurt feelings with love and compassion is a way to prevent this burying of emotions—this is discussed in the next section.

Lesson 6

IT IS POSSIBLE TO WORK THROUGH NEGATIVE EMOTIONS . . .

. . . by acknowledging them and using some simple tools.

How to express negative feelings and replace them with love

If someone hurts our feelings, it is easy to let that make us think that their actions define who we are. If we bury those emotions, we are allowing that to happen. Instead, if we allow ourselves to express our emotions (both positive and negative) it gives us strength and power to handle whatever we face in life.

* Meditate—inhaling light and love, and exhaling negative feelings.

* Yoga provides mental and physical stimulation. It is a positive way to experience and express emotions as the poses stimulate different parts of the nervous system, allowing our bodies to "work things out" for us.

Verbal/Emotional Release

Sometimes just being given the license and space to express themselves is what children need to release an emotion.

* You can use this every day as well as in response to negative situations. Take five minutes to review your child's day verbally. Ask her if anything was really Fun about the day and if anything is bothering her about the day. Making this a daily practice will help your child to feel free to express her feelings, which will prevent her from bottling them upg.

* Encourage your child to speak up (in an assertive, yet kind way) when she feels she is being mistreated. Help her make up and practice statements she can use when she is in an uncomfortable situation.

* HUG your child when he is feeling negative emotions. Physical touch is healing. Showing your love, allowing them to "feel" the love, activates his self-love, which helps him deal with the other emotions.

Physical Release

Some things that can help children to express their emotions instead of stuffing them are: throwing a ball against a wall when they are feeling angry, going outside and screaming at the top of their lungs, running really, really fast in the yard, CRYING(!), talking about it, hitting their pillow, and laying on the floor, kicking and screaming. Physical release is very positive and helps your child to express and get out what they are feeling. Then if you can follow this physical release with a loving and a short, loving reassurance that the feelings he had were okay, and that he can talk to you about it more if he needs to, it will reinforce that whatever upset him doesn't define him and he can move on.

By showing your child acceptance and giving him space to express how he feels, you give your child a tool that will help him to deal with his own negative emotions in the future. He will trust himself to release them on his own as he grows up because you showed that YOU trusted him to release them and were still there to love him afterward. This is a way of exhibiting unconditional, non-judgmental love. Allow your child the freedom to express and expel his negative feelings, and give himself love and self-acceptance in return.

We want to be clear here that we are not talking about expressing emotion through physical aggression towards other people. We are hoping for the opposite; we are hoping that as children find safe, non-aggressive ways to "get out" their feelings through physical expression, we will see fewer children resorting to fighting, kicking or hitting another child (or their parent in a tantrum), and more children finding that they can get those feelings of frustration out instead of burying them to fester.

Empathy breaks the cycle of negativity

Teaching your child to feel empathy towards the other person, especially when that other person is hurting his/her feelings, is a great way to replace hurt with love. For example, if someone is rude to you in a store, instead of acting rudely back, ask yourself:

I wonder what is going on in that person's day to make them treat others like that? Giving love to another person in this way, even as you feel anger at their actions, will help convert the anger to love. And the truth is that we do not usually know what stresses or negative experiences the other person has had prior to our interaction with them. By reacting with love and compassion . . . and not carrying the anger forward to another person, we break the cycle of negativity and replace it with love.

A thought about tantrums

Young children come in all kinds of different temperaments and ways of "acting out" their feelings. When it is your child that is throwing a titanic-proportioned tantrum in the middle of your grocery store, it can be easy to want to pick them up, sternly say to stop and remove them from the store. We suggest considering the following alternative. Start by realizing your child is not the first to act like this, and that it doesn't matter what the people around you are thinking . . . what matters is how you support and meet your child's needs in the moment. As we discussed above, children sometimes NEED that physical release of a tantrum so as long as they cannot injure themselves or others in their tantrum, consider stepping back a couple of feet, keeping your child in your arm's reach but giving them space. Say calmly, "I understand that something upset you, even if I do not agree. When you are finished getting it out, we can talk if you want or just move on and finish what we are doing." There is a good chance that once you remove the power struggle from the equation and give them license to express themselves, the tantrum will end very quickly. Then when they have calmed down, you can ask if they want to talk about it or wait until later to talk. You can then give them a quick hug (or whatever you do to show, and help them FEEL, your love) and tell them you are glad they got it out. Then try to move past it and continue shopping. In my experience with my child, she only threw a couple of these tantrums after I started handling them this way. She realized that

I really did care about what she was trying to tell me and got to the point of being able to explain her anger, sadness, and frustration with her words before getting to the boiling point.

Create a LOVE Journal

Encourage your child to keep a LOVE journal. For the small children this may be drawing pictures that show love. For the older children it may be that you ask them to look for love in their everyday experiences. Encourage them to write about the instances of love they see, or experiences of a *lack* of love. Then take a few minutes a day to discuss their experiences to help them process their understanding of love.

Help your children appreciate Who They Really Are

Explore the supplemental activity in the back of the book called "The Actual Truth, You are Special Just the Way You Are: Love." The Actual Truth addresses the perfection of every person and encourages the child to love him/her self and can help older children who may be struggling with self-esteem issues to understand that everything and everyone is made in perfection and that they are special just as they are.

Lesson 7

PUTTING IT ALL TOGETHER . . .

. . . Once your child starts to FEEL what love is, intuitively they will understand that Love is ALL there is! Every main emotion stems from love, making all of us Who We Really Are. Once your child learns, understands, and internalizes that these emotions are "feelings"—not just words—and that their negative emotions do not define Who They Are, they will begin to see a fuller picture of themselves as the manifestation of love. They will begin to know who they are with each emotion, how to express and expel that emotion instead of burying it, and how to move on in LOVE. Through this lesson we hope that you and your child will begin to feel Who You Really Are and then begin to know that you are everything—LOVE!

We all want our children to grow up with a full understanding and knowledge of their importance to us and to the world. Enriching them with the understanding that they are pure love will help them to understand their beingness as part of God and that they are perfect!

Chapter Seven

YOU DECIDE HOW LIFE FEELS

Conversations with God tells us that "you create your own reality." And this is one of the foundational teachings of the New Thought Movement and of contemporary spirituality. Yet until they reach a certain age, children might find it difficult to embrace such a notion. Or even to understand exactly what it means. So we have re-worded the concept here in language that children can relate to.

Children, of course, are all about feelings. They let their feelings be known to everyone around them just about all of the time. Yet children do *not* understand that they can actually *decide* how life is feeling to them. And that is because they have been unable to string together in their minds the reasons that whatever is happening to them, or whatever they are encountering, is occurring.

They have not been told about the world and how it works. They have not been told who they are (a spiritual being) and why they are here (their spiritual reason for being here), on the Earth. They think they are simply "smaller people" who have to listen to "bigger people" who everyone calls "adults" tell them what to do and what not to do, how to behave and how not to behave, what they're going to get and what they can't have, when to get up and when to go to sleep and what to do in between.

This is how most children—and especially younger children—experience most of life. They certainly don't see themselves as being *at choice* in these matters. Our job as parents is to bring them the experience of making their own choices as early in their lives as we possibly can. This includes the choice of how to feel about things.

We accomplish the latter by showing them how they can choose to feel a certain way, and even *different* ways about *the same thing* at different times.

Making the link

In adult terms the idea that you create your own reality has to do with how you and other souls collaboratively use the energy of life itself to produce physical and emotional manifestations in your exterior and interior reality.

Obviously, such a concept is far beyond the understanding of the average child. This does not mean, however, that children cannot make the link between how they think about things and how they feel about things. They can, in fact, easily make this link if you show them how. And this is the first step towards giving your children the most powerful tools they will ever have with which to negotiate life.

Here's a good example of how you can teach children how they can change the way they feel by changing the way they think.

Ask your child to imagine having only one piece of candy left in a bag of candy they've been given. Ask your child how he or she feels about having only one piece of candy left.

Now have your child pretend that they are walking down the street and there, right in front of them, is a child who has not had a piece of candy for over a year. Her parents can't afford candy. Her family is very poor. So she has not had a single piece in forever.

Say to your child: "This little girl sees that you are holding a bag of candy and does not know that there is only one piece left inside. She asks if she could have a piece. You know there is only one piece left. It's the last piece of candy you have. Do you think you would give this little girl your last piece of candy? And if you did, do you think you would feel good about it or bad about it?"

This offers a wonderful teaching and learning opportunity for you and your child. If described in the right way, you can show your child how a simple change in the way they think about something can change the way they feel about something.

Tell your children they can use the same exact tool to create, in the same exact way, how they feel about anything at all.

During the course of an average day, notice when your child is experiencing a particularly strong feeling. (It could be positive or negative.) Stop what you are doing and ask the child if there might be another way to feel about whatever is going on. You can even make it a little game, to see how many different ways there are to feel about something. Think about it with the child, and announce that the one who can think of the most different ways wins a prize.

They don't even have to change the way they are feeling, just think of the most different ways that they *can* if they *choose* to! When a child is three or four years old, this can make a big impression. They simply start to notice that there's more than one way to feel about something.

Give them an experience they will never forget

You can even, as a parent, be part of the same game, played at another time. For instance, suppose your child does something that would normally upset you—and that your child *knows* would normally upset you. You can say to your child, "Usually I get pretty upset about something like this, but can you think of another way, or even more than one other way, that I could feel right now?"

After your child gives you several alternatives to your being upset, ask your child which feeling they would choose for you to have now. Then, embrace that feeling, right then and there, in front of them! They are most probably not going to ask you to start really feeling angry or upset, so you'll have to be ready to let go of that reaction to what they have done. Nothing could be more powerful in their entire lives than seeing you exemplify the very thing you are seeking to teach them. They will remember these experiences for the rest of their lives.

They will have learned, by example from the person they love and look up to the most, the power they have within themselves to *decide how life feels*—or as we would say in adult terms, "create your own reality."

Now here, below, are some other ideas and strategies that you might find useful in sharing with your children the idea from *Conversations with God* that . . .

YOU DECIDE HOW LIFE FEELS.

The objective of the following teaching approach is to introduce the above concept to children by realizing Who They Really Are (an indivisible part of God) and their ability to *create* the life they wish to live.

Lesson 1

IN TEACHING CHILDREN THIS CONCEPT, YOU MAY WISH TO BEGIN BY . . .

. . . reminding your child that prior to coming to Earth, our souls, all part of the infinite God, knew pure perfection, peace, and love. However, in the purity of our spirit forms we realized that we couldn't truly *experience* those beautiful concepts because we had not known or encountered their opposites.

In other words, in order to appreciate love, we had to experience a lack of love. In order to appreciate peace, we had to know what living without peace felt like.

As divine souls in human bodies, we come to Earth to experience our God-Self in human form. As part of this process we choose to forget parts of our spiritual knowledge so that we can re-member it in the context of the human existence, but deep in our souls we have access to every part of our Being (God). Part of this being is the God-ability to create our own reality by deciding how we want life to feel. Your reality and my reality may be very different in the exact same situation—this is because we are creating our own experience of that situation as we go. This means we can control how we feel about situations and how they affect us. This strategy will begin by giving you tools to help children understand that they are part of God and so are truly the Creators of their own lives; that there is nothing pre-scripted about their existence. Next we will show you how to introduce the concept that children are in control of their own reactions to how others treat them and understand that while we cannot control how others act towards us, we can control how much (or little) we let in and how much it affects us.

Lesson 2

INVESTIGATE YOUR CHILD'S UNDERSTANDING OF THEIR BEINGNESS, PLACE IN THE WORLD . . .

. . . and their concept of God, through a conversation that includes the following discussion points.

What is God?

Ask your child to start thinking about his or her own relationship *with* or *to* God. Ask, "Who are you in relation to God?" Explore the concept that he or she IS God. Ask your child, "Why did YOU come here?"

For some children hearing that they are God will not seem new; for others it may seem strange, foreign, and unlikely. Allow your child freedom to express his initial reaction to your statement that HE or SHE IS GOD! Children and adults alike may have difficulty wrapping their minds around this concept of oneness with God, not only as offspring of God but as actual PART of God. Meet your child where he or she is. There are no wrong answers; everyone comes to understanding at their own time, and it is most important to allow them to assimilate these concepts naturally.

Who is God? Are you God? Is the plant God? Is your neighbor God?

❋ What does it mean to be God?

❋ What does it mean to create?

* What does it mean to decide?

* Who controls you, your actions, thoughts, and beliefs?

Lesson 3

GOD DWELLS WITHIN EACH OF US AND SINCE WE ARE ALL ONE, WE ARE ALL GOD . . .

. . . this can be a difficult concept so here are some learning strategies:

You are God—I am God

* Have your child picture a tree full of leaves. Every leaf helps make up the tree; otherwise, it would just be a trunk with sticks. It is the same with God.

* Use the Sun as an example of God. The sun is a swirling ball of energy and light. It sends off light that reaches far corners of the universe. That light is no less a part of the sun when it touches upon your face on Earth than when it "left" the sun. It is the same with God. Just because you have chosen to experience being separate from God (by coming to Earth), to experience the human existence, you (the light!) are still part of the whole of God.

* Move from a discussion of the sun and light to a more abstract discussion as God as a large body of energy with each soul being a particle of that energy. Even when that energy (soul) has left the original body of energy (to come to Earth) it is still part of it and connected to it.

* Show your child that everyone and everything is God. Go on a walk and point out that each plant, flower, bee, animal, cloud, and rock you see is part of God. Look at family pictures and point to each person (aunts,

grandparents, cousins, siblings, etc.) and remind your
child that each person is God.

※ Every person makes up part of God and without each
of us there would be no God. Discuss your own understanding of your God-Self.

Bringing it into your child's own body

Ask your child where she feels God inside. If she doesn't know,
back up and talk about where she feels love. My child points
to her breastbone when I ask her where love lives in her body.
I have then been able to use that concept to open a discussion
about her soul and where it "lives." Interestingly, she feels her
soul right next to where love lives! I thought that was an amazing
link, and we then were able to talk about the soul being PURE
love. I then took it the final step to explain that since the soul is
her God-Self, she had just found God inside her. Anything you
can do to similarly help your child make the connection from
the concept of God to the God residing in her body will be great!

Expand on love

Just as we feel love inside, love emanates from us to others in the
form of energy. We cannot always see this energy, but we can
imagine it as light coming out from our chest (where love lives)
to other people. Talk about that light as God and that we each
have our own ability to direct that love/light towards others to
help them feel God.

Meditation and yoga

Meditation and yoga are wonderful tools for dealing with life.
Emphasize the benefits of deep breathing, and that this type of
breath is an important tool he or she can use in many situations
to feel safe and secure. Tell your child that the warm, safe feeling
you get when you are breathing deeply, is a chance to connect
with your internal soul or God. Explain that when you are centered and grounded, it is easier to find inner peace and comfort

and deal more effectively with situations around you. Encourage your child to use this calm state to send questions out to the universe (or into her soul) about Who She Is, Why She Is Here, and how to harness her God-Self's power to create her own reality.

Teach children the value of a Journal as an avenue to their souls

Drawing

Ask your child to draw a picture of himself; then ask him to draw his soul, love, happiness, and/or God wherever he thinks they are on his body. At different ages you may see different interpretations. In younger children, the body might look like a blob and the heart might be a dot, but that does not diminish the exercise because as he is drawing and talking with you about it, some part of him is internalizing the wonderful message that He is GOD! Older children's pictures might be proportional and accurately drawn, or you might even have a child who goes more to the abstract; either is GREAT! The point is only to assist your child in visualizing his connection to (and his role as part of) God.

* Next, ask your child to draw a picture of himself with love coming out of his chest. This might look like hearts dancing out, streams of light, ocean waves, etc. There are no right or wrong answers here. The point is to assist your child in beginning to see his or her power and creative ability.

* Finally, ask your child to draw a picture of the universe in an energy/connectedness sense. Some children might draw intersecting lines; others might draw swirls of color and light. Again, each person will have his or her own conceptualization of connectedness and that is PERFECT!

Writing

Ask your child to write down some ideas he has about Who He Is and Why He Is Here.

* Ask him to write down a few goals for himself and how he plans to create them as reality.

* Ask your child to write about times when she has felt one with her own God-Self. Have her describe the feeling. If she hasn't felt such an experience yet, ask her to write about what she thinks it will feel like. Ask her to write about ways she thinks she might be able to begin connecting with her God-Self.

Lesson 4

HOW DO WE "DECIDE HOW LIFE FEELS?" (CREATE OUR OWN REALITY)

. . . The explanation of this can span from concrete to abstract explanations, but the understanding of this concept is crucial to living a fulfilled life.

Coming to Earth

We each choose to come to Earth to experience our God-Self within the constraints of the human body. *The Little Soul and the Sun* and *The Little Soul and the Earth* are wonderful parables that help to explain this process to children.

* Ask your child why she thinks she came to Earth. This might bring a different answer every day and that is perfect! The point is to begin to assist your child in finding introspection that will later aid her own Conversation with God. Even at a young age, you might be able to begin to help your child to make conscious decisions about who he is and why he is here. This

internal dialogue is what guides our everyday actions. It is very helpful to learn at a young age to choose your actions based on your own "big picture" of who you believe yourself to be so that later in life, when decisions are more complicated, you are well-practiced at knowing yourself and deciding actions based on that.

❋ Today the "who and why" could be a soccer player who scores a goal, and tomorrow he could be a nice friend who helps another child. Whatever his answers, giving him permission to have some autonomy and self-guidance in who he believes himself to be is a wonderful gift that will help him with self-guidance in the future!

What is my reality?

Discuss that your reality is tied to how you experience and view the world. That you may not be able to control the things that happen to or around you, but you can control how they affect you. Give your child examples from your own life to help them explain.

❋ Begin asking your child to give you examples from her own life of times she controlled her reaction to something in the environment. Putting her back in the driver's seat after giving your own examples and giving her a chance to compare her experience with yours may help the child to internalize the meanings, which is crucial if she is to apply them in her life.

❋ Show that people often see things from different perspectives. Open a book to a picture and have your child and yourself look at the picture for 5-10 seconds. Close the book and have each of your write down what you saw. Compare notes to see how similar/different your perspectives are. Even though it was the same exact picture, you each probably focused on different aspects and missed aspects the other saw.

❋ Role-play situations (positive and negative) in which you challenge your child to choose how life feels. Compare thoughts afterward about your different experiences. Use this to illustrate that we each see things differently and from different perspectives. This will show that each of our realities are truly constructs of our own minds.

As God we are Creators ... what does that mean?

Our perceptions of the world are up to our own interpretation and all thoughts are creative. With younger children, we again want to stay concrete in our presentation of the concept, but we can also start adding a few more abstract ideas to the discussion.

Creation

Playing with play-clay, ask your child to make a ball, an animal, whatever thing you think he would enjoy creating with the dough. Point out that he just "created" that object with his own hands. Tell him life is the same—he can be, do and have anything he wants if he just believes in his God-Self.

Role-playing

Role-play to understand how we create our own experience. Even as Creators, we cannot control the people around us in our life. Therefore, there may be times that your child experiences others being unkind or unfair. While we cannot control what people do AT us, we can control what those actions do TO us (in other words, how they affect us). Ask your child to pretend to take a toy away from you. Show the child a few different ways you can react to that same situation. Show the child that you can cry, yell, take the toy back, etc. (which all have to do with you being upset). OR you can say calmly, (something to the effect of), "That hurts my feelings, that wasn't nice, I don't like that," etc., and walk away to find something else with which to play. By making the latter choices, you have maintained control over yourself and not allowed another's actions to get inside you. This may be a hard concept, but if you continue to demonstrate it in real life, your child will begin to internalize it and draw strength from it that he is really the Creator of his own EXPERIENCE of how others treat him.

Manifesting the life we want

Begin introducing the idea that as Creators of our own reality (the deciders of how our lives feel) we can also begin creating/ manifesting the life we want to live. If I want to be a great base-ball player, I first have to BELIEVE in my ability to learn to be a great baseball player. Then I will have to put in lots of hard work. Then I can envision myself hitting the ball (catching, pitching, etc.) well. And then when I play baseball, I can play with con-fidence because I BELIEVE in myself, I have WORKED hard towards my goal, and I can SEE it happening in my mind. We believe that when children are taught to believe in themselves and their abilities and also gain an understanding that committing to their goals helps make them happen, children would grow up KNOWING themselves as Creators with limitless possibilities!

Gratitude

Introduce the idea of present gratitude as part of the manifesting process. This is a tough concept for adults, as well as children. Since in our soul form we HAVE everything, we ARE every-thing, and we can EXPERIENCE everything, we actually have that ability in our human form as well. We just have forgotten how to use that powerful ability of manifestation in the lim-ited human body. The act of WANTING something acknowl-edges and reinforces the lack of HAVING it at the current time (or in the current consciousness) and so then the power of our thoughts will continue to create the WANTING of it instead of the HAVING of it. Shifting your focus to feeling gratitude for the HAVING of it helps us to manifest the actual existence of it (because we have access to everything we want in our soul form already—we just need to make the leap from in-soul form to in the human form). So abstract—we know—but like many other concepts while we do not expect children to understand it completely right now, we feel laying the groundwork will help them to grow to understand later.

Part of God

Allowing your child to see his role as an indivisible part of God will help him to understand more of his role in the world AND his ability to control his own life. Teaching your child these hard concepts at a young age will assist them in avoiding confusion later over how to act and re-act in the world. It will also give them personal power and strength to understand that they have the ability to live and CREATE the life they want to live and accomplish the goals they set for themselves! Allowing your child to find the God-Self within at such a young age will also facilitate her to have an ongoing open communication with God that others struggle to find later in life!

Chapter Eight

YOU AFFECT EVERYONE

I have been asked many times since the *Conversations with God* books were published what I considered to be the most important message in the 3,000 pages of that extraordinary dialogue. My answer is always simple and always the same:

"Your life is not about you. It's about everyone whose life you touch, and the way in which you touch it."

This chapter is about teaching this extraordinary concept to children in an age-appropriate way.

Children, of course, think that life *is* about them. Especially in the very earliest months of their existence. We have heard much through the years about the so-called "terrible two's." This is that period of time about 24 months after children come into the world when they realize that they are not the Center of the universe, that other things—people, places, and events—can sometimes take precedence, and that they can't always get what they want when they want it, how they want it, and where they want it.

This can come as a shock to many children if they have learned during the first months of their lives that just the opposite is true. Now they have no idea why the world has turned against them, and they can begin to throw tantrums and have fits and cry and scream and suddenly use on you the same word they have heard you use on them. Namely . . .

. . . *No!*

Clarifying our terms

I would definitely not advise parents to try to teach their child that life is not about them, as the statement from *Conversations with God* says, because children tend to take things literally. They hear the words that are spoken and assume they mean exactly what was said. The above statement from the text of *Conversations with God,* however, must be interpreted on more than a surface level for it to be deeply and clearly understood.

"Your life is not about you" refers to what I call Little You—the part of you that is individuated as a single human being. However, *CwG* makes it clear that We Are All One. In that sense, your life is about you, because there is no one else it *could* be about. But it is about Big You, not Little You. It is about the part of you that knows itself to be connected with, and not in any way separated from, other human beings and all of life. It is not about the part of you that imagines itself to be "other than" or separate from other human beings.

The teaching of *Conversations with God* is that what you do for another you do for yourself, and what you fail to do for another you fail to do for yourself. In that sense, everything you do, you do for yourself.

In the more human use of the language, however, the lesson becomes clear: By extending yourself beyond the limitations of your own personal borders and boundaries; and by placing little or no attention on your Small Self and all of your focus on the needs of others as they perceive them, you will have invoked the Golden Rule that inevitably creates extraordinary and wonderful outcomes in the lives of those who follow this injunction.

The Golden Rule, as we all know, invites us to "do unto others as you would have it done unto you." *CwG* carefully explains what you do unto others *is* done unto you because there is no one else *but* you, simply expressing life in a variety of forms. This is another way of saying that what goes around comes around.

But all of these are very sophisticated concepts that I do not suggest you attempt to share with small children. So for the purposes of this parenting book, we have shifted the emphasis of this message to something that children can easily understand: "You affect everyone."

This is a smaller thought, a simpler version of "your life is about everyone whose life you touch and the way in which you touch it."

Our offspring can understand

As we begin to discuss this idea with children, it does not seem to me to be unwise to begin with the foundation of the Oneness, or Unity, of all of humanity—with itself and with God. To the contrary, it seems to me to be a very good tactic.

Can children understand this concept of unity and oneness? In my experience, yes. Children can be told of the unity of all of life, and they can understand it. They often feel it intuitively. In fact, very often it is the feeling of separation from life, from God, and from each other that they sense in adults that children don't understand.

Children seem to know at a cellular level that they are not separate from anything. They can therefore be told that they are not separate from God, but that they are like a wave is to the ocean—part of God, yet not the *same* as God, even as a wave is part of the ocean, yet not the same as the ocean. This is something they can graspg.

They can also be told that just as waves in the ocean affect each drop of water within the wave, so do we, in the wave of humanity, affect each person within humanity.

Each of us in the family affects each other, and that seems pretty clear (and can be demonstrated pretty clearly) to most children. The challenge for most parents is describing to children just how subtle this ability to affect others is. It is not just what a person does or what a person says that can affect others. It is a matter of energy, and the way in which a person moves through the space, that can affect the very air and atmosphere in a room. Even the mood of a person, where nothing is said or done overtly, can have a big effect on others—and it should not be difficult to find an example that makes this very obvious to a child.

It's all about 'being'

Once children understand at a very high level the ability that they and all of us have to affect other people, they can then be introduced to the idea of creating certain specific effects deliberately. They can also be introduced to the *reasons* why they might want to do this. ("Doesn't it feel nice to make Grandma feel good?") All they then have to do is connect reasons with particular ways of being.

This gets into a discussion of beingness—a concept which is at the heart of much of the *CwG* dialogues.

Conversations with God repeatedly places beingness at the core of the human experience. It is strongly suggested, if you are going to talk with your children or grandchildren about the fact that they affect everyone, that you read all of the passages you can find in the nine *CwG* books having to do with the spiritual implications of States of Being.

It is not suggested that you try to transfer this knowledge to your children at an early age, but the information can and should form the basis of your explanation to children that they can decide ahead of time how they wish to "be" when visiting their grandmother, sitting in class at school, having dinner with the family, or doing anything at all.

Children already know this

I can think of no information derived from the *CwG* material that would be more important to the psychological, emotional, and spiritual development of any child than the notion that they can and do affect everyone around them simply by the way they *are* in any given moment.

The truth is, children already know this. No one has to tell a child that the way they are being affects parents. They've understood this from the time they were three days old. The parents' job is to relate this deep interior understanding to a specific and intentional mental process by which the child decides the reason he would like a particular other person to feel a particular way, and then chooses a particular way of being in order to produce the desired outcome.

Important to this process is to make sure that your child does not begin to see it as a manipulation, but rather as a demonstration of who the child authentically is and what the child would genuinely like to experience through her authenticity.

Tell your children that other people can always tell when a person is acting a certain way just because they want something, or if that's the way they really and truly feel. Tell them it is best, then, not to pretend to be a certain way, but to choose a way of being that reveals how they genuinely feel—yet without making a "scene," without screaming or crying or throwing their body around the room or stamping loudly across the kitchen floor, etc.

Now here, below, are some other ideas and strategies that you might find useful in sharing with your children the idea from *Conversations with God* that . . .

YOU AFFECT EVERYONE.

The objective of the following teaching approach is to introduce the above concept to children so that they can understand how their actions affect others in the world.

Lesson 1

IN TEACHING CHILDREN THIS CONCEPT, YOU MAY WISH TO BEGIN BY . . .

. . . revisiting the idea that We Are All One. Reminding children that we are all indivisible parts of God will assist them in grasping that the self-awareness and introspection that accompanies a spiritual journey is a tool to experience our full beingness and actually leads us out of ourselves and into the whole, our connection to the All and each other. And once you accept your one-ness with all others, you begin to realize that your actions affect every other being instantaneously because you are all part of the same living organism, humanity. In other words, every one of our individual actions affects the others in the world.

Lesson 2

SOME QUESTIONS THAT CAN BE USED TO GUIDE THE DISCUSSION ARE . . .

How do you find your connection to God? Does that help you feel connection to others?

❋ What is the difference between you and me?

❋ Where do you end and where do I begin?

❋ How do your actions affect others?

❋ How do your actions' effects on others change you, yourself?

❋ Talk about how it feels when your child is actively connected to God.

 • Does she feel happy?

 • Does he feel like singing?

 • Does it make him feel like giving everyone he knows a hug?

 • Does she feel herself moving into a giving mood?

❋ What does "having" something mean? What does "giving" mean? What does "receiving" mean?

❋ What does it feel like to do something for another person's benefit?

 • Why does giving to others make us feel good?

 • Why does being nice to others make us feel good?

Lesson 3

SPEAK ABOUT HOW YOU AND YOUR CHILD EACH PREFER TO COMMUNICATE WITH GOD . . .

. . . Do you pray or meditate to find God, your soul, or connection to the universe? Explain that this connecting to God is essentially connecting to self and everyone else and vice versa—that since we are all one with God, there is really no difference or separation between any of us.

Please keep in mind as you move through this strategy that this is an attempt to simplify a very deep and complex topic. So as you move through the rest of this chapter, do not get discouraged if you get lost for a moment. Hang in there, even if you feel your thoughts are getting tripped up and jumbled, take a breath, read it again, and we think you will catch back up!

In *What God Said* it was written that, "It is in *giving* we demonstrate, and thus experience, what we *have*."

It would be easy to misinterpret the spiritual journey as, solely, one of self-enrichment, introspection, and self-betterment. Most of the time the good things in life materialize through our interactions with others. And while we may realize that nothing really exists outside of our own understanding, and that things and events only have the meaning that we give them, we can also come to understand that those experiences very often depend upon our interactions with others. So the circle is complete—my life is not about me and my goals; it is about how my actions in the world affect others, which comes back to me in how I experience myself in the world (and whether I accomplish my goals).

In other words: If I imagine myself to be a "giving" person, I would first choose to be "giving" (in concept), I would then wish to find a person to be "giving" *to* and perform some act of giving to that person (in action) in order to live out a life which exemplifies giving (back to me in concept). Even though it is a personal decision to be "one who is giving," I must focus the act of giving to someone else to complete the process. The dichotomy is that our selfless acts performed for selfless reasons actually come back to benefit us in how the acting of being makes us feel.

Lesson 4

SOME POSSIBLE DISCUSSIONS INCLUDE . . .

Read *The Little Soul and the Sun* together. It is based on a passage in *Conversations with God* in which the meaning/reason of life is explained.

In it, the little soul decides to come to Earth to experience "being forgiving" because in the perfection of heaven there is nothing to forgive. It explains that we all come to Earth to experience a specific *something,* and we make agreements to act out those experiences with other souls prior to coming.

Inherent in those agreements, then, is an understanding that we can be mutually beneficial with each other on Earth even while each soul has its own individual purpose.

Parent-Child Relationship

To bring this to your child's reality, take your parent-child relationshipg. In your current dynamic, you are the parent and your child is the child. Ask your child why it is that way. Ask your child what sort of things a parent does to help a child (for example, takes care of me when I am sick, cooks me healthy dinners, gives me lots of kisses and hugs). Ask your child why he or she thinks you, the parent, do those things. The child might start with answers like "it is your job" or "because you have to," after which you can begin to probe more deeply. (Some children who have been raised in the New Spirituality will skip these initial answers and get right into the more spiritual answers). Remind your child that he has previously learned that "there is nothing we have to do," "Love Is All There Is," and "We Are All One." Now ask your child with those things in mind, "Why would I CHOOSE to do things for you, my child, if I do not HAVE to?"

The answers might be varied, but most will be along the lines of "because you love me" or "because you want to help me." Next take it a bit further and ask your child to put herself in YOUR shoes: "How do you think it feels to ME when

I do those things for you?" "Because I choose to take care of you because it feels good!" (or makes me happy or feels positive or is effective/advantageous). The answer for many spiritual people might be that parents take care of their children because they chose to have them, knowing that they were also choosing to take on some "responsibilities." The word "responsibilities" does not mean it is something you don't want to do—the word has gotten a negative rapg. "Responsibilities" can mean things I agreed to do (chose for myself!) because I want what is best for you (safety, health, joy, etc.). And it is natural and important for children to understand that as their parents, we *feel good* (happy/ fulfilled) when we take care of our children.

☀ Recall the parenting partnership we discussed in Chapter 4. The more you do to solidify the trust and relationship with your partner, the more efficient your interactions will be, the more respectful and trusting your partner will be, and the easier your life will become.

☀ You can also reverse this process and help your child to explore their role as child in relation to your role as parent

Again, this is the dichotomy that it is not all about you and your self-fulfillment. It is about doing for another, which will in turn have a positive effect on you—in that doing for another allows you to fully experience a part of Who You Really Are (in the above example seeing yourself as parent).

Discuss positive and negative behavior

Ask your child to describe a time he did something positive for another person. Ask him how it felt inside to do that. If it felt good, ask why he thinks it felt good. Conversely, ask your child to describe a time she did something negative towards another person. Ask her how it felt inside to have done it. If it felt "bad" or yucky, ask her why she thinks she felt that way. Ask her what she did to try to make herself stop feeling "yucky." Did apologizing to the other person help? Allow your child to take this conversation in whatever direction feels natural.

Discuss Empathy

Empathy is defined as: the intellectual identification with or vicarious experiencing of the feelings, thoughts, or attitudes of another. [*http://dictionary.reference.com/browse/empathy*].

This means that a person can put himself in the other person's shoes and feel/understand the feelings of the other person. Empathy is a wonderful tool in spirituality because it helps us to understand how our actions can affect another person, and then we can choose our actions accordingly. If we understand that calling another person a mean word would hurt their feelings, we can choose NOT to call them that word. Conversely, if we understand that smiling at someone who is sad might help them feel better, we can actively choose to smile at them.

Lesson 5

GIVE YOUR CHILD THE OPPORTUNTIY TO PRACTICE WHAT IT IS LIKE TO MAKE YOUR ACTIONS ABOUT HOW OTHERS FEEL . . .

. . . through some simple activities.

Centering your thoughts

Read "I AM! (A Poetic Mantra)" by Emily A. Filmore with your child and discuss how the connectedness described there relates to how doing something for another helps yourself.

"I AM!" (A Poetic Mantra)
Written by Emily A. Filmore

"I AM!"

I am one.

I am one with the sun, its warmth and its light!

I am one with all the stars in the sky,
the fish in the sea and the sands of the beach.

I am one with the wind that blows my hair,
the rain that moistens my face and
the firm ground beneath my feet.

I am one.

I am one with the mountains reaching towards
the sky, the desert baking in the sun
and the flowers blooming all around.

I am one with all animals, the family
I love and the new people I meet.

I am one with God. The universe. The All.

We are ALL.

WE are all ONE.

I AM!

Connectedness

Practice meditation and yoga to feel connectedness and ground yourself in the desire to positively affect those around you.

A simple game

Play a simple game to show that our actions affect others. One way is to set up three different options. For instance: a glass of water, a piece of ice, and a warm towel . . . anything that will (safely) make a significant change in the feel of the child's hand in a short period of time. Ask the child, while you have your eyes closed, to touch their chosen item for 3-4 seconds, after which your child will touch your hand. Even though you didn't touch the ice, water, or warm towel, you can guess which item he or she chose because of the warmth, coldness, or wetness of the hand. Demonstrating that his or her *action* causes an *effect* when they touch you, you experience temperature change or water on your hand without directly feeling the causal object. Explain that our actions work and affect others in a similar way; people around us experience changes in their world based on what we do or say and how we act.

An exercise

You can also teach about how we are affected emotionally by others with a jar and some stones. This is similar to exercises in which people talk about filling each other's (emotional) "buckets" with nice words and actions, often used in team-building activities.

* Give your child an empty jar and explain that you want to show them how words can positively affect others.

* Begin by saying nice things to your child and accompanying the nice words with a small stone to put in the jar. Continue giving the child stones with kind statements for a couple of days until the jar has a few stones in it.

❋ Ask how it feels to *hear* the nice words and *see* the evidence of the nice words (the stones) accumulate in the jar. (You will probably get answers like loved, appreciated, good, and happy.)

❋ Tell your child he or she has the ability to make others feel happy, good, or appreciated by doing the same thing, and watch as your child tries to replicate what you did to others, including yourself (giving stones with compliments).

❋ Then ask your child how it felt to know that he or she was giving the gift of happiness to others.

❋ Explain that by being filled with love and compliments they then had that positive energy to give to others, which brought back more positivity to themselves and allowed them to experience themselves as both *having something to give*, and *giving*.

What we have tried to do here is to show children that how they treat others is important but not because they will be punished or rewarded by an outside source. What is important is that as we create our experiences we remember to create experiences that are in line with Who We Really Are. So if we imagine ourselves to BE love, then we would want to SHOW love in the world. If we imagine ourselves to BE understanding, then we would be a beacon of understanding and compassion in the world. And if we imagine ourselves to BE giving, then we would work to touch each life we encounter with a spirit of giving-ness. We affect everyone with our actions, and we can choose for that to be in a negative or positive way, both for ourselves and the others. We are what we experience and what we help others to experience in the world—so who you are in the world is not about YOU (and what you can get out of it); it is about how you allow others to experience you.

Chapter Nine

THERE ARE THREE PARTS TO YOU: BODY, MIND, AND SOUL

Take it from me, children wonder a lot about who they are, how they got here, and what's going on. Even in my seventh decade, I can easily remember lying in my bed at night as a child wondering about these things. How did I get here? Why am I different from a girl? How come my dog is different from me? How come my dog is smarter than my gold-fish? Why is my brother so much better than me at just about everything?

I didn't understand any of these things, and I longed to. I wanted to know more, more, *more* about my body and about my mind. I didn't even know that I had a soul until I went to elementary school and the sisters from the convent across the street came over to teach us not just reading, writing, and arithmetic, but about God and the soul and the temptations of the devil and the need to get back to heaven if I wanted to be happy after I died and not have to suffer in the everlasting fires of hell.

Hopefully, your children will not be exposed to such messages from their teachers. But even if they are not, they will pick up from other children many of these ideas, many of these notions, many of these stories. And you will want to have answers when they come to you with them.

The functions of our being

Conversations with God tells us that we are all Three-Part-Beings, made up of Body, Mind, and Soul. The best explanation (for adults) of these three aspects of ourselves that I have found, and the best description I have seen about their function and purpose and the way they interact and interrelate with each other, is contained in the book *The Only Thing That Matters*. This text is a further articulation of the *CwG* material, and I consider it the most important book in the entire cosmology after *Conversations with God, Book 1*.

Essentially, the Body is the localization and physicalization of spirit. The Mind is, basically, a databank. The soul is the individuation of Divinity—the presence of God in humans.

The function of the Body is to collect data from the environment in which it finds itself using its multiple and extraordinarily sensitive receptors, to send that data to the Mind along its neuro-pathways, then to translate the Mind's return messages (impulses) into physicalizations that reflect the Mind's choices and decisions.

The function of the Mind is to collect the data it receives from the Body, file and store the data according to category, retrieve the data and call it forward as the Body continually encounters new sensory data while it moves through life, compare its past data with the data presently being received, analyze that comparison to come up with an appropriate response to the incoming information, then send impulses to the Body generating physical actions in response to its analysis.

The function of the soul is to use the Body and the Mind as instruments or tools with which to express and experience the true identity of the Three-Part-Being as an individuation of Divinity.

Put simply, the Mind seeks to guarantee our survival, the Body seeks to facilitate this process, and the soul seeks to give it meaning and purpose.

The Mind's assignment is to keep us alive long enough to allow the soul to complete its agenda in entering the physical realm. We intuitively know this, and it is from this knowing that arises the notion of the so-called Survival Instinct.

The Body's assignment is to give the Mind sufficient data to allow the Mind to make the decisions it needs to make to ensure our survival, and then to instruct the Body in how to give expression to the Soul's Agenda.

The soul's assignment is to collaborate with all other souls in the joint creation of the perfect conditions, situations, circumstances, and events in which our Three-Part Being re-creates Itself anew in every moment of Now in the next grandest version of the greatest vision ever it held about who it is.

In other words, life is a process of the recreation of Divinity through the expression of physicality.

Most dictionaries define recreation as "the action or process of creating something again. A re-enactment or simulation of something."

Another definition of recreation is "activity done for enjoyment when one is not working."

Both of these definitions are accurate when describing the ultimate reason behind all of life. Life was never intended to be "work," and it never is when we know and experience that we are, at one and the same time, the literal recreation of God, and, literally, God's recreation.

This should not be confused with any sense of our being God's "plaything," or with God thinking of our lives as a "game." When it is said that we are God's recreation, what is meant is that we are God's greatest joy—even as the greatest joy of all parents is their children.

God's greatest joy is seeing that to which it has given birth giving birth to Itself as a rebirthing of Divinity. This is what is known as being born again.

And so it turns out that the basic instinct is not Survival, but the expression and experience of Divinity.

If our basic instinct was survival, we would run away from, and not into, the burning building to save the mother and child crying out from the second-story window.

In moments when life is on the line, we don't even think. We bypass the mind completely and respond intuitively and instantly from the place of Divinity within us.

The invitation we are receiving from life

Our job as parents is to find a way to explain all of this to our children in words they will understand, with examples they can grasp, using ideas with which they are familiar, and stories and illustrations to which they can relate.

Now here, below, are some specific ideas and strategies that you might find useful in sharing with your children the idea from *Conversations with God* that . . .

There are three parts to you:
BODY, MIND, AND SOUL.

The objective of the following teaching approach is to introduce the above concept to children so that they can view themselves as whole beings rather than in parts. The human existence can become confusing as children begin identifying themselves singularly as one of these: the physical attributes they see in the mirror, the intellectual or mental aspects they have been told about themselves, or the spiritual, meditative side that they feel inside. Teaching children this core concept will help assuage that confusion and help children to fully integrate themselves; such integration and working with all three parts in the same direction is the ultimate goal of life!

Lesson 1

IN TEACHING CHILDREN THIS CONCEPT, YOU MAY WISH TO BEGIN BY . . .

. . . understanding, for yourself, that the *mind-body-spirit is the totality of you* concept is another extension of We Are All One. Just like we are all parts of the whole of the universe, so are all of our parts indivisible segments of us; none can exist without the other. This is what we call the *Holy Trinity*.

Lesson 2

SOME QUESTIONS THAT CAN BE USED TO GUIDE THE DISCUSSION ARE . . .

Where do you feel your spirit? What is your body? Where is your mind?

❋ Can you be a mind without a body? Can you be a body without a spirit? Can your spirit exist without your mind?

❋ Why do you think you have three parts?

❋ Have you ever tried to align the action of your body, the thoughts in your mind, and the knowing in your soul into unified action?

Lesson 3

INTRODUCE THE THREE PARTS OF THE TOTALITY OF YOU . . .

. . . As stated above, you are not your Mind, you are not your Body, and you are not even your Soul. You are the indivisible combination of all three, the totality of you, made manifest in human form to experience life. But what does that mean?

The Body

What is the body? The body is the physical vehicle, the part of us most readily visible to the outside world. But it is so much more. All people and objects (matter) are made up of energy. The cells that make up the flesh, blood, and bones of the human body are comprised of molecules. Those molecules can be broken down to atoms. Atoms are made of pure energy, tiny particles that are positively and negatively charged and held together because as opposites they are attracted to each other. So a body is really a large energetic field of positively and negatively charged particles grouping together into an organized system, which we recognize as head, arms, torso, legs, etc.

The energetic Body travels along time and space with the Soul and the Mind. The physical attributes of the "body" are actually the least important aspect of the "body" because the energy holding it together is what "makes" your body "what it is." When the person leaves Earth at the end of a life, the organic matter that worked with energy to build a seeable body is left as a remnant to go back to the earth, but the Energetic Body lives on forever.

The Mind

What is the mind? The mind is the Earthly memory, thinking, analyzing and understanding part of you. It is not to be confused with the brain, which is part of the Physical Manifestation of the body. When we come to each earthly life, we choose to allow our minds to forget our pre-life soul's All-Knowingness so that we can experience the soul's greatest desire: "A Sacred Journey with a Divine Purpose." (*The Only Thing That Matters*).

Because the mind is limited to human understanding, attention span, and has given up the memory from pre-life, it is free to make decisions in the moment based on the immediate information presented it. The mind is the part of the system that coordinates, reads situations, and makes decisions based on the information that is presented to it within its limited human understanding.

The Mind travels along time and space with the soul and the Body. Every experience, memory and decision that the Mind has participated in will remain with the totality of you and become part of the soul's knowing.

The soul

What is the soul? The soul is the metaphysical, energetic Essence of you that is an indivisible spark of, and always connected to, the Source, God, or the universe.

The soul has perfect understanding and memory of everything you have ever experienced (both as an individual and as a Collective Consciousness—God). The soul is not the boss (all three parts of you are equal), but it is the storehouse of all emotions, thoughts, memories, and knowingness of all time and space and travels along with the Body and Mind infinitely.

* Each of the three indivisible parts of you is always with you, in every incarnation and experience *of* You. Energy can never be created nor destroyed, so all three are Essential Energies of You.

Lesson 4

WHEW! THAT'S BIG TO UNDERSTAND, HOW ABOUT A FEW EXAMPLES AND ILLUSTRATIONS . . .

. . . from the physical world to help us understand how the three parts can work together.

Consider a Hard-Boiled Egg

Eggs have three main parts that make a functional egg in terms of food for humans. It is easiest to use a hard-boiled egg as an example for children, since it is the egg's solid state. The shell is the porous, yet protective, outer coating which acts as a structure to hold everything together. The egg white (albumen) is the majority of the egg and surrounds the third part, the yolk, the yellow inner part; both the white and the yolk have dense nutritional qualities. When you boil an egg to eat, the liquid inside becomes solid, and yet when you take them apart, the individual pieces don't cease to be "egg." When you peel the shell to eat the inside, you don't think of it as less of an egg. If you only like to eat egg yolks, you don't consider the yolk to be less of an egg. If you use the egg shells to fertilize your garden, those shells are no less a part of the original "egg" because they have been separated.

In order for the object called an egg to exist, it must have all three parts, and the essence of each part remains even after the remnants are removed, because the totality of them all gave it its shape and being.

In the same way, the mind, body, and soul all must exist to create a whole being, the totality of you.

How can a lamp explain the Totality of you?

A lamp has to have a physical structure (body), an energy (soul), and an output of light (mind/consciousness) in order to be considered a lamp; without any of these pieces a lamp simply becomes a sculpture.

❋ You can easily illustrate this by unplugging the lamp
and flipping the switch. It still looks like a lamp, with
the light bulb intact, but without the energy coming
through the cord to ignite the bulb, it is unable to serve
its purpose. (You are not the totality of you without
your soul).

❋ You can remove the light bulb, plug in the lamp, and
flip the switch. It almost looks like a lamp, but not
quite because we know that lamps have bulbs of some
kind to emit the light that has been converted from
the energy. So a lamp without a bulb cannot serve its
purpose. (You are not the totality of you without your
Mind/consciousness)

❋ You can remove the light bulb and place it next to an
electrical receptacle, but it will not have an output of
light without the structure of the lamp to convert the
energy into the light bulb's illumination. (You are not
the totality of you without your Body).

What is a home?

One might say a home is merely the house in which you live. But
isn't the feeling of "home" a more complex process comprised of
the house or dwelling, activities, and the people living in it? One
could say that there are three indivisible parts to make a "Home."

❋ The dwelling is like your body. Home doesn't have to
occur in a house. It can occur in an apartment, a car, a
plane, a ship or even, in some cases, a cardboard box.
Home is the sense of being with your loved ones; and
even if the dwelling or container is moveable, it is crucial to a feeling of home to have a physical position,
location, or space.

❋ The household's energy (utilities, nourishment, and
water) is like the mind. A dwelling is just an empty
structure until you add energy to make it "work." You

might have utilities to light it, keep you safe from the elements, communicate with others, and wash your body. You might have food and nourishment to fuel your body. You might add music to calm you, TV to stay informed, and furniture to find comfort. Without energy and activity, a house is just a structure.

❉ The people and love in a home are like the soul. You can have a house with utilities and food; but until there is an emotional content, albeit through people living with you, guests, or family that helps you set up your dwelling, the house remains a shell in which you live. The goal of "home" is to feel a sense of presence, understanding, safety, and love.

In the same way, again, Mind, Body and Soul are working in concert with each other to make up the whole of you.

Lesson 5

WE ARE ALL ONE AND LIFE IS NEVER ENDING ARE BEAUTIFULLY EXPLAINED . . .

In *The Only Thing that Matters* will be found great examples to illustrate *We Are All One* and how our body, mind, and spirit stay together in a life-never-ending. We highly recommend you revisit those examples and share them with your children.

❉ An Ocean illustration of *We Are All One* can be found on pages 13-15.

❉ The concept that life is never-ending is illustrated in "The Parable of the Snowflake" and "The Truth of Trees" can be found starting on page 41.

❉ Pay close attention, as well, to the note about near-death experiences and the presence of the person's family members in their bodies from the most recent life. They look the same as in life (the energetic part of the body) but are lighter, having left behind the remnants, or organic matter, that the energetic body used to move through the world. (*The Only Thing That Matters*, pg. 43).

Lesson 6

SO WHAT IS THE GOAL OF THE TOTALITY OF YOU? WHY DO WE CARE ABOUT THE THREE PARTS?

First of all, it is important to remember, as we are told throughout *Conversations with God*, that there is nothing you have to do, nothing is required to be in "God's Graces," and there are no right or wrong paths. Additionally, since there is only one place to "go"—to the reunification of all souls in the collective—there is no way that you won't get there.

Then why do we care? And what does it matter for children? The entire mission of the soul, its Divine Purpose, is to integrate the needs and desires of the body, mind, and soul into one path. We call this completion. We can have moments of completion (complete harmony between the actions of the body, the thoughts of the minds, and the desires of the soul) multiple times per day, every day.

When the body is working on its own separate goal, the mind and the soul begin to feel disjointed. When the mind gets distracted by outer factors, and stops listening to the soul and the body, then unification of the totality of you is out of reach. When we allow our soul, mind and body to work together for a specific goal in any moment, to be going in the same direction, we can feel utter bliss. In that bliss, we get a glimpse and a remembrance of our oneness with the All.

So how can children learn that?

You can start by pointing out to them when you see them being their full, 100 percent, beingness. For instance, if your child "gets lost" in art, that is a moment of nirvana. If your child sees another child in pain and offers to give love, that is a moment of pure oneness with God.

Tell them to listen to their soul through meditation

Your soul knows exactly what it needs to know . . . and what really matters to it/you.

☀ Your soul is working hard for you . . . life loves you, supports you.

☀ Your inner voice is correct. Life does not have to be a series of crises.

☀ Your awareness rests in your soul and your attention rests in your mind.

- Encourage them to think for themselves. Don't go on the path that you were told to go, but rather go on the path your soul tells you to go . . .

- Invite them to think about and Feel *What really matters*, a result desired by the soul and the day-to-day moving towards a larger goal—communication, between all parts of you without judgment for how or how long it takes to get there.

Chapter Ten

EVERY DAY YOU CAN START OVER. WHO DO YOU DREAM YOURSELF TO BE TODAY?

As you move through this book you will come into an awareness of the amazing consistency—the vertical and lateral integration—of the material and the messages in the *Conversations with God* books.

There are nine texts in the *CwG* series, spanning over 3,000 pages, yet the through-line is remarkably congruous and unchanging.

The tenth idea from *Conversations with God* that you are invited through this book to place before your children is a prime example. We spoke in the last chapter about the fact that we are all Three-Part-Beings, made up of Body, Mind, and Soul—and that the purpose of the soul is to set the agenda by which the Totality of Our Being may experience Itself as an expression of its True Identity.

Now along comes Lesson 10, which is nothing more than a restatement of that message from *CwG*, in age-appropriate language for children.

When I began experiencing my conversations with God, now many years ago, I remembered that I had only one overriding question, one massive curiosity, one huge inquiry that I knew I had to have answered: What is the purpose of life?

God responded immediately, and with words so clear that they have stuck in my mind from that day two decades ago to this very moment:

"The purpose of life is to re-create yourself anew in every Golden Moment of Now in the next grandest version of the greatest vision ever you held about Who You Are."

Those words changed my life. They gave me a reason for living. They contextualized my experience. They colored my thinking and influenced my behaviors as no other words I had ever heard.

They provided for me a foundation. They supplied me with a motivation. They inspired me with a reason in the heavens for my journey here on Earth.

How I wish I had heard those words 30 years earlier. Even better, some version of them, fit for a child's ears, when I was 8 or 10 or 12.

The words above are just that! How wonderful it would have been for me to have heard: "Every day you can start over. Who do you dream yourself to be today?"

The good news is that your children do not have to wait half a century to hear those words. They can see their lives in this context even now, this very day.

Helping children understand

To make these words come alive for children (and adults, too, for that matter), we can talk in terms of growth—or, more poetically, becoming "larger."

In some families it is a tradition to make a tick mark in pencil on a door frame somewhere in the house—often the doorway to the closet in the child's bedroom, where the child will see it every day—evidencing the growth that is occurring.

We can tell our children that just as their body is becoming larger, so, too, can *who they are* become larger. They can dream themselves to be anyone they want to be. They can begin expressing themselves as who they want to be any time they are ready.

When I was a child I began pretending that I was a radio and TV announcer. I got very serious about this when I was twelve and thireen years old, and my way-older brother bought me a Webcor wire recorder (yes, children, they actually recorded voice on a wire that ran from one spool to another!) for me to practice on. I read "the news" from the front page of *The Milwaukee Journal* on my local radio station (WHRS Radio .

. . the "Walsch Home Radio Station"!) and played it back in the kitchen, and my mom would listen to it every day while she was preparing dinner, offering me encouragement and comments on how I was doing.

During those same early teen years I created a weekly family "newspaper" that I handed out at the dinner table each Friday evening. It was two pieces of typing paper scotch-taped together, complete with headlines that I penciled in and stories that I had typed on the wonderful shiny old Underwood typewriter that my father had given me. (Yes, children, there actually was a machine that transferred words to paper by punching keys that caused metal letters to be slammed against the paper through an inked-ribbon!) My family "paper" carried stories about the adventures of my mom, dad, and brothers . . . and our dog, "Jeep" . . . during the week. It carried headlines like DAD CUTS HAND DURING BASEMENT CARPENTRY PROJECT, and MOM MAKES FAMOUS SWEET 'N SOUR CUCUMBERS FOR TUES DINNER.

It should not be a surprise to anybody that I became a radio announcer, reading many a newscast across my 15 years in broadcasting, and a newspaper reporter and, ultimately, managing editor during more than a decade in the print media.

What we pretend to be as children, we often wind up being as adults, especially if we had particularly encouraging (and indulging!) parents—and I did. I was blessed with parents who saw my interests and talents in my very early years, and inspired me to keep heading for whatever it was I wanted to be when I grew up, whatever it was that brought me the most joy.

My father also instilled in me an absolute faith in my own ability to meet any life circumstance with the inner resources I need—and to accept my highest effort as Totally Satisfactory to life.

I can remember that whenever I went to my father with a dilemma, he would inevitably say, "Figure it out for yourself." If I told him that I had tried, but could not seem to produce an outcome that I thought others desired, his answer was always the same: "Did you do your best?" If I said yes, he would consistently respond: "That's all that matters."

In other ways as well, my father was constantly empowering. If he said to me once, he said to me 50 times: "You can be anything you want to be, son. You can do anything you want to do. Never let anything stop you. Just work hard, make yourself invaluable wherever you go, give 110 percent whatever you do, and you'll never be out of a job. You'll also never have to do very much you don't like."

That was one of the three best pieces of advice my father ever gave me. The other two?

"There's no such thing as a 'No Admittance' door."

. . . and . . . as I mentioned before . . .

"There's no 'right way' to do anything; there's only the way you're doing it. Make the way you're doing it 'the right way' and it will be."

Life's glorious opportunity

I have shared these anecdotes about my dad here because they offer what I consider to be a sterling example of how to teach children that their life knows no limitation—and that its very *purpose* is to demonstrate that. This is its invitation. And this is the glorious opportunity that it places before us.

This is at one and the same time both an opportunity and a challenge. The challenge is to embrace as perfect, and then release and forget, all of the "failures" of yesterday.

CwG reminds us very clearly in *Communion with God* that failure is one of The Ten Illusions of Humans. (See Item #18 in *1,000 Words That Would Change the World*, found in the *Preface* of this book.)

It is the First Illusion, on which all others are predicated. Scientists working in a laboratory understand that every so-called "failure" to produce a particular result is simply a stepping stone towards success.

That is why my father's words, when I tried to produce an outcome but did not, were so important to me—and served me for the rest of my life.

"Did you do your best?"

"Yes."

"That's all that matters."

Now it is the human tendency to always think that we did *not* do our best, that we could have done, or should have known, better. Yet the truth is that in every moment of our life, we did the best we could with the emotional, physical, and spiritual information at hand.

Nobody does anything awkwardly or badly deliberately. Each of us serves the agenda we have at hand in the best way we can think of. Sometimes it is the *only* way we can think of, because of our limited understanding, but at the time, in the moment, it was the resource we had available to us.

It is as the wonderful poet Maya Angelou said so eloquently: "When we know better, we do better."

It is when we accept the challenge of life to know better, move to the next level in our awareness, in our consciousness, and in our expression and experience of Who We Really Are, that we advance the soul's agenda. And that is precisely what we came here to do. We came here to experience and to express our Divinity, thereby giving God the experience of Itself.

All of this is wondrously explained in the *CwG* book, *The Only Thing That Matters.* I consider it the single most important book I have been given since *Conversations with God, Book 1*, and I strongly recommend it for reading.

Now here, below, are some specific ideas and strategies that you may find useful in sharing with your children the idea from *Conversations with God* that . . .

> *Every day you can start over.*
> *Who do you dream yourself to be today?*

The objective of the following teaching approach is to introduce the above concept to children so that they can let go of external expectations of themselves and start to truly live in the moment. Understanding that we can start over every day relieves us from crippling guilt, centers our decisions on who we picture ourselves to be, encourages us to make every day more fulfilling than the last, and allows us to always see ourselves with infinite potential, and unending ability to dream.

This teaching concept is the child friendly version of "The purpose of life is to re-create yourself anew in the next grandest version of the greatest vision you ever held about Who You Are."

Lesson 1

IN TEACHING CHILDREN THIS CONCEPT, YOU MAY WISH TO BEGIN BY . . .

. . . revisiting Chapter 4, "There Is Nothing You Have To Do," and Chapter 5, "There Is No Such Thing As Right And Wrong."

Now that you have the concept that God wants, expects, and requires nothing firmly rooted in your mind, you will get the chance to expand upon your child's understanding of God as partner, friend, and ourSELVES to embrace our purpose in life. That purpose is to make each day fuller, happier, and more authentic than the last.

The *CwG* material has used the phrase, "I am God, Godding myself." Godding means guiding, acting as, and embracing your beingness as an indivisible part of God. So when you see the word Godding below, you can also think of it as your soul guiding you.

Lesson 2

SOME QUESTIONS THAT CAN BE USED TO GUIDE THE DISCUSSION ARE . . .

Who are you, today? Who do you want to be?

* In your wildest dreams, what kind of person would you be?

* Does doing something, whether you consider it "good" or "bad," mean that you will be that (good or bad) for the rest of your life?

* Do you think you can choose differently how to act tomorrow than you did today?

* Think about your happiest moment. Do you know that you can be even happier?

* What does it mean to change?

Lesson 3

REMIND YOUR CHILDREN THAT WE ARE PERFECT, INDIVISIBLE PARTS OF GOD . . .

. . . As discussed in Chapter 1, We Are All One. This means that we each have the limitless potential to be anything we want to be, in any moment, because God is everything. What does that mean for a kid's understanding?

* Look all around you and ask: Where do you see God? We can see God in the trees, the flowers, the sky, the dirt, and each other. If God is everywhere, then is there any possibility that anything can be "bad"? No, because if any part of the universe is "bad" then God would be bad.

* God is recreated every day in our births, actions, conversations, planting of seeds, preparing of food, and going back to the source, etc.

* As an indivisible part of God, we have that same ability to be recreated (start over) every single day.

* Use guided and questioning meditations to explore this further.

Lesson 4

WHAT DOES IT MEAN TO START OVER EVERY DAY?

. . . Starting over every day (or in every moment) means:

* No action we take, no attitude or idea we have, and no feeling is permanent. We can choose to have a new experience of ourselves every day. That means that our current actions today do not have to define who we are tomorrow. In other words, doing something I think of as "bad" doesn't make me a bad person.

❋ When I wake up in the morning, I can choose how I present myself to the world, without guilt or regret about how I presented myself yesterday. This goes the same for moment to moment.

If I act one way in this second, I can choose to act differently in the next—being the best version of love I can be, in the moment. If we accept that we are unconditional love all the time, that is how we can effectively begin each day.

❋ Love has no boundaries when it comes to making choices for yourself. We will not have regret when we come from love because love is the ultimate preface for all actions.

❋ Even if a child is "mean" to another child, there is a part of that behavior that comes from love (love of him or herself); however, it is the opposite of *showing* love. He or she is possibly lashing out towards others in an effort to feel better about himself (self-love), but it is a sign of insecurity. It is possible to help them see that a more effective way to assuage their own insecurity is to show love to others, even when they don't want to because giving love to another is the highest form of *self-love*.

❋ By teaching this to your child, you help them to constantly reach for their own highest visions or biggest dreams about themselves (that which is pure love) by being and exhibiting love to others.

❋ The idea then is to not make the child feel regret or guilt for being mean to another, but to show them they are not separate, that they are the same as the other, that they are God, and that to love the other is to love themselves.

❋ This will help them understand that how you act towards others is what you believe yourself to be (and vice-versa), and that you can always change it in an instant.

Lesson 5

WHAT ROLE DO GUILT AND REGRET PLAY IN WHO YOU ARE?

Did you allow what someone else did to you to create the person that you are today? If so, how do we keep that from rubbing off on our children as we parent?

With each action through life we grow, we change, we understand, and we mature. Our soul's purpose is to see ourselves as divine, constantly giving ourselves the answers of life. If we teach our children to do what God would do for them to themselves and others, then how could any action be considered "wrong"?

Every action is an effort at self-discovery

And therefore, even if an action is harmful to another, it can be used for growth and understanding. A child only has to understand that they are "God, Godding themselves" from their soul, through their actions, interactions, choices, and decisions, etc. Armed with this amazing knowledge about themselves, the things that happen in life, both "good" and "bad" take on less meaning because we understand that any action, no matter how big it seems on Earth, is very small compared to the universe and our God-ness. Therefore, they have the opportunity to be less reactive to the events of life and can put themselves out into the world in the way they wish/dream to do so. Because there is no right or wrong, the decision to be "Godding" to themselves will change the way in which they face their everyday life.

So the answer is that Guilt and Regret have no place in your vocabulary.

Lesson 6

OUR PURPOSE, TO BE OUR FULLEST SELVES, DREAMING NEW DREAMS, EVERY DAY, IS UNAVOIDABLE . . .

Consider these examples from nature with your child:

❋ A spider comes to Earth with a specific purpose: to weave webs, to procreate, and to eat insects. It does what it does, without questioning it. It builds its home, catches its prey, drinks water from the dew drops caught on the web, it mates and lays its eggs, and it moves around from season to season. In other words, the spider is doing what it was put here to do—nothing more and nothing less. And all animals are the same; they have their instinctual goals and they do them. They don't sit around feeling guilt or questioning their actions. They feel their purpose and they act. They live their lives by "Godding" themselves, recreating something new each day on instinct.

❋ In the same way, birds "God" themselves in their songs and flight. Butterflies are "Godding" themselves when they emerge from caterpillar to butterfly.

❋ Animals are recreating themselves anew every day, being the best (most successful spider, bird, butterfly) they can be.

We are the same

We are merely just "Godding" ourselves through "Being" and then doing what we chose to come here and experience.

❋ Our instincts are the same, to be the best version of ourselves every new day, creating new experiences: To Love, Create, and Be.

Lesson 7

SO NOW WE CAN UNDERSTAND THAT . . .

. . . who we are today is not the same as who we were yesterday.

One way to understand constant change and the idea that every day is a chance to start over is to, again, have your child look around at nature.

* Think of the sun rising. Earth's process of rebirth begins every morning. The sun rises, flowers reach for it, the light expands and then contracts as the sun leaves our sight at dusk.

* Think about grass growing; a blade of grass is different every day, changing as it grows. Then it gets eaten by animals or bugs or cut by humans, but it is no less perfect as a blade of grass in any instance. We wouldn't call it something else because it is shorter or brown instead of green. It is still grass.

Another way to understand that things are constantly changing is to use the game of hide and seek as an example. That game, generally, has the same rules across the world. One person hides and the other closes his or her eyes and counts to 10. When the counting is over, we yell, "Ready or not, here I come!" and then we look high and low for the other players. Even though the game is always played the same *way*, it is never the same game twice. There are so many variables (location, personality, availability of hiding spots, and creativity) that change the process and outcome of each turn of the game that it is a new game every time it is played. The same can be said of life.

We are beings of constant change

* The cells of our bodies are always being born, dying, and/or multiplying; therefore, we are not physically the same as yesterday.

* Here is an activity you can do with your child to show them how things change from day to day.

  * Every morning for a week, month, or year, take a photo of your child.

  * Review those photos together, periodically, looking for the small and big changes that occur in your child's face, the way he or she wears his or her hair, etc.

  * Discuss what that means in terms of how if they look different from day to day, it can be freeing to know that their actions aren't permanent either.

* Our experiences build from one day (moment) to the next, so our mind and understanding is not the same from yesterday to today because the lens through which we see the world is always adjusting.

A decision you make today will be based on different factors than a decision you make tomorrow, even on the same question.

Even these paragraphs would have been different if they were written yesterday or tomorrow because the authors' understandings of the world are in constant evolution.

When we accept this fundamental truth, that our whole self changes every day, we can experience the freedom to be exactly who we dream ourselves to be in every single moment of every single day.

Fear of change, guilt, and regret are merely our minds and bodies playing tricks on us, clouding our present knowledge of our actual beingness, which our soul knows, with clutter. That beingness, again, is our God-ness.

Is change scary?

No! Change is beautiful; it is an opportunity for rebirth and dreaming bigger dreams than you ever did before!

* Facing each experience, question, and situation with love and positivity breeds more of the same. When you act out of love, you attract (and notice) more experiences of love. When you act in a positive way, you attract and see more positive instances in your life. And conversely, when you act out of fear and negativity, that is what you draw to yourself.

* Change is fun! It helps every day to be an adventure! You get the opportunity to learn, grow, and embrace new experiences when you allow yourself to dream bigger and bigger every day because the dreams build upon each other.

Lesson 8

WHAT DOES A BIG DREAM LOOK LIKE? HOW BIG CAN YOUR CHILD DREAM?

Love is the ultimate reality. It is the only. The all. The feeling of love is your experience of God. In highest Truth, love is all there is, all there was, and all there ever will be.

* From birth to adulthood to death, Love is the catalyst to your divine self. When you truly feel love, you overcome self-defeat, self-abuse, victimization, self-doubt, and poor treatment of others. Once the child understands their true purpose and the totality of themselves, they can begin to understand that love is more than a word; love is the soul aspect of God in you.

❋ Who are you? Divinity. What is Divinity, in two words? Unconditional Love.

Even with our social pressures, a parent can choose to translate their "soul's" words to their children and not their "mind's" words.

❋ The soul's words constantly come from unconditional love, the only thing that there is, influencing naturally how you see and experience the world.

❋ The mind's words, however, are clouded with motives, guilt, and fear.

❋ When you see and experience the world through love, you are then living in your highest potential.

❋ When we, as parents, always present ourselves to children as love, children get the opportunity to experience Divinity through us, which in turn, reminds them of how to be Divinity to others. Our souls know automatically how to be love, but the point is to clear the clutter of the mind and the constraints of the body to allow the soul to soar in our actions.

When we allow ourselves to truly live from our soul, we have enabled ourselves to live each day anew in our highest dream for ourselves.

The perfect way to start every day with your child is to ask: Do you choose love? Who do you choose to be in the world? How do you wish for others to see you? And what dreams and experiences do you wish for today?

Chapter Eleven

THERE IS NO SUCH PLACE AS HELL

Of all the damaging messages that our world has been sending to its children, none could be more destructive than the teaching that there is a place of eternal damnation called "hell."

The reason this is so damaging is that it creates in the mind of the child the idea that if he or she is not "good," there will be a horrible, horrible punishment. This places into the heart of the child an extraordinary fear.

First, the child becomes afraid of God—who is The One they have been told *sends* them to "hell" if they misbehave. Then they become afraid of themselves, of the things they themselves might do in a moment of weakness (like "stealing" a cookie from the cookie jar), and other things they often *wish* they could do, or *want* to do, even though they know it's "bad."

In this way, they become afraid of life itself—which seems to be filled with temptations. Soon, they become confused as to what really is "good" and "bad." Is it okay to steal a cookie? Even if Mommy says not to? "I see Daddy doing it sometimes," a child might say. "Why shouldn't I be able to do it?"

So they turn to others to give them this information. Not just about cookies, but about everything in life that seems to be labeled either "good" or "bad."

In this moment they cease to be their own authority. Rather, they transfer this authority to others. To their parents—who themselves are often confused (especially about things like cookies!). To their teachers. To all those who are older than they. And often, as they themselves grow older, to their religion—which is where their idea of "hell" and "right" and "wrong" got its start to begin with, and which they hope can offer the Final Word and be the Ultimate Authority, since everyone else seems to be pretty confused about all of it.

Is fear to be our child's teacher?

The challenge with turning to religion is that most religions deal in fear. This is bad enough if you're an adult, but it can be emotionally treacherous if you're still just a child if and when the views of some religions are placed before you (to say nothing of being foisted upon you).

No child should have to live in fear. Yet many children do. *Too* many children do.

We believe it is good, then, to teach your children as soon as you can, in age-appropriate ways, that there simply is no such place as "hell," and that while there is a Being in the universe that many people call God, this Being loves us so much that It would never do harm to us in any way, shape, manner, or form.

When I was a child, I lived in abject fear of being punished by God for all the things that I did that were "bad." Each night, lying in bed, I would say the prayer that I had been taught: With trembling lips the words flowed from my frightened heart . . .

"Now I lay me down to sleepg. I pray the Lord my soul to keepg. If I should die before I wake, I pray the Lord my soul to take."

I actually thought there was a possibility that if I died before the dawn, God might not take me back to heaven, and I would be cast in the everlasting fires of hell for all eternity.

I actually believed that.

And so I went to Confession faithfully every Saturday, so that I could receive Communion faithfully every Sunday, so that I could stumble through the week as best I could in my seven-, eight-, and nine-year-old way, hoping that I didn't offend God too mightily, that all of my "offenses" would be forgiven, and that if I had any really big sins on my soul, I could get back to Confession and have them absolved by the priest before I got hit by a car or fell sick or for some other unexpected reason, died.

Believe me, my mother didn't have to tell me to look both ways before crossing the street! I wasn't afraid of dying nearly so much as I was afraid of what God would do to me *after* I died.

No child should have to live in that kind of fear.

No child.

It's all simply untrue

Of course, there is no such place as hell, nor is there any reason to be afraid of "God's wrath"—and *Conversations with God* makes this very clear.

The inaccuracy of these ideas is also discussed in *God's Message to the World: You've Got Me All Wrong*, published in October 2014, in which it is observed that God has no reason to experience or express wrath.

When you *are* everything, *have* everything, *created* everything, *experience* everything, and can *express* everything that you wish to express, what can there be to be filled with rage about?

When you *want* nothing, *need* nothing, *require* nothing, *demand* nothing, and *command* nothing, what can there be for you to feel betrayed about?

Finally, when there is nothing else in *existence* except *You*, who is there for you to be angry *with?* Whom shall you punish? Shall the right hand slap the left?

The idea of a wrathful God rests on a notion that God cares what you do or don't do as one of billions of creatures in one of billions of moments on one of billions of planets in one of billions of sectors of a cosmos that is one billion trillion times the size of your home galaxy. And not only that God cares, but that God cares *so much* as to be *deeply wounded* and *grievously offended* if your behavior does not live up to what is expected—nay, *commanded*—of you.

That would be akin to saying that *you* are concerned with one grain of sand out of all the grains of sand on all the beaches in all the world. You may *love* the sand and *all* its grains because they are part of the wonder and beauty of all the world's beaches, but you certainly wouldn't be filled with wrath if one of those grains was not reflecting the sunlight the way it was designed to.

And you certainly wouldn't be furious if you knew that this was but a temporary condition in any event, lasting no more than a nanosecond in the eternal span of that grain of sand's existence.

So it seems to me that the job of the conscious parent is to make sure that their offspring's childhood experience is not besmirched with frightening tales of a God in the sky who is watching their every move and will punish them with everlasting hell and damnation if they step out of line.

Yet, how best to do that . . . ?

Well, here, below, are some ideas and strategies that you might find useful in sharing with your children the idea from *Conversations with God* that . . .

THERE IS NO SUCH PLACE AS HELL.

The objective of the following teaching approach is to ease children's fears about where we go when we leave our bodies or transition (A.K.A., when we die). Traditional religions and popular culture speak of hell as a place one goes for being "bad" during life. But there is no such place as hell. Hell, as a place, is a figment of human imagination, used as a mechanism of control of our behavior. There is no place to go other than back to God, to the collective of spirits of which we are made.

Lesson 1

IN TEACHING CHILDREN THIS CONCEPT, YOU MAY WISH TO BEGIN BY . . .

. . . remembering that there are no "rules," no objective standard of "right" and "wrong," and no sin or judgment set out by God. If there are none of these things, then there is nothing for which to be punished.

Our time on Earth is voluntary—we have the chance to feel what it is like to be alive, BE spiritual beings in physical form, and experience all of the things that we cannot when we are in the perfection of oneness with the source (such as fear, turmoil, lack of something, anger, etc.). By experiencing the opposite of perfection, we can appreciate our natural state even more.

In traditional religion the concept of heaven versus hell was invented to control the masses. People were told that they had to earn their way into heaven through a number of avenues (for example: good deeds, not sinning, and/or being baptized), and hell was where they went if they displeased God and were not forgiven. Or if they displeased God in a way that could *not* be forgiven under any circumstances.

The understanding of heaven found in the New Spirituality is discussed in *Conversations with God, Book 1* on page 98. There, God says that there is no separate place called heaven, that the entire *universe is heaven*, and that we don't have to strive for it, or "get there," because:

> "*Enlightenment is understanding that there is nowhere to go, nothing to do, and nobody you have to be except exactly who you're being right now.*
>
> You are on a journey to nowhere.
>
> heaven—as you call it—is nowhere. Let's just put some space between the *w* and the *h* in that word and you'll see that heaven is now . . . here." (*Cwg, Book 1*, pg. 98)

The Little Soul and the Sun and *The Little Soul and the Earth* are very helpful for this discussion and will be referenced in this chapter. If you have not read them, we think you would find it very beneficial to do so.

Lesson 2

SOME QUESTIONS THAT CAN BE USED TO GUIDE THE DISCUSSION ARE . . .

❋ What are fairy tales? Are they real?

❀ What does it mean to be separated from God?

❀ Where do you think you go when you leave this Earth?

❀ What does rebirth mean?

Lesson 3

REMIND YOUR CHILDREN THAT WE CAME TO EARTH BY CHOICE . . .

. . . Coming to Earth is a choice we make to help us experience our true nature as Divine beings. We came to experience a *perceived* separation from God. We wanted to see the fullness of life, but when we only knew love (in our perfect forms) we could not *experience love* fully.

Rules of the Game

We realized that in order to fully appreciate love, we needed to see what the lack of love felt like so we built a place called Earth, which you can think of like a video game. In this *game*, we made up rules (constructs) in order to be able to feel a lack of perfection.

❀ One rule we made is that you have to eat to nourish your body. But then we also made it so that it *could* be hard to find the food you needed. By doing so, we allowed ourselves to see what the opposite of perfection feels like. Being hungry is the opposite of perfection (hunger satisfaction).

❀ Another rule is that we all look different. Why aren't we all born six feet tall? Imagine for a second, if we were all born six feet tall, we would only know ourselves as six feet tall but wouldn't even really have an explanation or description for it because we wouldn't have anything to compare it to. So by having us all grow to different heights, we are able to appreciate what it means to be a certain height (and even measure it) whether it is 6 feet tall or 5'2". Because of that diversity those heights mean something to us.

☀ In the perfection of the communion of souls (some would call it heaven) there is only light, there is only love, and comfort.

☀ The overriding rule we set up on Earth is a rule of opposites and dichotomies. In order to appreciate all that was perfect when we were with God, we agreed to experience the opposites on Earth. We created darkness, fear, pain, anger, jealousy, suffering, illness, scarcity, selfishness, and hatred so that we could understand light, love, comfort, happiness, contentment, peace, health, abundance, gratitude, and acceptance.

What all of these "rules" in our game did for us was to produce a feeling of separation from God. In doing so, we created our own "hell" on Earth, hell being a lack of knowledge, understanding, and oneness with God. But, again, hell, as a place of punishment does not exist. It is merely a mental state.

This is explained very clearly in "The Little Soul" books. Here is a brief synopsis:

The little soul (in the Sun Book) was quite happy with God but God asked, and then the soul started to wonder if it really knew and understood everything there was to understand. If a soul is pure light and no darkness, how can a soul fully understand itself as light? It must encounter darkness to see that which it is not. God gave the soul a choice to stay in perfection or to go to Earth to experience being a human. The soul was hesitant to leave God and be apart but wanted to know more. God said, even if we are apart, I am always with you because we are one and you will always come back to me—so there is nothing to worry about. So the soul decided to take the journey and see what life was about. The soul knew itself as forgiving and wanted to experience giving forgiveness, but also understood that someone had to make it feel hurt in order to be able to give forgiveness. Before going to Earth, the soul spoke with another soul who agreed to meet it there and do something that would warrant being forgiven.

So if we accept that we make agreements about how we will treat each other before we come to Earth, how can anything we do here be bad enough to cause us to be permanently separated from God and the rest of the collective of souls? Especially when we understand that our souls are perfect and infallible in nature.

Lesson 4

WHAT ABOUT ALL THE "BAD" THINGS IN THE WORLD?

. . . You might be wondering if we think everything is roses, sunshine, and butterflies and that nothing happens that is "bad." Things happen on Earth that don't fit within ideas of love and acceptance, and things happen that are harmful to others. But those things do not change the validity and value of the person's soul, either the perpetrator or the person harmed. Those actions might influence how they are perceived and received in the human world, but once they leave Earth, their soul is untouched. This is because nothing occurs in this world without our prior agreement, based on our soul's purpose for this life. If we make agreements for everything that will happen, *the good, the bad, and the ugly*, then how can we expect someone to pay for it for all of eternity? Please reread that sentence again.

If we make agreements for everything that will happen, *the good, the bad and the ugly*, then how can we expect someone to pay for it for all of eternity?

Worldview and beliefs

No one does anything "bad" according to their own beliefs and worldview. In fact, it is the opposite; every person on Earth does the things they do because they believe those actions are "right" according to their beliefs, or because it is required of them by their God or their impulses, or because their influences taught them a certain way of living. Someone who steals food does it because they think they (or someone else) need it. Someone who embarks on a holy fatwa does it because she thinks her God demands it for entry into "heaven." Someone who causes harm to another does it to fill a void within himself. Someone who encamps and tries to exterminate a whole race of people because he thinks it will lead to a cleaner bloodline for his country does it because he truly believes he is doing the right thing, no matter how deplorable it may be to the rest of us. They do these things for the same reasons (just with different results) that people do philanthropic work, go into burning buildings to save someone, or who do any number of the "good" things in the world. They do it because it fits their view of the world.

The soul's purpose

If something terribly horrible, horrific or unfathomable has happened in your family, you might be reading this saying, "What the heck? Are you saying my child's molestation was okay or even worse, his or her fault? If so, I'm about to put this darn book in the fireplace."

We want to assure you a hundred percent that we are not in any way minimizing that harmful crimes can be devastating and significant to humans. We acknowledge that the human experience of being molested, or hurt in other ways, is hugely significant in a child's human life and in no way their "fault."

Nor are we saying that the incident does not deserve to be mourned and handled within the constructs we have set up as a lawful society including prosecution if appropriate; there are reasons that we have put those laws into place.

What we are saying is that there is some soul's purpose for every act and experience we have on Earth, and often that reason is far beyond our reach, memory, or understanding of why it would or could occur. Even though we may have made agreements prior to coming to Earth that lead to pain in our earthly existence, we do believe that when someone is harmed on Earth, they should rightfully allow themselves to *feel* the emotional pain and process it within the human understanding, for this is one of the things we came to Earth to do.

To experience, feel, and learn to overcome adversity is one of our soul's desires here on Earth and is one of the ways that we can come to appreciate the perfection of heaven. In other ways, our imperfections on Earth are the natural consequence of becoming human. Even if it feels "bad" on Earth, if it is a natural consequence of the earthly game/reality, then it can't be bad.

Why me, then?

Why would my child be harmed by another on such a profound level? Are you saying we chose that? Would the perpetrator really go to back to God with me? They don't go to hell? How is that possible?

It is possible because it is all an illusion, a game we set up to come to a fuller understanding of Who We Really Are.

And as stated above in the quote from *Conversations with God, Book 1*, what kind of God would we be if we created ourselves in an imperfect fashion and then expected ourselves to be perfect or face eternal damnation? In a word, it would be self-defeating. We could not create ourselves imperfectly and then hold ourselves to an unreachable standard.

Take the animal kingdom as an example. Lions kill water buffalo and gazelles, leopards kill road-runners and birds, cats and birds kill mice, and male polar bears sometimes kill polar bear cubs. We may be disturbed by these images, and we may even wonder why it has to be that way, but do we ever sit down and condemn the animal predators for doing what they came here to do? We see it as a natural cycle of life that some are the predators and some are the prey. Their souls are not tainted because they killed—they believed it to be necessary according to their own set of beliefs (needs).

Lesson 5

SINCE THE SOUL IS A PURE MANIFESTATION OF GOD, THERE IS NO PLACE FOR THE SOUL TO GO, BESIDES HEAVEN.

There is nothing that isn't God, and nothing that isn't perfect, even though sometimes on Earth we do not see things that way.

There are examples in nature to show that things can be there even when you do not see or know about them. Consider sharing the following with your children:

❋ A rainbow is a universal symbol of calm after a storm. We all know to look for a rainbow if the conditions are "right"—the sun is out during or immediately following rain. When we see a rainbow, we are actually seeing the full spectrum of color that is produced when light is fragmented. Those colors are always present in the light, but when they are traveling together on one path, they are seen as "light." When light bounces off water (rain and clouds) it produces the effect of a rainbow because water splits the light into separate rays. None of this matters, though, to our enjoyment of the rainbow. All we care about is the beauty and wonder of the light that's always present, just viewed in a different way.

❋ *Seeds in the ground.* Nature is in a constant state of growth and rebirth. Seeds can be growing in the ground long before we know of their existence. But our lack of knowledge does nothing to diminish their being there.

❋ *Pregnancy.* A fetus can grow in the uterus for weeks and months before the woman knows it is there. It follows its natural process of development using the mother's nutrients, and even if she isn't aware, her body is offering life-giving assistance. Her lack of knowledge will not change the fact that it is there, and eventually the female's body will show that a baby is growing inside through the form of a baby bumpg.

Our soul

Our soul is ever-present within us, even if we can't see it or don't always remember how to access it. Our soul is God. Therefore, God is always present in and around us.

❋ As discussed above, heaven is everywhere and there is nothing else. So even in places that look like hell, we are still in heaven. We may need to re-open our minds and understanding to recognize it as such, but it only takes one second to change your mind and transcend the moment from hellish conditions of pain and suffering into the joy of heaven.

❋ heaven, a state of bliss and oneness with God, is the experience of divine love no matter your physical location. Hell is merely a mindset and a tortuous place we put ourselves into which is derived from fear, not to be confused with the traditional scary "hell" with fire and a devil and eternal suffering. When we choose to view every situation with love, we can transport ourselves on the journey of the soul into eternal happiness; but when we allow fear and anger to consume us, we cause ourselves to be separate from God, which is the only manifestation of hell.

✲ In normal conversation, we often use the word heaven indiscriminately to mean very pleasurable, so that we can begin to confuse the meaning of the word.

✲ But what if any moment of bliss you have, is your manifestation of heaven in the moment? How amazing would life be if we understood that we could have heaven any time we want? Well guess what? We can!

✲ At this point of the book and your work with your children, they will probably already understand that love is all there is, their own true divine nature, their oneness with God and everyone, their ability to create their own reality, and the true totality of themselves, which is a balance of mind, body, and spirit—these understandings produce heaven in your life.

✲ In *CwG, Book 1*, God points out that if heaven is already on Earth, it would be ridiculous to think you could you go anywhere else when you die. Why would God make you leave heaven on earth to go to hell? She wouldn't.

Lesson 6

HELP YOUR CHILDREN TAKE CONTROL OF THEIR UNDERSTANDING OF THE CONCEPT . . .

. . . by using their imaginations and creativity.

✲ Have them write a short story about the difference between love and fear, what they look like in action, and how each emotion feels inside.

✲ Have them explain how love and fear can be related to the concepts of heaven and hell as explained in this chapter.

❋ You can even have them put on a play to show you how
to create a feeling of heaven on earth, even when things
are going "badly."

Changing our minds

Discuss ways that the next time they are in pain, for any reason,
they can change their mind in an instant, coming out of the
depths of hell into the beauty of a life lived in heaven.

❋ One such way is when someone is being mean to them,
instead of getting upset, they can choose to feel compassion for what is going on inside the other's world,
beliefs, and understanding. They can choose not to
internalize the feeling of being hurt and instead send
out love.

❋ They can also ask, "What hurts you so bad that you
feel you have to hurt me in order to heal it?" (from *The
Storm Before the Calm*)

❋ When they are down for any reason, or no reason at all,
they can take five minutes and write down five things
for which they are grateful. Expressing gratitude, even
in times of pain, can catapult you from hell to heaven.

❋ If you are feeling sad, find someone else who is also
sad and be kind to them. By helping another find a
moment of happiness, you will bring about your own
happiness.

❋ Teach them humor. It is very difficult to stay sad about
any situation, if you can reach inside yourself and find
a bit of humor. For instance, Emily has a potentially
fatal autoimmune disease, which causes chronic pain
and weakness, and is very difficult to deal with at times.
However, she has managed to have a beautiful life of
heaven on earth because she laughs, a lot. She laughs at

herself, she finds the humor in terrible situations, and refuses to allow her disease to control her.

☀ Kindness and humor can bring such relief to any situation.

Lesson 7

THERE IS NO ROOM FOR HELL IN A LIFE LIVED FULLY . . .

. . . Humans are the embodiment of love, light, and energy from God. When we truly remember this, we will have no need for fear. We will come to a complete knowledge of ourselves as worthy of experiencing heaven in every moment without exception. We wish that for you and your children.

Chapter Twelve

DEATH IS THE SAME AS BIRTH

Most people have a fear of dying. Even those who hold a belief that true death does not exist (in the sense that all souls live forever) often fear the end of *this* life, in *this* form, in the physical realm, because if nothing else, it means the end of this particular experience—and they have enjoyed this experience very much.

(Even if they have not enjoyed it, it is the only experience they've had [that most can remember], and often for that reason alone they don't want it to end.)*

The fastest and most effective way to eliminate the fear of death in your children is to eliminate the fear of death in yourself. And the fastest way to do that is to have death itself explained to you, thoroughly.

The ninth and final book in the *Conversations with God* series, titled *Home with God in a Life That Never Ends*, does a marvelous job of doing exactly that from a spiritual point of view. Many have said it is the most extraordinary book produced on the topic of death in the past 100 years.

Maybe the past 1,000.

Maybe forever.

I feel I can report this point of view with impunity because I'm very clear that I did not write the book in question. Nor did I write, in the sense of having *authored* the material, any of the *Conversations with God* books. Rather, all I did after posing my questions was take dictation. And I am certain now, in retrospect, that even my questions were inspired by Divinity. God knew just what I needed to ask in order for God to share just what God desired to share.

A new definition of death

In *Home With God*, I asked God directly: What is this experience that human beings call "death?" And God gave me an answer that I never heard before: "Death is simply a process of re-identification."

It is a process by which we come to know the Totality of Who We Really Are. In short, we realize that we are each an Individuation of Divinity. A singularization of The Singularity. An aspect of God.

Then we are told that what we call death is part of a larger process: the Eternal Journey of the Soul. This larger process is a never-ending passage through the realms in the Kingdom of God.

There are three such realms, we are told. These are: the Realm of the Spiritual, the Realm of the Physical, and the Realm of Pure Being (which also could be whimsically called the Realm of the "Spirisical"—making up a word that indicates and describes the other two realms combined.)

The movement from the Realm of the Physical to the Realm of the Spiritual that we call "death" is taken through the Realm of Pure Being. The movement from the Realm of the Spiritual to the Realm of the Physical is called "birth."

From Pure Being we have come, and to Pure Being we shall return. It is in this place that we know God in its purest, non-differentiated form. And so it could be said that from God we have come and to God we shall return.

Yet what *is* this "God" to whom we so often refer?

If we might be allowed to use physics and human biology as an analogy, God could be considered the stem cell of the universe. Stem cells, as we know, are the undifferentiated foundational cells of the body. The raw material of our biology. The not-yet-identified nor specified Energy Units of life itself.

I call these cellular units Particles of God. Some people call them souls.

Helping children to understand

Now the above is a much more sophisticated look at things than we would place before our children at the age of four, seven, or even ten. So we are advised to find a simpler analogy.

One of the most wonderful ways to explain death to children is to explain birth to children.

Most children can be brought an understanding of the miracle of birth at a relatively young age. Children who have seen Mommy bring a baby home from the hospital have no doubt already asked many questions about this impending event. Children who have witnessed the birth of a pet's litter will likewise have been exposed to a marvelous experience, which can be explained to them by a parent in loving and gentle ways.

Once a child has experienced and understands birth, a bridge to understanding death has been built. Death, it can be explained, is not the end of anything, but the beginning of a new life, in a different place—just as birth is the beginning of new life in this place that we call Earth.

We may not be able to see the person who has died in their physical form, but we can still see them in our Mind by closing our eyes and remembering what they looked like, what they sounded like, and what they did with us when they were with us in this place.

Just as birth is a happy time, death is a happy time, too, for the person who is experiencing it. This can be explained to children in age-appropriate ways, and that can make them much less afraid of death. Of their own death, and of the death of others.

It need not be difficult to explain to children that even though death may be the end of something for us, it is not the end of something for the person who has died. It is just the opposite. It is the beginning of something. The beginning of something wonderful and joyful and happy.

And so, even though we will miss that person being in our lives in a physical way, we can be happy that they are having such a wonderful time. And we can also be happy knowing that we will see them again, when it is our turn to go to the place in which they now live.

Now here, below, are some other ideas and strategies that you might find useful in sharing with your children the idea from *Conversations with God* that . . .

DEATH IS THE SAME AS BIRTH.

The objective of the following teaching approach is to help you ease children's fears about death and what happens to us when we leave this earthly life and rejoin God in the collective of all that is. Death is the same as rebirth because we are moving from one reality (physical) to another (spiritual).

By understanding that we never die, we can stop feeling pain and fear about death and embrace life in a new and more dynamic way. What's more, by releasing the fear of the process of "death" and coming to a new appreciation of it as a rebirth into the freedom of the spiritual world, children can come to view death as a beautiful gift, something, not only to *not fear*, but something to celebrate and look forward to with excitement.

This doesn't mean that children should look for opportunities to die; it means that earthly life is very short, and they will get there no matter what, but in celebrating death as a wonderful part of life, they can come to embrace their life even more fully.

We can also help children to feel happy for the soul of a person who dies, even while feeling sad that they will be missed.

Lesson 1

IN TEACHING CHILDREN THIS CONCEPT, YOU MAY WISH TO BEGIN BY . . .

. . . reminding your children what they learned in Chapter 9: There are three parts to you: mind, body, and soul. Remind them that these parts are all equally important and that the experience of *you* comes from how they work together both on Earth and when we are with God "on the other side."

Lesson 2

SOME QUESTIONS THAT CAN BE USED TO GUIDE THE DISCUSSION ARE . . .

☀ What happens when a person dies?

☀ Are you scared of death?

☀ What does rebirth mean?

* Can you still feel people who have passed on before you?

* If you can let go of a fear of death, what other fears will go away?

Lesson 3

"DEATH" IS REALLY A CONTINUATION OF LIFE . . .

. . . in the spiritual realm. It brings us to a beingness of oneness and complete unity with everyone that has ever, or will ever, live.

In *Home with God in a Life that Never Ends*, God helps us to remember that "Home with God" is not a place. It is everywhere, all things, all the time and that there is no "Away from God." The complete oneness of Now—meaning that there is no time—and the unending process of life through these constructs we call "birth" and "death" is explained beautifully by the "Applorange" metaphor. We think it would be helpful to use that metaphor in a concrete fashion to share with your children.

* Take an orange and an apple and cut them both into four quarters from top to bottom through the core/center. Setting aside a 1/4 slice of each, sit your child down for a healthy snack for the body, mind, and soul! (Okay, we mean feed the three extra slices of each, the orange and the apple to your child while you use one of each to demonstrate.) Put one apple and one orange slice together using a toothpick so they become a half of a piece of fruit we will call the Applorange.

* Where the two slices meet will be called the core, which is where we experience Absolute Reality, Total Awareness, and Oneness with God and Everything. The side made of apple will be called the physical life, and the side made of orange will be called spiritual life. Every soul on a life journey passes through the core to go from

the spiritual to the physical (what we call birth) and to go from the physical to the spiritual (what we call death).

❋ Show your children the toothpick going through the Applorange and ask them to imagine this toothpick is a tunnel. Then tell them that they can travel, at will, through this tunnel to either side (physical or spiritual); even backward and forward, up and down, side to side, and around the core.

❋ Explain to them that while they are traveling through the tunnel (living life in the physical or spiritual sides) they can do and see whatever they want, whenever they want. When they "die" in human terms, they aren't really dying; they are merely traveling from one world/ awareness (physical) to another (spiritual). When they are "born" in human terms, they are also simply traveling from one world/awareness (spiritual) to another (physical). In both directions, they only have to decide to enter the core to experience the feeling of oneness and transition between the worlds.

So what is the process we call death?

Using the "Applorange" we can picture death (and also birth, by the way) as a three-part doorway into the Core's state of Absolute Oneness.

First Doorway

The first doorway is the one in which we shed our human vehicle, how we identify with our physical body.

In this time we realize that the body is only something we have; it is not who we are. During this time we adjust to not having the physical restrictions we had in the physical realm. We might have trouble knowing that we have left Earth, and be confused as we shed our body. We can enter and leave this space back to "physical life" many times as we adjust to having left our bodies. Many people enter here before the hour of their human "death."

For a concrete example, you can relate the body to the clothes we wear. When we put on a new outfit, we feel something—hot, cold, comfortable, dressed up, sporty, pretty, handsome, relaxed, glamorous, artsy, etc. When we shed our body through the first stage of death, it is similar to shedding your clothes. Whatever physical feeling we had in relation to our clothes goes away when we remove the clothes. It is the same with shedding our body. The things having that body told us about ourselves—short, tall, blond, brunette, athletic, more cerebral, healthy, ill, strong, weak, etc.—are shed with the body, and we are able to experience ourselves as Who We Really Are instead of being tied to a particular body type to define ourselves.

Second Doorway

The second doorway allows us to shed our human mind, beliefs, thoughts, and our mental identity.

This is the time in which we learn that our minds and thoughts are no more *us* than our bodies, and that the thoughts we think about ourselves may have limited our full knowledge and expression of Who We Really Are. During this segment, we can take as long or as short of a "time" as we wish it to, depending on how much processing we have to do to kind of get over our preconceived fears and beliefs about how "death" will feel as well as getting over the stories we told ourselves about who we were in life.

For a concrete example, you can relate the mind and thoughts to a song or script playing over and over in our heads, which is finally switched off in the second stage of death. Many times what we tell ourselves in our mind has roots in what parents, friends, and strangers have said to us, about us. In other words, we take on the scripts about Who We Are, the purpose of life, what God Wants, and how we will (or will not) be judged from what people tell us. The second stage allows us to turn that radio off and quiet those intrusive thoughts and begin to know Who We Really Are, at our soul. This enables us to overcome sour mental constructs (fears) about death and see it for what it really is, a beautiful transition from one world/awareness to another.

Third Doorway

The third doorway is the shedding of the soul (our understanding of us as an individual, separate from God).

Yes! We even shed this as we begin to remember that we are not separate from God but are Completely One with God and Everything, and we desire to feel that oneness again. As we become aware of the presence of God (within, all around us, and in an all-encompassing of everything) we begin to see a light at the end of the tunnel. As we travel along the tunnel towards the light, we become more and more aware of the unmistakable love, comfort, and warmth of the Core, and we realize we want to be there. As we become more aware of these things, we shed the final vestiges of our individual identity (our knowingness as us being a separate being) and remember that God's love and light is "All there is." *Home with God*, pg. 225. In full understanding that we are one with all that is, we embrace our place in the light . . . we merge back into God, into the Essence of the universe, the All. We, in a beautiful instant have complete love, knowing, openness, belonging, and peace. We melt into the Essence as if we are Home, and in that moment, we finally remember that we have never really left God. We just blocked part of our conscious understanding of our oneness so that we could experience life. And in that moment, we also release any individual desires.

Examples of moments of Completion on Earth:

* How do your children *feel* when they are doing something they love? Whether it is playing a sport, dancing, swimming, singing, doing a piece of art, or reading a really interesting book, how does it feel? It's that feeling of just *getting* something so fully that you could scream

"Yahoo!," cry with gratitude, jump up and down, or smile from ear to ear.

* How do your children feel when they walk with nature, meditate, smell a field of flowers, or skip a rock along the water? Do they feel a supreme moment of calm, an inexplicable welling up of love and joy?

* How do they feel when they meet a new friend but just can't imagine they haven't known the person all along? Have they ever made a new friend who was a fast and loyal friend from the start? Did their heart sing when they met? The moment when you make one of these new/lifelong friends is a moment of pure joy because you can feel your souls recognizing each other through the costume of your human form.

These are moments of Completion on Earth—when your soul is working in concert with the universe to be just where and what you are meant to be for that second. These moments, that are most similar to shedding your soul and experiencing oneness with God, can be had anytime either in death or life. They are the moments when we "shed" our facades and embrace our soul's purpose, to be One with the All.

We are God

Through the shedding of the identities of the mind, body, and soul we remember totally and completely Who We Really Are. We Are God!

When we merge with God, we have the opportunity to have a "life review" in which we can watch a "show" of the human life we just departed. This can be similar to walking through a gallery of photos from your life, listening to a song or a prayer that highlights all of your experiences, watching a movie of the important incidences, or even swimming in a flowing river of the feelings you had washing away all the doubts you ever knew.

That review (however it is characterized for you) is powerful and meaningful as we finally understand why and how everything occurred in life. We have a much fuller knowing of life and its meanings as we see everything from both the perspective of the observed and the observer.

With that knowledge we get to make the most creative decision of all, "What do I want to be, next?" And then God asks the Holiest Question of All, The Holy Inquiry: "Do you want to stay in the spiritual or go back to your life?" Yes, you can "come back to life" after "death."

How is that possible?

* It is possible because time does not exist, time is all happening in one moment, and in that moment we can go to, be, do, have anything we have ever wanted to. We can, at the "hour of our death" reverse death and be alive again.

* If we feel we have completed everything we wanted to do in that life, we will say, "Yes, I want to stay, I am ready to move on." But if at the moment of "death" we feel we have unfinished business, we can go back to our body in the moment just prior to "death" and *be alive again*, without anyone on Earth ever being the wiser.

* Much like you can rewind a DVD to a specific place in a movie that you want to relive/revisit, we can "rewind" life and go back to an exact spot to pick up and try again.

* Much like when you are playing a game like tag or hide and seek, and you can ask your friend for a "do-over," the Holy Question is your chance to give yourself a "do-over" for your life! But there is no way that You-God won't grant it to yourself, because You-God always want You to succeed!

In fact, God says we all do this repeatedly throughout a lifetime. This is how we can say that, "no one ever dies at a moment they have not chosen." Because you always have the chance to come back to the physical world if you are not finished or if you just want to continue. When you are, finally, there in the "core," having achieved mergence with God, and can answer the Holy Question with, "I am complete and ready to move on," then and only then will you choose not to go back to life. So again, on a spiritual level, you choose whether you live or die, always. Always your choice. Always and forever your own choice.

Death doesn't happen to you

You choose the moment of your "death." You don't have to fear death because you can always choose to come back.

In the moment that you say, "Yes, I have completed what I came here to do," you have the opportunity to make a new choice. Be Born into the spiritual realm, stay in oneness and complete symphony with God. Or go back to the physical world for a "new" birth, or even the same one over again. So even in the ending of your previous physical life, you get to choose what to do next, i.e., what movie to watch/participate in next.

There is no way to *ever* fail to get where you are "going" because there is *nowhere else to go because we are already here!* Here—and everywhere—is oneness, creativeness, and God-ness.

Lesson 4

WHEN YOU UNDERSTAND THE NATURE OF DEATH—AS BIRTH—YOU CAN STOP BEING AFRAID OF EVERYTHING . . .

. . . and anything . . . from here to eternity.

There is absolutely nothing to fear because when even death is a beautiful, intentional act of the rebirth of the soul, then *nothing else can ever hurt us without our consent.* We are in complete control of our destiny even if we aren't always aware of it in the human existence.

We acknowledge that this seems like a big concept for children to understand, so Emily asked her daughter, Sage, who is eight years old, what happens when you leave Earth. (They had previous conversations saying that death was a beautiful rejoining of the All and God, but had never spoken directly about the actual process of death.) Sage's answer shows that children remember more than we give them credit for. She said, "When you die, you are reborn. You get a new life. That's all. Can I have some ice cream now?" She has a complete understanding of the process—birth and death are one in the same and was bored with the idea, ready to move on.

Lesson 5

IF WE HAVE SUCH A CHOICE, THEN WHY COME BACK TO EARTH AT ALL?

We might wonder why we would ever leave the all-encompassing comfort and light of mergence with God. We don't have to; we can choose to remain in completion for all of eternity, which again, is only occurring in the moment of now. But God says that if we stay there forever, we will lose the desire to experience because the love and feeling of home is so complete. When we do decide to leave the collective to give Earth another shot, it is because we crave that contextual experience that can only occur in the physical form. And so we take on a physical body, our tool for the earthly experience. We come to Earth to experience human love, touch, and even all of the negative aspects of the human existence.

It's kind of like standing upright sometimes and standing on our head other times. If you had to stand upright, all day every day, you would get bored and tired and wonder why you can't try something different. So, if you are the adventurous type, which you are . . . because you are God . . . you might try standing on your head for a totally new perspective. But then, again, you will get tired and bored with that and want to try something new. Neither perspective is wrong or shows you a false view of the world (or your nature); they just aren't, either, something you want to do all day every day for the rest of your life (or eternity).

Lesson 6

THE REASON WE DON'T WANT OTHERS TO DIE . . .

. . . is we think that death severs our physical connection to them. We think we are mourning their opportunity to *live, taste, touch, and feel human love;* but in actuality, we are mourning our ability to see them readily.

In that moment of the mergence with God that occurs in the core, every member of our life (past, present and future) is there to greet and celebrate our spiritual birth. Because there is no time, and all time is occurring in one moment, the "time" we are apart when one of us stays behind on Earth is really just a blink. Just as we are never really separated from God (we only tell ourselves we are) we are never really separated from our loved ones either.

An example you can use to help your child see what separation is, and why it is an illusion, is "homesickness." When kids spend the night at a friend or relative's house, they often wake in the middle of the night, disoriented and missing home. They know where their parents are physically, and they feel separated from them, even if only by a few blocks or miles. But children also know that their parents are available and would come comfort them if they were scared.

It is the same with God; even though we may not see God in our conscious sight, we know God would never leave us to be alone and scared.

Children can even come to understand that souls of people we love, whether they have already passed or not, can actually be "with" them any time they need. Think about when a mom calls a child out of the blue because she felt something was "wrong." This is an instance of her soul being with the child through their spiritual connection, thereby allowing her to actually be with the child (through a call) when the child needed it. Souls that have already passed can do the same thing, because all of the past and the future are occurring in this moment, and souls have perfect awareness of everything, all the time.

If we can get children to understand that a person being reborn into the spiritual realm does not truly take the person away from us, and we can actually make them more available to "be there" for us, holding our hand, comforting us in a spiritual sense, then children will be able to feel less fear about death. Call it a "soul phone call!" Our dearly departed are never really away from us at all.

We can even help children come to an understanding of "death" as a wonderful celebration, the continuation of a soul's life purpose, to rejoin God in the most beautiful hug you can ever imagine. By doing so, we can remove the fear of death from children's lives and assist them in truly living life fully, again reminding them that even after "death" we can have contact with our loved ones at any time because there really is no difference of space or time.

By helping children understand the process of birth into the physical realm, we can also assist them in relieving their fears of death.

    ❀ Children watch others coming "into" life and see it as a joyous occasion. They understand that the person wasn't here and now is. The same is occurring in the opposite direction. The person is here and then "is not." These are just flipped sides of the same coin. Death is a rebirth into the spiritual, and birth is a kind of death from spiritual to physical.

❈ The reason we are so excited about birth is because the baby is getting the opportunity to experience what we came here to do, feel, touch, love and be . . . and we can feel, touch, love and be with that baby by virtue of their birth, fulfilling one of our own soul's desires.

Lesson 7

THE PROCESS OF BIRTH AND DEATH (OR CREATING OURSELVES) IS NEVER-ENDING.

We can continue this process of traveling along the pathways of the Applorange forever, until we decide to stopg. And even the decision to stop and "rest" in the collective is a process of creation of its own because it is a decision about who we are in that moment.

A tree and its seeds are a great example of how life never ends. A tree sprouts from a seed, it grows to be mighty and strong, and then it drops its seeds, which can grow again. When the old tree withers and dies, its energy is preserved and passed on to the next tree. The essence that is "Tree" never really dies; even as one incarnation of it rots on the ground, its matter feeds the new tree. And this can go on for generation of tree after generation of tree. Life is never-ending in the same way. We are "born," grow, build a life, plant the seeds of understanding and existence, and eventually shed those understandings in "death," only to reap the benefits of our experience in the spiritual world as well as our next physical life. And on and on.

Lesson 8

THEN WHY DO WE DIE? WHY CAN'T WE JUST STAY ALIVE FOREVER?

. . . The answer is that we don't ever really die because our essence, the part of us that exists across all space and time, lives forever. But we understand that children will still want to know why we have to leave Earth, the only thing that we can remember about our existence.

To put it simply, for children to understand, we come to Earth with a little checklist of things we wish to accomplish, no matter how few or many years it takes to do them. The soul is keeping track of this list, and the list probably doesn't even have anything to do with us as individuals.

Once the soul has checked all of its tasks off the list, it is ready to rejoin the collective and experience the mergence with God discussed above. The soul is always allowed to stay, or come back, but it will probably choose to have a new experience so that it can continue recreating itself in the next grandest version of the highest vision it ever held about itself. Or in child-friendly terms, it wants to experience a new day, with a new bigger dream!

Once we have left the physical realm and gone back to the spiritual realm, we have the pleasure of reviewing the things we experienced in the physical, but our understanding is of clearer, broader regard. We can see things we couldn't before, make connections between incidences to see their full value, and bask in the greatness of knowledge and understanding that we can only have in the spiritual. . . and then we will remember what our soul already knows. We are infinite beings, with an infinite number of opportunities, and an infinite amount of love to give and receive.

Chapter Thirteen

THERE ARE NO GOOD GUYS AND NO BAD GUYS

It is sad that we have raised our children in an "us against them" culture. They encounter this paradigm everywhere—in the media, in television shows, in movies, in video games, in comic books, in children's board games, in competitions (like which school class can sell the most fund-raising candy bars, or which Girl Scout Troop can sell the most cookies), and in sports.

In all of these contexts, children see themselves as the ones they are "for" and the others as the ones they are "against." For children it can be just a short emotional step from there to: "The Good Guys and the Bad Guys."

It should not be surprising then, given this upbringing, that this Good Guy/Bad Guy mentality pretty much permeates human society. As adults it's Conservatives vs. Liberals (or vice-versa), Democrats vs. Republicans (or vice-versa), Whites vs. Blacks (or vice-versa), Straights vs. Gays (or vice-versa), Christians vs. Non-Christians (or vice-versa), Muslims vs. non-Muslims (or vice-versa), Jews vs. non-Jews (or vice-versa), Believers vs. Non-believers (or vice-versa), Poor vs. Rich, (or vice-versa), Young vs. Old (or vice-versa), Male vs. Female (or vice-versa), even Healthy vs. Unhealthy (or vice-versa).

Just as we did as children, we tend to line up, metaphorically, wearing the jersey and the colors of "our team," and working to defeat "their team." The truth is, there are no inherently Good Guys and no inherently Bad Guys, but simply people who are trying to make their way through life, each person trying to get what he hopes he can get of what he imagines that he needs to be happy, and each person trying to avoid what she hopes she can avoid of what she imagines would make her unhappy.

It is what makes us happy or unhappy—as individuals and as groups—that is going to have to fundamentally change if we are ever to change human society, and finally civilize civilization.

The way out of all this

The escape from this maze is open to us—but it won't happen overnight. Its process is slow, but it is sure: Simply teach our children a new story.

Shift the emphasis that is placed on all our human endeavors from "winning" or "losing" to "doing our best." Make *that* what makes us happy. And teach our children to find their happiness in knowing they excelled and did better than they thought they could do—or that they did before—rather than that they did better than "the others."

Doing better than "ourselves" rather than doing better than "the others" is the key.

Eliminate, as well, the idea in our children that "failure" exists. Teach them that "failure" is an illusion. (See: *The Ten Illusions of Humans*, as found and deeply explored in *Communion with God*, and listed here as Item #18 in *1,000 Words That Would Change the World*, found in the Preface of this book.)

With the elimination of the idea of "failure," the activity that we call "competition" would become a whole new experience for children (and, ultimately, for the adults they will become).

Teach your children that while some kinds of competition can be fun (Little League baseball, certain classroom or school contests, etc.), life itself is not about producing winners and losers—and, in fact, there is *no such thing as a loser.*

Even not scoring the most runs, even not selling the most candy bars, is not "losing." It is another winning outcome, when "winning" is defined as "having the fun of doing something stimulating and invigorating."

"The minute you attempt *anything* that you're interested in, you have won," we should tell our children. "Because what you have 'won' is the joy and the exhilaration and the elation of the activity itself, not the outcome."

Tell them—and *show them*—that it is the *process*, not the *product*, of every endeavor where life's delight and pleasure will be found.

We'll then remove our offspring from the Victory/Defeat, Benefit/Detriment, Reward/Punishment, Recognized/Ignored, Success/Failure, Profit/Loss scenarios that currently dot the landscape of childhood's emotional journey.

Stop setting the stage for dysfunctional and non-beneficial adult expectations, encounters and experiences, and create instead a New Cultural Story to share with your children that will result in a whole different set of ideas of what life is really about—and what it is *for*.

Clarifying our terms

Once "failure" is eradicated as a term to be used regarding certain aspects of the human experience, and once the experience that we now call "competition" is not seen as "us against them," but simply us working to enhance and improve our own performance, the next step is the elimination of the "Our Side/Their Side-Good Guy/Bad Guy" labels that go along with the old way of seeing things.

We can eradicate these labels through sharing with our children that *every* person is a "good person"—even people who support goals or objectives different from ours.

And at some point in your child's later development—perhaps in their teenage years—there may come a time to bring up a much larger idea for discussion and exploration: The idea that everything that any human being does originates as an act of love. In this sense there *are* no Good Guys and Bad Guys, only people trying to express their love.

Some people don't know how to do that without hurting others, but that doesn't mean they are inherently bad or evil; it means they are emotionally embryonic, ill-equipped, unknowing and undeveloped, psychologically immature, and spiritually unaware. They may even be psychiatrically disabled. But they are not pernicious, wicked, monstrous, or villainous at their core. They are simply severely emotionally handicapped.

This is far too complex a notion to place before young children, of course. (It is even difficult for many adults to understand or accept). Yet at some point those who closely examine human nature and human response and human interactions come to observe that everything that human beings do—even those things that most humans judge to be terribly wrong—is done out of someone's love for something or someone (including, in some cases, themselves). That love may be being expressed in a horribly dysfunctional way, but it is love nonetheless that sponsored their destructive act.

This doesn't make the action "right." This doesn't condone it or approve of it. But it does make it, at a minimum, understandable. People act out love in many ways, and sometimes those ways are distorted and dysfunctional, demonstrating the exact opposite of love.

A person steals because he loves what he doesn't have and wants to have it. A person cheats because she loves and wants something she doesn't think she can get any other way. A person lies because he loves being thought of in a certain way and doesn't want the truth to come out. Even a person or a group committing violence or terrorism does so out of love for a principle or a person, which sometimes—far too often—tragically translates into hatred for some other principle or person, not least because of our centuries-old "Our Side/Their Side-Good Guy/Bad Guy" labeling habits.

Again, this doesn't condone the action, but it makes it easier for us to understand "how they could have done such a thing," and to pardon or forgive at least some of the lesser offenses of which so many righteously accuse each other . . . and for which we seek revenge, retribution, and the harshest punishment.

Even our criminal justice system recognizes innocence by reason of diminished capacity.

Teach your children well

If humans were trained in childhood to know that life is not about "them against us"—not even in sports or other kinds of competitions—but that life is really about expressing the truth of our Oneness with God and with each other, they would have a whole different set of values to carry into adulthood.

If humans were taught in childhood that all so-called "competitions" are really about challenging ourselves to put out our next best effort, and in that sense to continue to better ourselves, they would have a whole different set of values to carry into adulthood.

If humans were treated in childhood as if there were no winners and no losers, but only participants in life's many opportunities and experiences, each at the highest level they wish to or are able to express, they would have a whole different set of values to carry into adulthood.

If our childhood "entertainments" did not center around Good vs. Evil, Nice People vs. Bad People, White Hats vs. Black Hats, our children would have a whole different set of values to carry into adulthood.

These are some things that you could teach your children. These are some of the values you could invite them to embrace.

There are other ideas and strategies that you might find useful as well as you seek to share with your children the idea from *Conversations with God* that . . .

THERE ARE NO GOOD GUYS AND NO BAD GUYS.

The objective of the following teaching approach is to relieve children of the fear that anyone can do anything to cause them real harm.

We can also invite your children to come away with the perspective of the masters, that while sometimes people do things "to us" on this Earth that make us uncomfortable, we can choose to view them through the lens of the soul. We do not have to suffer for another's actions; through the idea that we create our own reality (You decide how life feels, Chapter 7), we can view every "bad" circumstance as an opportunity for growth, understanding, and forgiveness. We can also come to understand that since we all come here with the same soul's purpose (to be who we really are—Divinity expressed), we can view our role in a "hurtful" situation as a chance to be an angel for others. This can manifest in our being forgiving, helping the other to come to a new realization about themselves, and even supplying them with something they need in that moment (for example, being a supplier of food to someone who steals from us).

"In the spiritual sense, there are no victims and no villains in the world, although in the human sense it appears that there surely are. Yet because you are Divine, nothing can happen against your will." (*What God Said*, pg. 290)

Lesson 1

IN TEACHING CHILDREN THIS CONCEPT, YOU MAY WISH TO BEGIN BY . . .

. . . reminding your children about the concept of Chapter 5: There is no such thing as right and wrong, there is only that which works and that which does not work, that which is effective and that which is not effective, given what it is we are wishing to do. Since there is no right and wrong, there is no good or bad. The idea that there are no "good guys" or "bad guys" is a direct outgrowth of this understanding. The identical purpose with which everyone comes to Earth includes the ways in which we will interact with others to help them achieve this single purpose.

Lesson 2

SOME QUESTIONS THAT CAN BE USED TO GUIDE THE DISCUSSION ARE . . .

* What does it mean to be "good" in your mind? What does it mean to be "bad"?

* What does it mean to "suffer"?

* Can you think of a time when you hurt someone else's feelings by accident, or by forgetting to do something? Does that make you bad?

* Can you think of a time that you did something on purpose that wound up hurting someone's feelings, even though you didn't intend for them to be hurt?

* How can we avoid being attacked, functionally, physically, mentally, or spiritually?

* If you step on a bug and smash it, does that make you "bad"?

* What would happen if you stopped looking at people as having power over your life? What if you gave love to others even when they were being hurtful? What, if anything, might it change for you? What, if anything, might it change for the other person?

Lesson 3

UNDERSTANDING WHO WE ARE
AND WHY WE ARE HERE . . .

. . . Humans! What is a human? Why do we come here? Who are we? Who do we want to be? Why do we behave the way we do? Why are some people mean? Why do we get hurt feelings? How do we be happy? Why do we want stuff? Why do we treat some people nicely and others differently if we are all human? Why do humans have a more evolved brain than any other animal or species? These questions can go on and on!

Humans are a species, a form of energy just like any other energy in the universe. Humans are Divinity, all one, created in the likeness of God, coming from God and each other. We *are* The All And The Everything. Then why does it feel like humans are sometimes harmful to others? Why do I sometimes feel like people are out to harm me? Out to harm themselves?

We all share a single purpose when we come to the physical world, to be and express Who We Really Are—Divinity individualized. But we each choose a different aspect of the Whole beingness of God to express . . . so we look like we all have different reasons for being here. Some of us want to express what it is to be forgiving, while others want to express what it is to be forgiven. Some wish to express hunger so they can appreciate being full, while others come to express being giving to those who are hungry. The beautiful reality of our planet is that we come to Earth in, from a spiritual point of view, a perfectly symbiotic relationshipg. Every person who needs something will meet the person who has it to give. Every person who does not understand how to express love in a way which is not hurtful to others (while trying to truly understand the magnificence of love) will meet someone willing to experience the pain that the person lacking an understanding of love will have to give.

  ※ Again, the children's books *The Little Soul and the Sun* and *The Little Soul and the Earth* are helpful parables to understand the diverse, yet fully connected purposes for which we come to Earth.

  ※ Can anything happen against your will? The answer is no, not from a spiritual perspective. "Against my will" means being unwilling to do something. In the human experience, we, and our children, worry that we are losing control all the time. But from a spiritual perspective, there is no such thing as against your will. You are Divine, and God cannot have anything done to her that she hasn't decided upon.

Changing how we think/evolving

We often say, "What humans believe [about themselves] is what makes this planet what it is today."

Think about that for a moment. If the human race (species) didn't have an evolved brain, where would this planet (Earth) be? We wouldn't have travel from continent to continent by airplane. We wouldn't be able to talk to (and see!) other humans all over the world through technology. So, the human brain has a purpose! But the flip side is that we have also chosen to use that brain to create unrest and war. If we were operating from our soul's purpose and from a complete understanding of love and how it is most wonderfully expressed, we wouldn't be in wars with weapons of such mass destruction, and we wouldn't be killing each other in our schools and streets.

The evolution of the human race is ongoing, but "mind matters" of jealousy, scarcity, and a desire to be "right" rather than "nice" sometimes influence it. We are not different from God and yet we, collectively, create something that looks very separate from God. Instead of lamenting this fact, though, we can find our way through it, together. We can realize that no *one person or group* has caused our reality to be as it is; there are no "Bad Guys" who have gotten us here. We have all collectively contributed to the present state of our being. And that means we can also, collectively, find a solution to the problems we have created. The goal is to see that human life inherently brings that which we think is true to our reality, so if we believe ourselves to be innovators, we will be. If we see ourselves as at war, we will continue to be so. If we see ourselves as peacemakers, we can bring about peace.

Lesson 4

WHY DO WE EVEN HAVE WORDS SUCH AS "GOOD GUYS" AND "BAD GUYS?"

. . . You can remind your children that while there are no external rules about what is good or bad, and no sin or judgment, we do have the ability as humans to decide *for ourselves* what we choose to call "good" or "bad" within our own framework and understanding of Who We Are and what we want to accomplish in this life. In fact, we are constantly making these decisions to help us navigate our own behavior. Therefore, from a completely human perspective, when we forget that we are making all the rules as we go along, it may look as if there is good vs. bad. Yet when we step back and ask ourselves, "What is the other person's true motivation for doing the things they just did?" our perspectives about right and wrong can change drastically. This is one of the most powerful things we can do.

The role of good guys & bad guys

Consider the idea that as referenced above, a good guy (victim) and a bad guy (villain) express those aspects because, on a soul level, we wished to come here to express love in the highest and grandest way; yet in our state of temporary amnesia, and given that we all have Free Will, some of us do this and some of us do not. Thus, we may wind up being what is called a "victim" or a "villain," or even, in one lifetime, both. Yet each role eventually leads us to understanding who we truly are.

A victim is someone who may choose to experience victimization in order to help another soul remember who they really are through the playing out of who they are not. In this, the physical realm, you can't be in the position that others call being a victim unless you, of your own free will, *allow* yourself to be. You make this decision, of course, at a soul level. That is, at a metaphysical level. It is not something that you choose at the level of your conscious Mind.

If you wanted to help someone else experience themselves as, say, "forgiving," you could reverse roles and play what some call the villain. In this way you would give another soul something and someone to forgive. We have the spiritual opportunity to be both victims and villains all the time. Yes, we really do. Most of the time we just don't consider ourselves to be that.

You can go even further and stop considering yourself a good guy or bad guy (and those around you as well) altogether. You can begin to see all interactions as merely opportunities to help ourselves, and another, be and express a certain aspect or part of Divinity, realizing that all experiences as humans are temporary (remember, even *death* is reversible!) and that it is we who "decide how life feels." When we take control of how we each see the world through our own eyes, terrible circumstances can lose their terrible-ness and become new chances for growth and remembrance. We can look into the eye of every storm and find the gift it is bringing us (which can often include the wonderful chance of giving a gift to another), rather than seeing anything as a tragedy.

Your idea about yourself as a "good guy" or victim is determined by a judgment you make about the situation. Sometimes things happen that look bad, but we characterize them differently based on how we judge the situation and the "aggressor's" motives. Children might find the following examples helpful:

Something Drastic

When we experience something drastic, such as being robbed, we might call ourselves victims because it feels very vulnerable to be robbed. It feels like something we should be able to control or stop from happening.

In fact, because no one *wants* to be robbed, we try to say that someone *should not* rob another through the laws we have written. And then when someone violates those laws, we call them a "bad guy."

The person who robs another on the street may turn around and feed his family with the loot, thereby making the person (victim) who got robbed an angel to the family who lacked food. The person who looks like the "bad guy" can also be a victim, in this set of circumstances, because they feel a type of suffering—perhaps from lack of work or life experience, perhaps suffering from a physical condition that creates an inability to work, perhaps suffering from a mental condition (sadness or depression), or perhaps even spiritual suffering (feeling separate from, or abandoned by, God).

The person who got robbed could even decide to turn the whole situation around and use it as a reason to be grateful for the things that he or she has.

Even something small like being stung by a bee could make us feel like victims (and the bee as a villain or bad guy). So why doesn't being stung have the same effect as being robbed? We don't ascribe the same judgment to situations that seem *uncontrollable*, like being stung by a bee, and we don't assign negative motives to the bee. We don't feel singled out or persecuted when a bee stings us. We accept that the nature of a bee is to sting when alarmed, and we realize that, other than avoiding the outdoors altogether, there is no way to avoid being around bees. On the other hand, when a person steals from us, we take it personally.

And yet, to our souls, being stung is no different than being robbed, because the person doing the robbing might be, like the bee, acting out a natural response to their circumstance (in this case, believing they need what we have, and then "stinging us" by taking it from us). It just looks and feels different . . . because the emotional content we assign to each situation makes each feel different.

Perspective and Perception

Perspective determines your perception, and perception is everything in this life. In other words, you see events through the lens of your own attitude, experience, and expectations, and you make judgments and decisions upon them.

If you believe that the bee is merely fearing its safety and trying to protect itself, you will not experience it as a mean, willful attack.

If you believe that a robber is trying to take something that is yours because he doesn't want you to have it, or because he doesn't like you, or because he is simply greedy and wants the money he can get from selling your possessions, then you will perceive it as a personal attack. Conversely, if you accept that he is acting within his understanding of how to respond to his needs (such as the need to feed himself or his family), then you will not perceive his robbing you as being directed at you personally. You may not even perceive it as an "attack" so much as a call for helpg.

One can even view a suicide bomber in this light. If you understand that terrorists are often acting out of a desire to please their conceptualization of God, with the threat of eternal separation from that God if they fail to act in a certain way, you might have more compassion for the actions than if you just see them as bloodthirsty "bad guys."

Similarly, if you can look upon a rapist or murderer and understand that their actions are based in fear and feeling abandoned or a lack of connection to anyone (including their God, by whom they may feel abandoned), you can look at them with compassion instead of hatred.

✻ I said, "If one person attacks another, it's because that first person is suffering." (*The Storm Before the Calm*, page 110)

✻ A way you can help your child distinguish between willfully hurting something and just doing something for another reason that ends up causing "harm" is to use a terrarium to capture a frog or a bug and watch its reaction to being in the container. Ask your child, "Do you think the bug is feeling like a victim being captured and kept away from its home? Or do you think it is just scared and wants to get out?"

✻ Another way is to speak about the foods we eat that come from animals. Does your child intend to hurt the animal that ends up on your table? No, not likely! But we eat the animals because we know they have nutrients that we can use, and maybe even need, to grow strong healthy bodies. And we can share with our children that life serves and supports life through the process of life giving life to life itself. We honor, at our table, the animal who gave its physical life so that we may have ours, and we acknowledge that no life ever ends, but only changes form. This is not just true of humans, but of every life form in the universe.

What about rules and laws?

Does this mean that we shouldn't have rules, laws and contracts for how we treat each other? Should we just allow—or worse, celebrate—a murder, a bombing, or a theft?

No, we aren't saying that at all. Laws and rules are helpful to create a contextual framework in which to live.

We will all feel human emotions surrounding tragedy; we will feel the loss of the contact with the person, or the loss of the feeling of safety. Helping children embrace and then overcome those feelings of loss are part of the human experience. The point is that we do not have to feel hatred towards the perpetrator. Further, our hatred doesn't even serve to hurt the other person; it only hurts ourselves. We do not have to "damn" them for their actions because in the fullness of Divinity, in the spiritual realm, we know that actions that have occurred in the physical life cannot touch us. The things we endure on Earth do not change our true Divine nature. They only add to the rich tapestry of the experience of our soul.

Children can understand that the emotions we hold about situations do have an impact on us because our thoughts are creative, and what we put out, we draw to ourselves. If we feel negatively towards someone, we will get negativity back. If we feel and express positivity towards someone, we will get positivity back. This knowledge actually helps children to be more effective Creators of their own lives. Once we stop feeling like someone can victimize us, because we are Divine and nothing that happens here can change our soul's beingness, we can come to an even deeper understanding of who we are and how to express it.

Instead of damning the person doing a "bad" action, we can teach our children to choose to send them compassion, love, and wishes for a better future. Instead of hating them and adding more negativity to the world, we can meet their negative energy with positivity. This is what all the world's masters have taught; compassion, love, acceptance, understanding, and forgiveness are the traits of Divinity, and they enrich your life with more of the same.

Lesson 5

WHAT IS SUFFERING ALL ABOUT ANYWAY?
AND HOW CAN I STOP IT?

Suffering is something that occurs when we feel out of control of our situation and allow the circumstances of life to rule our emotions. It is best explained thusly: " . . . from a spiritual perspective we understand that 'suffering' is experienced only when we do not fully comprehend what, exactly, is occurring in our lives and why. When we see the *reason* for the occurrence, suffering ends." (*What God Said,* pg. 292-293) It is pointed out that while childbirth can sometimes be very painful, women gladly do it over and over again because they don't see the pain as the end result; they see the baby as worth the pain. Pain doesn't have to cause suffering. What we call "suffering" is the emotional response to a lack of understanding about the pain. It is the outcome of our decision that what is happening should not be happening. (*What God Said,* pg. 293)

What does this mean for children? It means that children can, through your guidance and by watching your example, end their suffering (their misunderstanding of, or resistance to, pain) in an instant. How can they do that? By realizing that pain, and *all* of the human existence, is just a temporary condition that the soul has chosen to experience. We can change our minds about pain (and end our suffering) by choosing to look for the positive in every situation, by reminding ourselves to feel gratitude, and by living a life of love and acceptance rather than jealousy, suspicion, and victimization. This will end our feelings of unfairness, of being violated by others, and of a lack of control, thus opening the door for us to be our most creative selves, living the lives we want to live!

Chapter Fourteen

THERE IS NO SUCH THING AS FAILURE

Why we humans ever decided to teach our children that a thing called "failure" exists is beyond me. It is surely one of the most damaging notions we could ever plant in the brain of our offspring. And sadly, many, many parents do so when their children are at a very early age.

The fact is that it is impossible to "fail" at anything. Most dictionaries define "failure" as "lack of success" at something. But what is "success"? Most dictionaries define "success" as "the accomplishment of an aim or purpose."

And there is a larger question here. What *is* the aim or purpose of life? And how does one achieve one's aim or purpose? Is trying, over and over again, improving on one's efforts every step along the way, one part of that process? And if it is, how can any of those steps be considered anything other than a "success"? If an action, choice, or decision leads you ultimately to your aim or purpose, how is that action a "failure"?

Isn't everything that leads to success a *part* of that success?

The answer to all of these questions is self-apparent. A child who does not achieve 100 percent on a test of multiplication tables, for instance, has not failed at anything, but merely taken a step towards her success. A scientist in his laboratory who runs a number of experiments—perhaps hundreds of experiments—has not failed at anything, but merely taken a step towards his success. A medical researcher who, working to find a cure for something, takes years to do so has not failed at anything, but merely taken a step towards her success.

Every step that leads to success is by definition a success in itself, in that it gets one where one is wishing to go.

Knowing your destination is important

Now there are those who will say, "I've taken all the steps I know how to take, and I *still* cannot seem to achieve success."

This is the experience of those who have not become clear on what their desired destination is. They may think that their desired destination is a certain physical experience (i.e., the right job, the perfect mate, the noticed achievement, the applause of others, the recognition of the world), but that is because of what they have been raised to *think of* as "success."

As parents we have the opportunity to highly impact, to greatly assist in shaping and forming, our children's definition of "success." And that is the point of this chapter.

If children are raised to think that "success" is the achieving of a particular exterior outcome—some physical result in the material world outside of themselves—they may very well be among those who later in life utter the plaintive words above.

If, on the other hand, children are raised to believe that "success" is the producing of an *interior* experience—the experience of joyful expression and fun, completely disassociated with any eventual exterior outcome—they may very well be among those who later in life talk about how much "fun" their life has been, *whether or not* they achieved fame or fortune, recognition or applause from others.

My mother was a wonderful example of this. It was evident to me as I grew older that some kind of *interior* satisfaction was driving her, because she was clearly not receiving widespread public acknowledgment for being The Best Mom In The World.

She was that, of course. But very few people knew it. So how could she be so happy, and so positive in the face of life, without the exterior *accouterment* of "success"?

Ah! She was *defining "success" differently from most human beings.*
Aha!
And where and how did she learn to do that?
Yes, of course. In her childhood.

So it is important to share with your children their true identity (as an aspect of Divinity), their true purpose (to experience this identity), and their true successes in life (whenever they feel themselves being close to God by closely *resembling* God).

I have written a book titled *The Only Thing That Matters*, which I highly recommend that all parents read and then discuss with their children in age-appropriate language as their offspring mature.

The book begins with a startling assertion that "98 percent of the world's people are spending 98 percent of their time on things that don't matter." It goes on from there, suggesting what really does matter to the human soul, but first telling us that we are *not* merely a Body with a Mind, but that we are Three-Part-Beings, made up of Body, Mind, and Soul.

This recontextualization of our entire understanding of Self, based on an expanded awareness of our true identity, can change everything in the way we encounter, express, and experience life.

It can change everything for our children as well.

A striking example

Once we understand what we are trying to do, what our destination is, we can see that *every* step is a step towards our innermost desired experience of the fearless and joyful expression of life itself.

Let me put this into practical terms.

A participant at one of my spiritual renewal retreats a few years ago told me that his company throws a big office party, complete with awards and congratulations, whenever any employee does something that causes the company to lose a big contract or sustain a major financial loss.

The bosses want their employees to innovate, to take chances, to try new approaches, and to risk being "wrong" about something, rather than playing it safe at every turn. So when an employee creates an outcome not originally desired, the company celebrates the knowing of what *not* to do next time.

The owners of the firm completely understand that this is not unimportant or useless information. Quite to the contrary, it is *extremely* valuable— and so an award is given by the company to the employee for "Outstanding Achievement in Creating a Pathway to our Highest Outcome."

Now that is what is called enlightened thinking. There's nobody in the firm who is "afraid of the boss" or "paralyzed by nervousness about making a mistake." The boss is clear that there is no such thing as a mistake, but only steps towards the company's objectives.

(God, by the way, is very clear about the same thing regarding *us*.)

He is also clear that it should be *fun* for his employees to reach for those goals—and that the joy is in the process, not in the product.

(God, by the way, is also very clear about *this* regarding us.)

A parent's most powerful tool

Our opportunity as parents, then, is to take the idea of "failure" out of the minds of our children, and to re-cast the experience of not initially achieving one's goal as an important step in doing so.

The adage "if at first you don't succeed, try and try again" is a first step in doing so, but it doesn't go nearly far enough, and it falls on the deaf ears of a child who is crying because he did not achieve what he set out to do—much less a child whose parents *tell her* that she has "failed" at something and cause her to feel devastated by it.

Nothing is more potent during early childhood than a parent's approval. And nothing is more devastating to a child than a parent's disapproval. Children will first be crushed by it. And then—if it occurs repeatedly—will resent it and revolt against it.

You cannot easily or gently modify a child's behavior by pointing out to the child what he is doing wrong. You may (or may not, actually) produce a short-term adjustment in the child's interactions, but the unwanted choices being made by the child will return—if only as a means of the child asserting herself, or expressing her anger at being "made wrong" and at repeatedly losing the approval (and what seems to the child as the love) of the only security figures she has ever known.

Misbehavior is a natural response

Remember that a child seeks security more than anything else. This has been the child's deep inner quest since exiting the warmth and utter safety of the womb. From that moment on the only security a child has ever known is the love of his parents (or very first caregivers).

When that is taken away (or *seems* like it is being taken away), the child has lost his footing, and will fight back in response to the rapidly rising fear inside of him. *It is a natural mammalian response.*

This has nothing to do with the personality of an individual child. A child's particular personality may cause this response to be *expressed* in a particular way, but the response *itself* is a built-in mechanical reaction in virtually all life forms.

"Growing up" is about controlling this response, assessing whether love has really been taken away, and adjusting to fluctuations in the feeling of being loved, without harming the self or others.

It is important, therefore, to remember that the early years of a child's life are, and must be, devoted to finding oneself, defining oneself, declaring oneself, and positioning oneself in the world in a way that feels *safe*. It is a world that the child had no idea he was going to be entering. She has no idea how she got here, much less who she is and what she can do about finding out. The child obviously does not understand his behaviors in this way, but the parent must, or the child is done a great disservice.

Our job as parents is to supply answers to every child's internal quests and questions. The child cannot and will not actually articulate any of these. The vocabulary is simply not available. Rather, the child will use *behaviors* as a means of communication.

Remember this always: Behaviors are a child's vocabulary. You can clearly hear what a child is saying by watching what a child is doing.

(You may find it beneficial to consider that this is true with adults as well. The statement that "actions speak louder than words" did not become widely used without good reason.)

What many parents don't understand

The suggestion here is not that a parent remove disapproval completely and entirely from a child's life. Yet precisely because parental disapproval *is* such a powerful tool, and has such a huge impact on a child, it should be used sparingly. Perhaps only when the child's safety is being immediately imperiled.

And when disapproval *is* used, every effort should be made to help the child understand that it is a particular *behavior* that is being disapproved of—not the child herself.

This may seem obvious to most readers here, but it is nonetheless remarkable how many parents forget this recommendation when disciplining their children. The parents' own anger and frustration often takes control—and now you have two human beings *experiencing the same thing*.

This does not create the best chemistry.

Except in the case when the immediate halting of a behavior is necessary to protect a child's safety (*"Don't touch that stove!"* . . . *"No! Stop! Don't move! Don't cross the street!"*), offering an alternative that immediately produces the experience of feeling *safe* is better than disapproving of a behavior.

Remember, loud and abject disapproval from a parent threatens the child at the level of *safety*. This is something that many parents do not correlate. They simply do not see the connection. But I assure you, the child feels it.

At once.

And from that moment on, fear dictates the child's response.

When a mammal is afraid, a mammal lashes out. The unevolved mammal (most animals) and the immature mammal (most children) know of no other choice.

A wonderful formula

I'm going to give you now Seven Magic Words that can allow every child to feel that love has not been taken away, even as certain choices with regard to behavior are being removed. ("It's not okay to talk to your mother like that" . . . "It doesn't work for you to be so loud in this restaurant" . . . "No putting your muddy shoes on the furniture" . . .)

The Seven Magic Words are: "I see what you're trying to do."

This makes the child feel immediately understood. Suddenly his actions are not being seen as "misbehaviors," but simply as exactly what they are in the child's mind: The only way he knows to be, do, or have what he wants.

And in the still developing mind of the child, being *understood* is no small achievement. (Neither is it in the mind of an adult.) This removes the feeling of "failure," of having done something "wrong," from the child's experience.

Then the wise parent asks: "Can I show you a way that might get you what you want faster?" *Or* . . . "easier?" Now the child feels *helped* (which translates to feeling loved), rather than *admonished* (which can translate in a child's mind to feeling unloved.)

So here is one formula, one hint, one tool: *Help, don't admonish.*

There are others as well. Below are more ideas and strategies that you might find useful in sharing with your children the idea from *Conversations with God* that . . .

THERE IS NO SUCH THING AS FAILURE.

The objective of the following teaching approach is to relieve children and parents of the perceived need to "succeed" or "avoid failure" in society's eyes. Many of the ideas discussed in this concept are rooted in the preceding chapters so you may notice that we are referring back more. This is because as we get to the deeper understanding that this and the following concepts reach, they all have bits and pieces of other concepts within them.

Lesson 1

IN TEACHING CHILDREN THIS CONCEPT, YOU MAY WISH TO BEGIN BY . . .

. . . reminding your children about the concepts of "There is no such thing as right and wrong," "There is nothing you have to do," "Death is the same as rebirth," and "Every day you get to start over." What we want your children to bring forward from the previous concepts is that there are no expectations for us as humans so there is no way we can get any of it wrong. *This is so important that it bears repeating: There is no way you can get any of it wrong! Ever.*

Even your death cannot happen differently than you choose. Since death is merely a beautiful rebirth, and you have an infinite number of chances to get it the way you want, how can you ever fail at anything else? *You can't!*

Lesson 2

SOME QUESTIONS THAT CAN BE USED TO GUIDE THE DISCUSSION ARE . . .

* What does it mean if you don't get something "right" the first time?

* Are you scared of "failure"?

* What do you think "failure" means?

* If something ends (you quit a sports team, your parents get divorced, you stop being friends with someone), does it change who you are?

* If you behave "poorly," does it change who you are inside? (The quick answer is, "No! Because you are divine and nothing can change that and you can choose a different action in the very next moment.")

* If you don't get the things you wish for (or ask for), is that failure? Does it mean you are unworthy?

Lesson 3

PARENTS CANNOT FAIL THEIR CHILDREN . . .

. . . Even if you get divorced, even if you sometimes react in anger, and even if your child grows up with emotional or physical problems, you have not failed them. You cannot fail them because they are here with their own purpose and their own life to live.

This doesn't mean, "Well, I have no responsibility to their future so I can stop trying, because none of it matters anyway." It means that when you are living and parenting in a loving way and doing your best to live each day in the next highest version of the grandest vision you ever held about yourself, you cannot fail. That is to say, you can parent to your best ability, but give up any attachment to the results. You can only give your children the tools to grow; it is their responsibility to find who they are and how they want to be in the world. And even though it is very difficult to take in this next statement because of how society judges each other, how your child *is* doesn't reflect on who you *are* as a parent (at a soul level).

If our children have human actions that are not conducive with what society expects, it is often seen as a parental failure, so we strive as parents to do everything we can to ensure our "success," but the consequence of trying to be the "perfect" parent is that we can becoming controlling, create a need to over-achieve in our children, and cause anxiety, anger, and frustration in them as they continually try to please us instead of being and expressing who they really are.

Partnership and parenting

We have spoken about the parenting partnership before so remember that the parent and the child are in this together! We all came from the same light, yet with the opportunity to create different outcomes. So while it may feel like a separation of energy, you really are still singular parts of the same whole, just different expressions of it. When a parent and a child have conflict, for instance a difference of opinion, we could fall into the trap of viewing our relationship as a failure. However, there can be no failure when the entire reason for life is to find new expressions and experiences. Because we are all sparks of light from the same divine energy, each creating our own experience (and

outcome), we are always living out the perfection of the soul . . .
no parenting can ever be a failure.

Some of you might be reading this saying, it is all well and
good in theory, but how do I accept when my two-year-old is
hitting, biting and spitting at others? Do I just allow it?

Your child, at a young age is testing their boundaries and
how far outside of themselves they can act without consequence.
They are really trying to figure out "what is me and what is you?"
Physical aggression is often a way that people (not just toddlers)
show a perceived need for something. It could be that your child,
in not understanding that biting hurts another person, is just
trying to increase physical contact. Rough housing and rough
play are similar in that they give us a physical reaction of body
contact. If your child is doing things that hurt other children, it
might be most effective if you say, "Ouch, that really hurts me.
I'd rather if you hug me to feel close."

If you really feel that your child needs to expend a rougher
kind of energy, you can show them how to throw pillows, jump
into a pile of blankets, etc. But if the child continues to bite, hit,
or spit you still don't have to take it on as your failure because
it is coming from inside of them. The more you can reinforce,
"let's show our love in gentle ways," the more they will come to
understand it.

Lesson 4

HERE ARE A FEW CONCRETE EXAMPLES . . .

. . . to help make it clear to children that failure is not a possibility.

Quitting

In Chapter 5, we dispelled the concept of "being a quitter." If
you revisit that discussion about teams and "obligations" you
will see that when you live in the moment and make conscious
decisions about who you wish to be and what you want to do,

"quitting" loses its negative value. It is perfectly natural to try something out and find it isn't for you. There is no compulsion that you *have to complete what you started* in order to be whole. It is actually your chance to decide freely that you can start each day anew with a bigger and bigger dream. You do not fail by deciding that something is no longer working for you. You actually gain a new level of understanding and respect for yourself when you make a decision to stop doing an activity that isn't within your idea of yourself. We will get more into this decision-making process in Chapter 15 when we assess whether our actions are working for us, whether we can change to make it work, and whether we can continue doing that action until it stops working for us.

Conflict

When your child is facing a conflict with another person, whether it is a family member, a teacher, or a friend, you can equip them to handle it in a way which allows them to know that they cannot fail.

Let's say a child feels their teacher isn't treating them the way they wish to be treated. At first it might be natural to get protective and try to handle it for your child. And if you feel this is necessary, then you should trust your gut. But if you think the child has an opportunity to express themselves and learn a new way to be in the world (able to ask for what they need and not allow another's actions to penetrate their soul), you, as the parent, might choose to coach them on how to kindly assert themselves and express what they are feeling. You can do this by asking "If you could tell the teacher anything to make the situation better, what would you tell him or her?" Then follow it up with helping the child to formulate a script of what they would like to say, even role-playing and practicing it so they are not scared when the time comes. By doing this, you allow your child to step into their own creative power and learn how to speak their truth while helping them to do it in a more effective way than just walking around upset.

You can instill a sense of autonomy in your child by doing this and also give them the security that you will help them through any situation. If for some reason, the interaction doesn't go as your child had hoped, you can show them that you are always there to back them up by intervening and helping them handle it directly. There is no way to fail in asserting your truth, especially when you know that your parent is there to help you figure it out.

In the event your interventions are not effective, you can always choose to take the more drastic step, if available to you, of removing your child from the negative situation. This will clearly show your child that you will always help her or him and illustrate well that there is no such thing as failure.

Another example is when your child draws a picture and then says it isn't good enough, or they don't like it. A loving response to teach them that there is no failure would be: "I love the picture just the way it is because it was created by you, but you are free to try again if that makes you happy to do so." Again, there is no "bad" drawing (or anything) but you always have the choice to recreate it (and yourself) anew!

Life is an opportunity for constant change, or infinite "re-do's." Much like a game in which you can choose to replay a move because it didn't go "well," life is also full of infinite possibilities to change your situation. Even if you cannot replay that exact situation again, you will have a new opportunity tomorrow! This is why we say there is no failure because you, in every moment, have the opportunity to change your mind, change your actions, and be who you wish to be.

Even if you feel like a "failure" in any given situations, "You create your own reality" or in child's terms, "you get to decide how life feels" so even if something FEELS like a failure, you can always change your mind about it and see the value in, and learn from, the experience. Doing so makes it a success, no matter what.

Lesson 5

WHY DO WE EVEN HAVE A WORD SUCH AS FAILURE?

As mentioned in the Preface, somewhere along the way, we decided we were separate from God.

In that separateness we also decided to perceive ourselves as inferior beings. In making ourselves inferior, we made God B-I-G, and because we believed God was so big, we started a vicious cycle of making God bigger and bigger and making ourselves smaller and smaller in our understanding. Consequently, we didn't think we could keep up with God, that we could never match her abilities, and that we could never be enough to please him. That is when we found what we call failure.

It is helpful and can change everything about your perception of the world if you remember that God would not create anyone as a failure. God only has the ability to create perfection in its many forms . . . and perfection is just being. It is true that your light, in human form, can grow as big and bright as you wish it to be because you are the light of God. Conversely, you can shrink your light to be as small as you wish it to be if that serves you in the present moment. But none of that changes who you are because you are always and will forever be the light of God.

Why do we choose to see our mistakes, decisions, actions and behaviors as failures? We see ourselves as failures because we do not trust our understanding that we are as big as God, but even more, that we *are* God. If our children can remember themselves *as God in physical form*, then they will know that nothing they can ever do is a failure because God is the definition of perfect creativity. What's more, when children (and adults for that matter) truly know themselves as an indivisible part of God, they will never again do anything to themselves (or another) that is harmful.

If you don't get the things you wish, or ask for, is that failure? No! "Since you noticed that you could fail to obtain all the things that you imagined you need to be happy, you have declared that the same is true for God . . . From this illusion you have created a cultural story which teaches that the outcome of life is in doubt." (*Communion with God*, pg. 35) The paradox here is that by understanding ourselves as fallible and able to fail, we actually have shrunk God's beingness because since we are God, shrinking ourselves shrinks God. We would say we made a self-fulfilling prophecy that we created ourselves as "children of a lesser God." When in actuality since there is no other place to go other than back to Oneness, mergence, and completion with God, there is absolutely no way we can ever fail.

Chapter Fifteen

ALL CHOICES CAN SERVE
THE HIGHEST GOOD

This is a marvelous concept to teach children! It is a re-stating of the remarkable insight in *Conversations with God* which reveals to us that there are Three Basic Principles of Life: *Functionality, Adaptability,* and *Sustainability.*

We explored this earlier, in Chapter Five of the present document, when we looked at the *CwG* messages that "there is no such thing as Right and Wrong." Now we'll take a closer look at the foundational concepts surrounding Functionality, Adaptability, and Sustainability. Because we cannot expect ourselves to be ready to teach these ideas to our children if we do not fully understand and embrace the concept, when stated in adult terms, ourselves.

There is a way for all the choices that children (and we, as adults!) make to serve the highest good—and that is for us to teach our children (and ourselves!) to "check in" to see if the choice we are making in any given situation does not violate life's basic principles.

The principles again, straight from *Conversations with God*, are Functionality, Adaptability, and Sustainability. So how can we encourage children to consider their own choices and decisions inside of this very sophisticated paradigm?

Well, we might simply invite them to ask themselves three questions that can be very helpful in making any decision: Will the decision work for me? Can I make it work? Can I keep doing it this way?

But let's back up now and take a look at the Basic Life Principles that would sponsor such questions . . .

What the source material tells us

Conversations with God has revealed to us that there are three principles that undergird all of life in the physical universe. Life, in every one of its endless expressions, always and eternally reflects Functionality, Adaptability, and Sustainability.

We begin our understanding of this wisdom by embracing the notion that all of life is *intelligent*. Every life form, from the smallest to the biggest, from the most primitive to the most advanced, is comprised of energy expressing in ways that demonstrate *awareness of the outcome of its actions*. Or, if you please, basic native intelligence.

The fundamental impulse of life is always to produce the Highest Good. And what is that? The Highest Good is defined and understood by life to be the endless and uninterrupted expression and experience of life itself.

A flower bends to the sun automatically, "knowing" that from this source does it receive its life-giving energy. White blood cells "know" to rush to any location in the human body where bacterial or fungal invasion has occurred, as first responders to microbial infection. Single-cell organisms, believed to be the oldest form of life, possibly existing 3.8 billion years ago, "know" that they must carry out all life processes in order to survive. And even the simplest multi-cellular organisms interact with each other *automatically* in ways that they "know" they must in order to continue the life cycle.

This is what is called, in *Conversations with God*, "Functionality." Life inherently *knows* how to best function. Functionality is *built into* every form of life.

So, too, is "Adaptability." This is the process by which life forms shift and/or change their configurations or expressions in some way or another in order to lengthen, as much as possible, their present and particular physical expression. (In human beings and other mammals, we call this the Survival Instinct. The truth is, it is built into life at every level.)

When the expression of any life essence in its present form is no longer possible to maintain, it will adapt its expression, taking on a new and different form. In this way, all life forms guarantee the Sustainability of life itself.

It is possible to observe life on the miniscule scale of simple cells, and life on the massive scale of the universe, engaging in this identical process.

Again the parable of Sara the Snowflake, from the book *The Only Thing That Matters*, describes this process with childhood simplicity and childhood eloquence.

There was never a time when You were not. There will never be a time when You will not Be. You appear from the heavens, physicalized as individual aspects of All That Is. While each physicalization is absolutely and gloriously non-identical, they are nevertheless All the Same Thing. And so they merge into a single essence, a particular life expression that you call "humans."

Then to the heavens each Essence returns, once more "invisible-ized." You are not "no longer here." You are simply "no longer visible." Yet You exist, fully self-conscious and fully self-aware, until You return again to total visibility through full physicalization.

And here is a great secret. You are never not "physical." You are sometimes simply less physical. Even as a snowflake is never not physical. When it is snow, it is physical. When it is water, it is physical. When it is steam, it is physical. When it is vapor, it is physical. When it is moisture, it is physical. When it is unseen and utterly invisible, it is physical.

When it falls from the clouds as rain, it is physical. And when it hits the freezing temperature beneath the sunlit clouds, it crystallizes, becoming a snowflake once again.

What a journey the snowflake has taken! Changing form, changing form, evermore changing form, finally returning as another snowflake, magnificently different from its earlier version, but still, in essence, the same.

And what a journey you have taken. It is a Sacred Journey, with a Divine Purpose.

Applying this formula to individual decisions

The Divine Purpose of life is to express and to experience Divinity eternally. You can thus count on the fact that life will always support life through the process of life itself. Again, it does this by being in all cases Functional, Adaptable, and Sustainable.

The fact that it is Adaptable is what renders it Sustainable, and the fact that it is Sustainable is what guarantees that it is forever Functional. You can be assured, then, that whenever the functionality of life in its present expression is in any way threatened, it will immediately adapt its expression.

Now the wonder is that this overarching formula can be applied to life's individual moments. It can be overlaid on every choice and decision, response and reaction that any moment invites. And when it is, mastery in living can be achieved.

This is what we wish to assist our children in experiencing, is it not?

And so, we are encouraged to reduce the formula to proportions that may be easily grasped by inviting children to ask a series of simple questions as they experience any particular moment and consider a decision or choice that the moment sponsors.

Through these simple inquiries we seek to bring to the child an *awareness of the outcome of its actions.* We open the child to its basic native intelligence.

The questions we invite the child to ask and answer, then, are: Will the decision work for me? (Is it Functional?) Can I make it work? (Is it Adaptable?) Can I keep doing it this way? (Is it Sustainable?)

The outcome is always the same

When the answer to the last question is *yes,* a decision serves the highest good. Which is to say that it allows life to serve the Divine Purpose of Life through the process of life itself. You can easily know if any choice or decision has served life's Divine Purpose because it always produces the same interior experience: Joy.

Is what you're now thinking, doing, or saying producing Joy? Is how you are changing producing Joy? Is the way you are continuing to experience your life producing Joy? Then you have served the Highest Good.

Yet "going for the joy" in life can take great courage—and this, too, you will want to teach your children.

People on Earth have pretty much decided that life was meant to be a struggle. At the very least, it's meant to be a school, and the lessons we've come to learn are very difficult.

Nothing could be further from the truth.

Conversations with God tells us that life is *not* a school, and that we came here with nothing to learn. We came here to express and to demonstrate, thus to experience, *everything that we already know* about Who We Are.

We do this through the process of remembering.

The book *Happier Than God* (which I sincerely and highly recommend that all parents put on their immediate reading list) makes it very clear that *life was meant to be happy.* It is true that it often doesn't look that way . . . but this is inevitably and always when we have forgotten Who We Really Are.

Who we *really* are (as opposed to who we imagine ourselves to be, based on our limited view of ourselves until we remember our True Identity) always and automatically holds thoughts, makes decisions, adopts behaviors, and undertakes actions that both produce and sustain Joy.

Now here, below, are some specific ideas and strategies that you might find useful in sharing with your children the idea from *Conversations with God* that . . .

ALL CHOICES CAN SERVE THE HIGHEST GOOD.

The objective of the following teaching approach is to help children move past the limited decision-making style of society based on "right or wrong" and to embrace the awareness that there are Three Basic Principles of Life: *Functionality, Adaptability,* and *Sustainability.*

Lesson 1

IN TEACHING CHILDREN THIS CONCEPT, YOU MAY WISH TO BEGIN BY . . .

. . . informing your children that you wish for them to make decisions with rationality and an eye towards what outcomes and natural consequences the decisions will create in their lives, given who they imagine themselves to be. Our intention for this lesson is that your children will be strong decision makers and grow up equipped with critical thinking skills. This will lead them to make positive choices in their lives, which work for them, and to be able to adapt if and when those decisions stop working; that is, stop producing the outcome for which they were designed, which is Joy.

Lesson 2

SOME QUESTIONS THAT CAN BE USED TO GUIDE THE DISCUSSION

❋ Ask your children how they know whether an object (toy, pen, automobile, machine, etc.) works.

❋ What does "works" mean?

❋ What does "broken" mean? (This will help you with explaining functionality later.)

❋ Do you ever feel stuck in a rut? Like you just can't change your circumstance?

❋ What would it look like to decide newly, every day, Who You Are and how you wish to live?

❋ Would that mean freedom? What would you base your decisions on?

❋ What does acting in "love" mean?

❋ What does "beneficial" mean?

❋ How do you know if your actions "worked" or didn't in a particular situation?

❋ Instincts can present in many different ways in various people; some people get a feeling in their stomach, some get a light feeling in their head, some get a weighty feeling in their arms. Where do you feel your gut instinct, your intuition, or God talking to you?

❋ If you do something that doesn't "feel good" to you, where do you feel it and how do you learn from it?

Lesson 3

WHAT DOES EACH OF THE HELPFUL WAYS TO MAKE DECISIONS ENTAIL?

Remember that a child-friendly restating of the concept that "all choices can serve the highest good" is to tell your offspring that a helpful way to make decisions is to ask:

1. Will the decision work for me? (*Functionality*)

2. Can I make it work? (*Adaptability*)

3. Can I keep doing it this way? (*Sustainability*)

The Three Questions

The helpful way to make decisions is a fluid process in which, based on life experience, we can move from one question to another, repeatedly. What works for me today may continue to work tomorrow, so life is a continual journey of discovery, both about the world and about ourselves. Here is how the above questions work:

Functionality

Will the decision work for me? This phase focuses on assessing your life and determining if your actions are "working" or serving Who You Really Are. Those which do not serve your highest purpose are disposed of; while things that do *function*, within the space of the person you believe yourself to be, are retained, repeated, and enlarged into your repertoire of actions . . . until they do not serve you anymore. It is really about understanding spiritual *cause and effect.*

Adaptability

Can I make it work for me? This phase focuses on the ability to change your ideas and tactics about what works or doesn't work in the scope of who you believe yourself to be, as life evolves. This expands upon the spiritual *cause and effect* with a little bit of *problem solving* thrown in.

Sustainability

Can I keep doing it this way? This phase focuses on the implementation of and the adherence to a set of principles you design for yourself for as long as they continue to work within your idea of who you are. Spirituality accepts that as life situations change, so will your principles. Your ideals will work for you until they do not. Some ideals that you develop for yourself may not be completely altered over time, but they will mature and adjust to fit some new understanding or knowledge that you have acquired. Periodically, you may revisit, reassess, and change your ideas of what "works" and what "doesn't work." This leads back, of course, to assessing functionality, applying adaptability, and arriving, again, at sustainability.

Grey areas

The three basic principles of life are fluid, intermixed, and, sometimes, overlapping. Children may start out with very sharply defined understandings of right and wrong, but those lines can blur and find grey areas as children mature. This is a good example of how the three principles will be revisited. They may choose to change course to adjust to new information and new ideas they have about themselves.

Lesson 4

IT IS POSSIBLE TO BRING THIS TO CHILDREN IN AN UNDERSTANDABLE WAY, EVEN THOUGH . . .

. . . the concept is very deep and has far-reaching consequences in how we live our lives. As such, we have sought here to simplify how to demonstrate the concept with a very short explanation. We feel that starting with a simple approach will enable you to open an ongoing conversation with your child.

To teach this very fluid and abstract idea to children involves some patience. It is probably not something children can learn in one sitting, but is more of a continuing lifestyle choice, which will last throughout their childhood. Please feel free to use our examples as jumping off points, adapting them to topics your children will find interesting. It helps with younger children to start with concrete demonstrations to show them cause and effect.

For instance . . .

. . . imagine your child wants to build a block castle, but is doing it hastily and keeps knocking over the structure.

Think about how you would approach them to help them problem solve why the blocks are not staying upg. You can ask, "What works about how you are trying to build it?" If they are unsure, you can guide them to the answer with prompts such as, "Well, I like how you are doing this (insert example of how their approach is working)."

Then you can help them problem-solve by asking, "What isn't working about how you are trying to build it? What do you think is causing the structure to fall?" Next, you might ask them what could be a more effective strategy.

Then, using what you talked about together, help them rebuild the castle, giving them the lead, letting them guide you as you both stack the blocks, using what you both learned about what "worked" and what didn't. Following upon the conversation with actually *producing an outcome* will help them to make the connection between the abstract conversation and the concrete *doing*.

Think back to our pre-assessment questions about cars. The evolution of the automobile is a good example of how needs, knowledge, and technology change over time as well as how those changes produce new results.

Discuss the following:

❈ How do cars work? Do you think they are the same now as they were when they were first invented?

❈ Why were those changes made?

❈ Can you suggest improvements to cars as they are now? How long do you think your improvements will be good enough before new ones are desired or necessary?

❈ Are they long-lasting improvements that are easy to maintain and use every day?

❈ Or, are they fun, fashionable changes that will need to be changed again in the near future?

Spiritual progress

The fact that changes have been made in automotive engineering over the last 30+ years does not mean that the cars of the 1970s were not useful to the people of that time; it just means that once the first ideas about building cars no longer reflected the highest level of Functionality, the industry adapted to new needs and desires, and created a "new norm." This is how progress works in technology, and how it can also work in spirituality—and thus, of course, in everyday life.

As children get older, you can expand this conversation into the more sophisticated articulations of Functionality, Adaptability, and Sustainability.

For instance, imagine your child has an experience with friends that is upsetting. You can approach the situation in much the same way as the building blocks, asking probing questions and guiding the child to understanding his or her feelings/reactions within the context of what works and what doesn't. If the child became upset or feelings were hurt as a result of interactions with a friend, you can help him or her explore the friendship and whether it is serving his or her highest good. This does not necessarily mean that after one small disagreement you will advocate ending the friendship, but helping the child to look at relationships honestly early on will assist him or her in maintaining friendships that are beneficial and choosing, in a healthy way, not to have friendships that aren't.

> ✸ *For example*: Imagine a friend is lying to you. You could start by asking yourself, "Has this relationship served me in the past? What has changed?" Then you can proceed with, "How is this friendship currently functional? How is it serving me? How is it working, or not? Do I want to continue with the friendship?" If so, "What can be done to change the relationship for the better? Will these changes be sustainable? Will they last? Can I keep making them? Or do I think they will, at least, be useful for a short time?" Then the important question: "Are they coming from a place of love?"

Helping the child problem-solve about how he or she can handle a similar situation in the future is the essence of adaptability, the application of which, to your life, is the sustainability aspect of this topic.

These types of discussions, even if they have to be repeated throughout childhood, will help the child learn to *think* about his or her actions, rather than follow a set of rules (or "in group" constructs, or societal "norms") regardless of how they work.

There is, of course, no guarantee that our children will not do the things we hope they don't, and, conversely, only do the things we hope they do. Accepting that your children are on their own path and have their own life to live (which does not reflect on you) is a huge step in your parenting journey.

But beyond that, when children are encouraged to look inside and feel the connection to others, find their inner, cellular *knowing* that love is all there is, and embrace the knowledge that they are the Creator of their own destiny, the likelihood is that they will live a life filled with love and respect. Helping them to understand that making decisions from a place of love (and that asking what works and doesn't work within their idea of themselves *is* what making a decision from a place of love is all about) allows them to replace the Old Cultural Story's *external control through fear* with an internal sense of control and accountability to themselves and their own ideals. As *CwG* says, no one does anything inappropriate, given his or her model of the world. No person intentionally does things that contradict their worldview and their own internal sense of "right and wrong." The trick, then, is in assisting your child in creating a worldview that supports the notion that all choices *can* serve the Highest Good.

As part of this process, it is very beneficial to assist your child in understanding that his or her *current* decisions do not invalidate prior ones. Evolution is not about invalidation, rather it is about adaptation.

Remember, the evolution of the way cars are made didn't invalidate earlier versions of cars. The decision that a relationship is no longer working does not invalidate how the relationship began, or the whole relationship experience. Adaptation merely acknowledges that circumstances have changed, and that we are changing with them.

Helping your child to understand that flexibility (adaptability) is really the hallmark of this concept is what will aid him or her best. Help him or her understand that living their life in a way that is consistent with "Who You Really Are" may change from year to year. Indeed, it would be amazing if it didn't.

✴ The main idea behind this concept is the acceptance that life is ever-changing and that your best asset is your own ability to flex and adapt, then sustain that way of being until it doesn't work anymore, and then willingly and joyfully start the whole process over again.

In all of this we should make it clear that, in spirituality, *sustainability* does not imply *permanence*. It simply creates continued *functionality* in one particular way—as long as it does.

The concept only suggests that you will choose to *sustain* a particular course as long as it works within the highest ideas you hold about yourself.

Perhaps, the most important idea you will *sustain* (hold onto) for yourself is the idea that life, attitudes, and circumstances are ever-changing, and that spirituality encourages you to allow life, and your ideas about how you should live your life, to *flow*.

In this sense, sustainability is only "sustainable" so long as it produces functionality. When it does not, we cycle back to adaptability once again—as does all of life, from the micro to the macro level.

Lesson 5

YOU CAN PROCEED WITH GREAT HOPE FOR THE FUTURE!

By giving your children these critical thinking tools early in life, you will assist them in creating life-long decision-making skills. Through this lens, they can assess situations for *functionality*; learn to *adapt* to make situations work better within their idea of who they really are, and then *sustain* a life-path until it no longer serves them.

The best you can do for your children is to be there to listen and help them process life as it occurs; to assure them that life is ever-evolving and that there is no reason to *fear* change; to let them know, instead, life is more fulfilling when they embrace change as an opportunity for growth.

Chapter Sixteen

THE WONDERFUL WAYS TO BE ARE TRUTHFUL, AWARE, AND RESPONSIBLE

This is a longer chapter than usual because I think this topic could be the most important in the book. Surely, in terms of what we hope to share with our children from *Conversations with God*, it is going to be among the most critical.

Let's start with this: I think that the fact that there are States of Being (or, as we might put it to a child, "ways to be") is one of the biggest insights we can give to our children.

And the fact that we can *choose* to be certain things just because we *decide* to be is one of life's greatest secrets. It's such a secret, in fact, that many adults don't even know it. (Or if they do, they don't do anything about it.)

So "States of Being" (or "ways of acting," if you wish) are pivotal—indeed, crucial—to the ability of humans to experience a happy, peaceful, and fulfilling life. And the fact that we are *in charge* of how we are being, and even how we are *going* to be in the future, is the single most empowering truth of our existence.

Getting straight about 'beingness'

Because how we are "being" in any given moment is often thought of as something that is tied to our emotions, many people imagine that what we are being is outside of our control. This concept arises out of our belief that our emotions arise within us more or less spontaneously in response to external events or internal memories or projections.

We learn from the *Conversations with God* cosmology, on the other hand, that emotions do not arise spontaneously, but are *chosen*. Yes, we come to understand, the choice is made in a nanosecond—so lightning fast that it feels as if it *is* a spontaneous eruption—but it is the product of conscious choice, in fact.

How the Mind makes this choice is explained with wonderful clarity in the book *When Everything Changes, Change Everything*, which describes the mechanics of the mind, showing us the pathway of our mental energy from the time that any exterior event occurs to the moment when we put that energy into motion (e=motion) about it. So I won't go into all of that here. But just know that an emotion is something we *choose*, not something to which we are subjected.

Why this is important

Knowing this can change your life—and the life of your child. Because if emotions are chosen, that means we can be in total control of them. The secret is in *how far in advance we decide on them.*

That is something that not many children have been told or taught. But when they are, not only will their lives change—the whole world can change. Because right now the world is being run by people who believe that emotions are *reactions* rather than *creations*. As long as we accept that they are reactions, we do not have to take any responsibility for them. But as soon as we acknowledge that they are creations, everything changes. We become not only responsible, but *empowered*. We're no longer in the passenger seat of life. We're in the driver's seat.

Because if we can control our emotions, we can control the outcomes that our emotions create.

What? What's this? Emotions create outcomes?

Yes. Every outcome in life is created by energy. Indeed, all of *life* is energy. And energy is a physical phenomenon that impacts upon itself. *And* the *strongest* energy is the energy of emotion. Its power is in its amplification of the ordinary energies of life.

Emotion is *life*, writ *large*.

So now, what if we could decide on what emotion we are going to express far, far in *advance* of life's events, rather than a billionth of a second *after* those events? Would that, could that, make a difference?

Um . . . it could make all the difference in the world. And would.

How life makes this possible

Of course, the only way it would be possible for us to choose our emotions far in advance of events would be for us to be able to know in advance that those events are going to be.

And that is where one of life's most beneficial characteristics plays its effect. That characteristic? It is something called *Reliable Repetition*.

Let's turn to the pages of *The Only Thing That Matters*, where this is all described thoroughly. There it says that you can depend on life to be repetitious. Very few events or situations arising in your life will be much of a surprise to you after a certain age. Not in the sense of your never having experienced anything like them before.

Within an astonishingly short period of time following your birth, you came into contact with—then analyzed, assembled, and stored—a monumental amount of data about your exterior world. You did this so efficiently that after only a few years on this planet, it became almost impossible for you to encounter any new experiences. New events, yes. New experiences, no.

You have already experienced love, and you will no doubt experience it again. You have already experienced animosity, and you will no doubt experience it again. You have already experienced commitment, and you will no doubt experience it again. You have already experienced betrayal, and you will no doubt experience it again.

You have already experienced disappointment and excitement, agony and ecstasy, frustration and exhilaration, exasperation and exaltation, anger and joy, agitation and peace, loss and gain, fear and fearlessness, cowardice and courage, ignorance and wisdom, blahs and bliss, confusion and clarity, and just about every other emotional polarity that one could describe or imagine.

How you are going to react—how you usually react—can therefore actually be anticipated by you. This means that you can reject your prior decisions about such events or situations if you wish. And that is one of life's great secrets. The "secret" is not the Law of Attraction, but the Law of RE-traction.

This is a tool used to retract old decisions and make new ones, instantly. That is what true creation is all about. When you bear witness to your responses to life's current events and immediately retract what you decided in the past about similar events, you give yourself almost unimaginable power—including the power to end struggle and suffering forever.

Buddha demonstrated this precisely, and taught it.

And so now you are clear that the way we are being is not something that erupts within us spontaneously, but something that we decide upon consciously. The only question that remains is, do we choose to decide upon it long in advance of life's totally predictable events? Or in the immediate aftermath of them? That is, do we choose to *create,* or to *react?*

And what do we choose to teach our children about this?

A wonderful little tool

Our suggestion is that you tell your children that life is *designed* to offer them repeated chances—literally millions of chances—to *respond differently* to what is going on around them should they choose to . . . and that when they choose to, they put themselves in life's driver's seat. They become "the boss" of the way they are going to BE. (And of how much fun *life* is going to BE as a result!)

Children who get into repeated crying fits or tantrums or other negative behavior patterns know very well that these moments are not happy for them. They just don't know how to self-adjust to avoid them. They seemingly "can't stop themselves" when the moment comes.

One clever way to give your children some tools is to invite them—at a time when they are happy and things are going very well in the house—to play a little game called *Glad-Sad-Mad: Here We Go Again!*

Get out a paper and pencil (that's really "yesterday," isn't it . . . okay, get out an iPad) and say to the kids: "Think of three things that you absolutely know are going to happen over and over again—they could be things that make you glad or things that make you sad or things that make you mad—and make a list of them."

Then you do the same. Say, "I'm going to make my list, too. And the person who finishes their list faster gets to have this special treat." (Make it a treat that works well in your home for your children to have.) Say, "Okay, I'll go first." (Have some kind of timer ready, so that you can be timed making your list and your child can be timed making hers or his.)

Be imaginative when making your list, and make sure that every item on the list happens a lot in your house, to let your child get the idea. Also, take *plenty of time* creating your list, so that your child can easily beat you! You might say something like . . .

"Okay . . . things that happen over and over again . . . things that happen a lot . . . that make me glad, sad, and mad . . . okay, 'glad' first . . . hmmmm . . . it makes me glad when . . . um . . . it makes me glad when you give me a great big hug! That makes me *really* glad . . . (write it down or type it out on the iPad) . . . and . . . uh . . . (take plenty of time to 'think' about it) . . . it makes me *sad* when . . . hmmm . . . oh, yes . . . I have to say the same thing to someone two or three times and nobody listens to me . . . yeah, that makes me sad . . . (make a note of this one, too) . . . and . . . hmmmm . . . this is a hard one . . . let's see . . . something that makes me *mad* that keeps happening over and over again . . . hmmm . . . (think about it) . . . oh, yeah! . . . it makes me mad when somebody moves my stuff from where I put it . . . and I can't find stuff . . . and I'm *sure* I know where I left it . . . that makes me mad . . . (write it down, and take your time doing so)."

Look at your timer. "Okay, that took me almost three minutes. Not very long. Think you can beat that? Okay, your turn. You get to think of things that happen over and over again. One thing that makes you glad, one thing that makes you sad, and one thing that makes you mad."

Your child does this. Now see who took the least amount of time. If you played it right, your child should be able to easily beat your time. Your child gets the treat.

However it turns out, make sure there are not "winners" and "losers" in a "glad" or "sad" sense. Make sure that the person who took longer making their list also gets a treat. A smaller portion, maybe, but a little treat nonetheless. "Nobody 'loses' in our games! Isn't that great? Everybody gets *something*, just for playing!"

Then announce: "Now Ladies and Gentlemen, it's time to play *Round 2* of Glad-Sad-Mad. Round 2 is called 'Choose to BE'. In this round, you get to choose *ahead of time* to 'be' any way it feels *better* to be the next time the same things happen over and over again. Everybody who finds a way they could feel *better* when the same thing happens again gets a special prize!"

(The "prize" can be any number of things. A special "Good Goin' Certificate" you have made up in advance. You can have five or six different ones, and they get the first one off the top of the "deck" after you mix 'em upg.

(Maybe one Good Goin' Certificate says someone can stay up a Half Hour Longer after bedtime is announced . . . maybe one says that the holder gets to watch whatever *they* want to watch from the approved list of television shows or movies *right now* [even if you're in the middle of something you want to watch!] . . . maybe one certificate says: Good For One Game Of [list their favorite game] with Mommy or Daddy . . . and maybe one could say Good For One Sweet Treat Right Now—even if it *is* right before dinner!)

Be imaginative. These kinds of things can be lots of fun, and bring joy into your kids' daily life (and into your own). It shouldn't be difficult to come up with special "prizes" that you know would make your children happy. And their being able to *present* these Good Goin' Certificates later, whenever they want to, will give them a sense of having their own power, too. (Not a bad thing to give them experiences of, in controlled quantities and controlled ways.)

Okay, so now go over the same list you both created the first time around, and think of a better way to BE when the same things happen again. You might say . . .

"Okay, when you give me a great big hug, an even better way to BE than 'glad' would be for me to be *sooooo* happy that I forget about every bad thing that's happened for the past *two days*, and decide to be in a really good mood for the rest of the day! . . . all just because I got a great big hug from *you!*

"And if I have to say the same thing to someone two or three times and nobody listens to me . . . let's see . . . instead of being sad . . . a *better* way to BE might be for me to BE . . . um . . . patient! Yeah, that's it! I could be *patient.* I could give that person another chance to hear me. I could stop whatever I was doing and just go to that person, give *them* a big hug, and say, 'Hey, Sweetie, maybe you didn't hear me. Let me say something again.' Then I would say it *again*, and ask them if they heard me! And I bet that would make things *better* for *both of us!*

"And if somebody moved my stuff instead of leaving it where I put it . . . I could choose not to be mad, but to be . . . hmmm . . . I could choose to be *curious* where my stuff might be. I could even make a little game out of it. I could give myself a Good Goin' Certificate if I guessed where my stuff is and found my stuff within three minutes or less! Hey, you know what? That could even be *fun.* That could turn a 'mad' moment into a 'glad' moment! Wow, hey . . . I *like* that idea!"

Then I would say, "Okay, so I get THREE Good Goin' Certificates *right now*, 'cause I thought of three ways to BE that were even BETTER than Glad, Sad, or Mad."

Then have your children do the same thing with *their* list.

Guys, this could turn into a game that's *lots of fun.* And you'll learn a lot about what feelings your children go through during their experiences in the house. AND . . . you'll be giving your children a direct experience of the truth that human beings are *called* human "beings" because they can choose ahead of time to "be" whatever they want to be in any situation.

Wait . . . there's more to come

And it doesn't even have to end *there.* You can announce *Round 3* of this game! Say, "Okay, this is the Challenge Round! This is when we get to see if we can find a *better* way to be than 'sad' or 'mad.' That's the tough part. This is only for those who want to Go For The Gold.

"If any of us can actually BE a better way to BE than 'sad' or 'mad' when one of these things happen that's on your sad or mad list, we get a really BIG prize!"

Think of something that your child would really, really, *really* love. Going to the movies? Heading out for pizza tonight? A trip to the Indoor Amusement Park, or the bowling alley? You know right now what your children think is *really special.*

So make up Golden Prize Envelopes (get cool yellow ones from a stationery place), and keep them on top of the refrigerator . . . and every time *anyone* in the family changes from being sad or mad and finds a *better* way to be . . . give them a Golden Prize Envelope!

Let them have the fun of opening it up and seeing what it is!

And now, to the *CwG* concept here

That's just one little suggestion on how you can show your children that they (and you) can decide ahead of time how you're going to "be" when certain things that always happen, happen again.

Now you can introduce your children to a very big idea. You might say to them that "there are three very *special* ways of 'being' that Mommy and Daddy and Grandma and Grandpa and Aunt Mary and Uncle Gene and all adults try to be as often as they can. Would you like to know what they are?"

Now talk with them about three very special ways they can "be"— Truthful, Aware, and Responsible—if they really want their day, or any moment, to go well.

Why these three in particular?

Conversations with God tells us that Honesty, Awareness, and Responsibility are the Three Core Concepts of Holistic Living. We are then advised that if we live according to these precepts, "self-anger will disappear from your life."

I've come to these pages to suggest that if this is true for adults (and it is), it will be true to an even higher degree for children—who experience self-anger more than most adults might suspect.

Children may be angry with themselves for a wide variety of reasons. If a parent has left the home for good as the result of a relationship break-up, children often see it as their fault. If parents often quarrel, children may again feel that *they* must have done something wrong. And if parents are highly and constantly critical, or even gently but overly correcting, of a child, self-loathing will very frequently follow in the child's mind.

Children's thoughts include many self-recriminations—*Why can't I get it right!?; Why do I always DO that?!!; Nobody likes me!;* and *It's all my fault!* among them.

It does sometimes seem that children exhibit the same "bad behavior" over and over again—not listening, talking back, throwing tantrums if not getting their way, etc.—and these repeated behaviors are difficult for children to change, mostly because they don't have the tools to change the self-anger that produces so many of them.

Their internalized self-anger and self-criticism at never being "good enough" turns into moments of actual self-hatred—which, of course, no human being, child or adult, can long endure. This negativity is, therefore, inevitably turned outward.

"I *hate* you!" a child might shout at his mother—and then hate himself for saying it . . . which makes him even more angry with *her*, because he *can't* keep on being angry with himself.

Sometimes a child will express this inner turmoil in dramatic terms, startling parents with statements like, "I just want to die!"; or, "Maybe I'll just go kill myself." These kinds of outbursts make it clear that a little mind is struggling mightily for self-approval—without the tools with which to build it.

The adult tools of Honesty, Awareness, and Responsibility can work with equal effectiveness for children—but they must, of course, be given these tools in age-appropriate ways and language.

Before you could be convinced to give them these tools, you would have to be convinced that the tools themselves are really important. The concepts themselves are explored in wonderful detail in the book *What God Said.* I encourage people everywhere to read that text from cover to cover. Yet if you have not had a chance to, turn to the Addenda at the back of this book, where you will find a lengthy passage from the previous title that explores, from an adult point of view, the Core Concepts of Holistic Living, making it clear why they are vitally important for all children to come to understand.

Teaching our children about these concepts may be one of the most important things we will do in our lives. Most parents that I observe seek to teach their children about honesty fairly early. The concepts of awareness and responsibility were not shared with me in my childhood until rather late in the game.

It was only then that my dad tried to make me more "aware" of how I was affecting other people. Nobody ever taught me to be more "aware" of how other people, and life in general, was affecting me. That is, to pay more attention to what I was feeling, and why I was feeling it. It was only when I was an adult, and in actual counseling with a psychologist, that I was made aware of being more aware, so to speak. We shouldn't have to wait until our adult years to be given this tool.

Likewise, it was not until I was nearing puberty that I was invited to take responsibility for outcomes in my life in any kind of personal way. I think if a direct line had been drawn for me between my thoughts, my words, and my actions and the exterior circumstances and events that kept presenting themselves in my life, I would have been a bit more circumspect in my decisions and behaviors between 7 and 12 or 13.

It's important, however, not to confuse "responsibility" with "fault" in a child's mind. There were plenty of times that I was told that something or other was "your own fault" . . . but that is not at all the same as teaching someone about their metaphysical and spiritual responsibility in the matter of how their lives are being experienced.

So now, below, here are some specific suggestions and strategies that you might find useful in sharing with your children the idea from *Conversations with God* that . . .

THE WONDERFUL WAYS TO BE ARE
TRUTHFUL, AWARE, AND RESPONSIBLE.

The objective of the following teaching approach is to show children how to be Who They Really Are so that they are able to be fully truthful, aware, and responsible. This will allow them to let go of anger towards themselves and embrace self-love and acceptance.

Lesson 1

IN TEACHING CHILDREN THIS CONCEPT, YOU MAY WISH TO BEGIN BY . . .

. . . reminding your children that while "there is nothing you have to do" to please God, you might choose to be certain ways (truthful, aware, and responsible) to please yourself. The adult conceptualization of this idea is: *The three core concepts of holistic living are honesty, awareness, and responsibility.*

Lesson 2

SOME QUESTIONS THAT CAN BE USED TO GUIDE THE DISCUSSION ARE . . .

❋ Why would a child tell a made-up story and pretend to make it truth?

❋ Is lying harmful? What scares you about telling the truth? What happens when you tell the truth to someone even when you don't want to?

❋ What happens when you pay attention to what is happening around you? Does being more aware make your decisions easier or harder?

❋ If you were to walk around owning your part of every interaction and decision, how would it change your reality or world? Does being responsible for your own actions seem hard or easy?

❋ Do you ever feel "yucky" or "bad" inside after you do something? Why do you think that is?

Lesson 3

FIVE THINGS YOU CAN DO TO HELP YOUR CHILD UNDERSTAND THE IMPORTANCE OF HONESTY, AWARENESS, AND RESPONSIBILITY

1. Always tell the truth yourself to your children—about everything, in age-appropriate detail.

2. Eliminate innocuous "little white lies" and fanciful "stories" about where babies come from, or what happened to the pet that died, etc., in situations that you think are too complicated to tell children about honestly.

3. Invite children to explore the difference between a "lie" and the "truth" by playing The Untruth Game. Make up a series of statements about something the child knows about—some that could "almost" be true and some that are true. Invite your child to tell you which is which.

4. Take your child into the kitchen and play The Awareness Game. Ask him or her to tell you at least three things they see that might not be very good for the family in the kitchen and the living room. (Set up five things in advance. A grape on the floor. A glass too close to the edge of the counter. A knife out in the open. The refrigerator door slightly ajar. A jar of mayonnaise left open on the kitchen counter. A pair of skates by the stairs, etc.) Ask the child to identify not only the things that don't seem like a good idea . . . but also why. Explain to the child the "why's" if they do not identify them themselves. Teach the child about "awareness" in this way. Then relate awareness to being "self" aware regarding the child's own behavior and how it affects others.

5. Ask the child if they can remember ever having their feelings hurt by another child, and invite the child to tell you what they told THEM about their OWN

behaviors in the future, and how they will treat other children who are their friends, etc. Even though forgiveness is not necessary for the soul's wellness, you can teach your children that saying, "I'm sorry" when they treat others poorly is a wonderful way to take responsibility.

Lesson 4

BEING ANGRY AT OR JUDGING YOURSELF IS A NON-HELPFUL EMOTION BECAUSE . . .

. . . it keeps you from being your true self.

Children who judge themselves for past actions limit their own understanding of their potential because they can begin to see themselves as imperfect, as someone who can fail. Self-judgment keeps them from remembering Who They Really Are—an indivisible part of Divinity. Negativity comes from doing things that, while not "wrong" by some external definition or judgment, *feel wrong* within their own conceptualization of how they want to live in the world.

Children can begin to forget their nature as they get angrier and angrier with themselves. One way you can begin helping your child to remember their true self, and not have self-judgment, is to have a nightly discussion about what actions they did that felt "good" that day and what felt "bad."

After they give you a few examples, you can ask follow-up questions like, "When you kicked the dog, did it feel like something that was based in love?" Or, "When you smiled at me first thing this morning (thanked someone, drew a picture for someone, etc.), where did it come from?"

Next you, the parent, can list more examples of things they did that day that were "loving" or "positive." The point is to help them see that one or two (or twenty) negative interactions do not change their nature, that they always show more love in their daily activities than negativity, on the whole, and that they are not defined by the negative actions. Some days this may feel like a stretch, when it has been a particularly contentious day. But there is always a way to find the "good" in your child.

If you have a terrible, rotten, catastrophic day that cannot be salvaged, you can comfort children by saying, "Okay, so we had a rough day. You may have said/done things you wish you hadn't and so did I. No matter what you ever do, I will always love you unconditionally, because you are a beautiful, precious being of light."

Even in the middle of an argument you can stop and say, "Nothing about this fight makes me feel differently about you. I love you unconditionally, and I want you to feel better/safe/ heard. What can I do right now to help you feel that? Would a hug help? Would a walk around the block together help? Would jumping jacks help? Do you need a moment to yourself to work out your feelings?"

The process will become more effective if you begin with a morning conversation.

First of all, be aware of your own morning disposition.

- ☀ Are you greeting your child with smiles, excitement for the day, and lots of affection? If so, that will help them to greet the day in a positive way.

- ☀ Are you greeting your child with a frown, dread of the day and stress? If so, they may use that to color their own experience of the day.

- ☀ It might be helpful to remind yourself, before your first encounter, three things you love about your children so that you will be ready to smile to open their day.

- ☀ In the same way, you can teach your children to do the same. If one of them wakes up grumpy and dreading the day, you can ask them to tell you something they are grateful for this morning. You can ask if they are looking forward to anything at school, etc. You can remind them of the open possibilities of the day. Through this conversation, children will feel valued and heard; and as a bonus, they may open up and tell you something which is bothering or worrying them that wouldn't have happened in passing. This gives you the opportunity to help them work through their worries.

❉ By opening the day with positivity and love, you will possibly help your children to change their minds about the upcoming day. You will remind them how wonderful it is to be part of a family. And you will aid them in remembering that they are beings of light.

Embracing and living life according to the wonderful ways to be will set up an internal dialogue in which we can make decisions based on if the action is truthful, aware, and responsible. These aren't edicts and commandments. These are tips we can use to Be our full selves. Again, not doing them, or doing the opposite of them (lying, avoiding awareness, and not taking responsibility for our own actions), will not result in punishment or condemnation from God. They will only result in our own internal unrest, a discomfort that tells us that we may not be being our authentic selves—that which is pure love and Divinity.

Lesson 5

LET'S LOOK AT EACH OF THE WONDERFUL WAYS TO BE AND HOW THEY CAN BE USED IN A CHILD'S LIFE!

. . . These "ways to be" all work together like a beautiful symphony of complementary music.

As a parent, the goal is to get your children to feel so comfortable with themselves that they will automatically, naturally, tell the truth, be aware, and be responsible.

When kids tell the truth to themselves and everyone else, they naturally become aware of everything around them and that, in turn, makes them responsible in every moment. Once they are more aware, they will only feel comfortable telling the truth. Once they have accepted responsibility, they are more likely to be aware of how their actions affect the world.

> **Please note, as cited below, some of the following passages are taken directly from a newsletter written in 2007 for the ReCreation Foundation's CwG Bulletin, #227. We reprint them here because they are such clear explanations of the wonderful ways to be, and we will build on them for children's applications.*

If we desire for our children to be fully truthful, awake/ aware, and responsible as pathways to their true selves, we, as parents are the best teachers through demonstration.

If we walk around skirting the truth, acting as if we didn't know something was a logical outcome to our actions, or failing to take responsibility for ourselves, they will learn that way of being.

However, if we take ownership of our actions, tell the truth (soothed with love), and are always aware of how our actions affect the world around us, children will learn to do the same.

All it takes is a conscious decision to stop lying, to stop hiding behind not knowing, and to stop blaming others for our mistakes.

* That conscious decision needs to be made on an individual basis, every day.

* Returning to this material might be a good reminder for the parent, as well as to remind children.

To help your family remember to be their highest selves, you can place sticky notes with affirmations and messages around your house:

❊ I am love.

❊ I am Divinity.

❊ I am grateful.

❊ I am truthful.

❊ It feels good to think about others.

❊ I admit when I act differently than I chose.

❊ I own up to my actions.

❊ I make conscious decisions about my actions.

For this concept to be applicable in our lives, children need to be able to trust their parents, implicitly, in all ways.

They also need to know that they will not get "in trouble" for being honest. It is very important that children understand that there is no such thing as right and wrong, and that we love them unconditionally—that nothing they can ever do will change how we feel about them.

If they do not have these thoughts firmly planted in their minds, they might be afraid of being truthful, aware, and responsible. Living this concept out means understanding that since nothing you ever do is "wrong" unless you believe it to be, you can always own your actions, and their consequences, without reproach from another.

If your child does tell you the truth about doing something that is "against the rules" you can have a frank discussion with them about it while still thanking them for their honesty.

❊ Turning around and yelling at them will teach them not to trust you.

❊ Speaking calmly about what different choices they could make next time will lead them to trust you more.

❋ Encouraging them to continue to be open with you will change the dynamic of your relationship from ones in the Old Cultural Story. Instead of your parenting relationship being one of strife, struggle and hidden agendas, you can foster an understanding of a partnership, teamwork, transparency, trust and fairness.

This can begin at birth. When parents show their children that they trust them, the children choose to rise to the occasion and be trustworthy.

❋ When parents allow children to make some minor decisions, we allow them to understand their own responsibility.

❋ For instance, we can allow our children to trust their own bodies and in the process teach them how to be truthful.

❋ Consider allowing your child to determine how much she eats at a meal. Children are born with the ability to eat the right amount, but making them "clean their plates" overrides that natural instinct to only eat until full.

Picture this: A family dinner table, an antsy four-year-old wriggling in the seat. Child says, "I'm done."

❋ You can ask, "Are you full or do you just want to get up so you can play?" This gives the child an opportunity to learn about being honest.

❋ If the child says, "I am full" you can answer with, "Okay, we can leave your plate here in case you get hungry again."

❋ If the child says, "I want to play but I'm not really full," you can ask how many more bites will it take to be full and make a game about taking those bites.

* If you value dinner table time, you can say, "Wow, we really enjoy our family time at the table., I wish you would stay two more minutes to finish this conversation before you leave us."

You have accomplished three goals by doing the above:

1. By not making this situation into a fight, you have increased your child's ability to distinguish between truth and non-truth.

2. You have shown them that you respect their decision-making, which increases their trust in you.

3. You've continued to encourage them to listen to themselves, their bodies, and their intuition in decision-making.

Meditation might also be an effective tool as you help your children look at the wonderful ways to be.

Honesty (Truth)

From the CwG Bulletin #227:
"This simply means that we tell the truth at all times. We are truthful. That is, we are full of truth. It means that, first, we tell the truth to ourselves about ourselves. Next, we tell the truth to ourselves about others. Third, we tell the truth about ourselves to others. Then, we tell the truth about others to those others. Finally, we tell the truth to everyone about everything.

"I have found that this is not easy to do. It's a real training. It requires a certain level of recklessness, a certain kind of abandon. What I have to abandon is my own safety—and my own need for safety.

"Honesty means, simply, that we stop lying.

"In a world full of lies, based on lies, run by lies, both large and small, this can be very difficult. People do not expect you to tell the truth anymore. In some cases they would rather have you lie.

"Sometimes, a lie can be told without saying anything. Keeping quiet can be a lie. Honesty means saying everything that you know needs to be said in order for others—in order for someone else—to be holding the same number of cards that you have.

"Honesty means telling the truth about that of which you are Aware. Awareness means being conscious about everything that you know and not pretending that you 'don't know that' or 'didn't know that.'"

Applying it with your children

Children who feel safe with their parents, who know that they cannot "lose" parental love, know that being honest is a positive action that keeps the line of communication open. Children who fear their parents are afraid to be truthful because they do not know how their parents will react.

Being truthful, for a child, is a natural thing! They only learn to lie because it accomplishes an objective for them, usually to stay out of trouble. But giving children full acceptance of who they are, no matter what, helps them to want to be honest with you. They want you to know *them* and they trust you to love them even when they do things they deem as "bad."

How often do we say these things to our kids? "Don't tell Aunt Betty that her meatloaf is terrible" or, "Please don't say anything to Susie about having a cold." Rather it would be more helpful to embrace that children are naturally truthful and we can encourage our children that it is okay to say how they feel. For instance, "Aunt Betty, I don't like meatloaf," and, "Susie, I have a runny nose;, I just wanted you to know." If we want to truly help our children form positive patterns, we must teach them that telling the truth is important even if it stops you or them from experiencing something fun, like a field trip, or a party, etc.

We can all worry that our children's honesty will be hurtful to another person. If your children have been learning and growing through the process of this book you can speak to them about telling the truth with loving words, "How would love say this?"

✳ We may not want to say to another person "I don't like you" because that is hurtful, but saying, "I don't think we have enough in common to be friends" is truth, soothed with love.

✳ Truth coated with love is an artful science, to be sure. It can be difficult to find the balance in which you are being truthful and not hurtful.

Brainstorm, with your child, ways in which you can tell your truth to another while soothing your words with love. In the end, it is the other person's job to decide how to feel about what you say; you cannot control their reaction. But if you are speaking in an authentically loving way, you can rest easy with yourself that you did your "best."

You can make the difference between make believe, imagination and story-telling, and actual dishonesty clear for your children. Talk about these scenarios with your child:

✳ Do we ever make things up to feel better about ourselves, to look better to others, to get attention, to hide something, or to get someone to do what we want them to do? These are a few types of lies.

✳ On the other hand, playing a game of pretend, telling stories using your imagination (when the other person knows that you are purely telling a story) are not lies.

✳ We stop being truthful when we start trying to convince others of something we know is not true.

✳ From a very young age, children are aware of the difference between real and made-up stories. You can easily teach them that it is most beneficial to tell the truth, in part, because we want people to value our opinion and our observations. When we stop being truthful in some aspects of our lives, people may start to doubt us in all situations.

❊ But then again, that is just the outward result of telling an un-truth. It is even more important that children see themselves as truthful, so that when they look at themselves in the mirror they can feel they are being their very best selves.

Many children have a good sense of what a "gut feeling" is. You can ask them to think of a time when they told a lie. Ask,

❊ What was the lie?

❊ What did you think you would gain by telling the lie?

❊ Did you accomplish that goal?

❊ How did it feel when you were telling that lie?

❊ How did you feel in your gut afterwards?

❊ Did telling a lie create a positive or negative experience?

Discussions

❊ Discuss so-called "white lies." Is there really any such thing? Is there any lie that is really harmless? Even if it seems harmless on the outside, is it harmless to your internal dialogue about yourself?

❊ Discuss exaggeration as a type of lie. We often exaggerate for the same reasons we lie—to get attention, to hide a truth, to look a certain way, or to accomplish a particular objective. Ask your child to remember a time he or she exaggerated, the reason, and the outcome. Work through how he or she felt before, during, and after the exaggeration.

❊ Tell your child a made-up story (*in this case, don't be afraid to exaggerate!*) and then ask them to tell it back to you. Ask: How could that look to someone else? How does it feel inside to be saying something you know isn't true? How do you know it isn't true? Ask them why that would be considered a lie if you told it as if it were real.

Role-play

You, the parent, tell a truthful story versus a non-truthful story. Discuss how the child felt to hear each story. Ask them how they knew what was true and what wasn't. Reverse the role-play and ask the child to tell a truthful story and a non-truthful story. Ask them how they felt to be telling the one that was a lie?

Awareness (Aware)

From Neale's CwG Bulletin #227:

"This [being aware] simply means that we make ourselves aware of everything. We are awake. We are no longer 'sleep-walking' through life. We open our eyes and see what is going on, exactly as it is, with no illusions about it, with no false thoughts or crazy ideas. We fight to get those out of our system and see things as they really are. We don't kid ourselves or delude ourselves or lie to ourselves or keep ourselves from looking at anything.

"Awareness means that we 'walk in awareness.' That we ignore nothing. That we never pretend or claim that we 'do not understand,' or 'could not have known,' or 'did not realize.' It means that we own up to what it is reasonable to expect ourselves to understand, know and realize—and then raising the bar higher.

"Awareness means that we look deep inside before and after every meaningful action and interaction, that we listen to ourselves tell ourselves about that, and that we close our ears to nothing that we are hearing from our Highest Self. It means having a conscience. It means being fully conscious, rather than walking around as if we were unconscious. It means knowing, and knowing that we know. It means knowing that we know that we know, and admitting that we know what we know.

"It means stopping playing dumb, if we ever started. It means never again hiding behind the shield of ignorance. It means playing life at a very high level, being sensitive to every nuance, noticing quickly every signal, seeing clearly every potential outcome. It means knowing what hurts others, and knowing why it might hurt others, even though we are not technically responsible for the hurt that others may choose to feel. It means looking down the long road as well as the short, seeing distant effects as well as near-term, and choosing our thoughts, words, and actions with all of that in mind.

"Awareness means looking deeply into every moment, noticing what the moment has to give to you, and seeing what the moment asks of you. It means being fully awake, not just partially awake. It means being fully present, not just partially present. It means being fully engaged, not just partially involved.

"It means bringing all of your perceptions to This Moment Now, stretching them out to also cover as much of the Past and the Future as you can, and using those perceptions to recreate yourself anew in the next grandest version of the greatest vision ever you held about Who You Are.

"That is what Awareness is, and if you are Aware, then you are aware of what Awareness is, and need no further explanation."

Applying it with your children

Play a game to show what awareness means. You can use the example in Section three of this chapter.

* You can place 15 objects on a table and have each family member look at them for one minute, then cover it upg. Next, you have each family member make a list of objects to see how much they remember. If you play this game often, you will actually see your awareness of your surroundings increase.

❋ This is regarding spatial awareness, but it will help make the following discussions more understandable about the abstract awareness of our actions affecting others.

When children do something that breaks an object or makes a mess (for example, breaking a vase on their grandmother's hearth), it is important for them to understand that they did nothing wrong. Accidents happen. Being aware of themselves and the consequences of their actions, means being able to come forward and admit that they did something that might upset someone.

A child who is aware would choose to tell the grandma what happened and why. Putting being aware and truthful together leads us to both understand what we have done and how it might be upsetting to another; it also leads us to choose to be honest and forthcoming about how it happened, never choosing to hide or lie about it. (Which brings in being responsible, from the next section.)

So the way to encourage this with your children is to simply tell them that we appreciate their honesty and their awareness that their actions might have hurt someone.

❋ We can teach them from the outset to understand that accidents happen and that they are not "bad" for having something go wrong.

❋ We can encourage them to feel safe to always come get us, in any situation and say, "I need to talk to you, please." And commit that when they do so, we will take them seriously.

❋ If we are in a situation where our child looks upset or like something just happened, we can approach them privately, and ask, "What is going on? Are you okay?"

❋ And then, once they have told us what happened, we have to stay true to our word, be kind to the child, and help them handle the situation with the injured/harmed person, without becoming judgmental ourselves.

Being aware means understanding the impact we have on others around us, and taking that into consideration in our decisions. (Remember Chapter 8: You Affect Everyone.)

We can talk to our children about making choices that serve the highest good of a situation, whatever that looks like in the moment. We can encourage them to think about other people's feelings before acting.

Awareness helps us to find balance in the life we are creating. When we are aware, we can better assess all of our actions to see if they are serving us, if they are having the intended consequences, and if they are in alignment with who we imagine ourselves to be.

* Teach children to ask, "Am I being consistent?"

* You can ask them, "Why did you do that? What did you hope to accomplish? What was the result?"

* They may or may not immediately know the answer. But all of this is with the intention of teaching them to think through their decisions

* Initially, we want them to reflect after they do something.

* But eventually we want them to ask those questions before acting.

Having awareness also helps us to make adjustments when we feel that we are not acting in the ways we wish to. The example above about stopping in the middle of an argument works here as well. We want children to know that just because you start down one path of action (arguing), doesn't mean you have to be stuck on that path. You can always choose differently (hug and stop fighting, find a peaceful compromise) the moment you realize you are not being who you want to be.

Our children have a keen sense of what is going on around them and us.

Sometimes they fear being aware of circumstances because they feel helpless, or, perhaps afraid of the outcome. But be assured, they are very aware of everything, from relationships to the world around them. And they actually gain security and a feeling of safety from the consistency of their life and the actions of people around them.

Children like to know, "If I do this action, another action (consequence) will result."

They like to know that they will see the same result each time. When they cannot anticipate a result, they get uncomfortable.

For instance, if you accept that a child made a mess one day and act like it is no big deal, but when it happens the next day "blow your top," the child will start to feel that he or she doesn't know what to expect from you. This awareness in the child leads to confusion and insecurity.

If children become overwhelmed with the inconsistencies of people around them or begin to feel lost in their own decision-making, they can begin to push back from awareness and hide, retreating inside, to a place where they don't feel so insecure.

Children who are choosing to give up awareness might become a "problem child," perhaps not do well in school, act out, etc. It is a type of being un-aware, or avoiding reality. Through being consistent we can teach our children to listen and to trust what we have to say. They can then gain wisdom from both us and their experiences and "mistakes." They will become more aware that they are their own decision and choice makers.

Help your children problem-solve when they experience an inconsistent situation. Encourage them to not retreat inside, but to voice their concerns to you. And allow them to do so safely without anger or judgment on your part. This will allow them to assess situations with full awareness.

Being aware means refusing to try to "fool" yourself. Trying to fool yourself is silly—you are not fooling anyone. Being awake means looking at every situation honestly and with integrity.

Children will sometimes act as though they had no part in an incident (bullying, making fun of another child, etc.). They will say things like, "I was just standing there, and I didn't say/do anything!" acting as though they had no role in what took place.

As parents, it is important to let your child know that by simply being there and not acting *against* the bullying or name calling, they allowed themselves to become a part of the issue. Both the people doing the bullying and the person being mistreated might think that their silence was agreement. Whereas, if they were being fully aware in the moment (and not acting in fear) they would probably have spoken out against the acts and worked to stop them.

Brainstorm ways that your children could handle themselves in such a situation. Give them tools like, go get a teacher or parent, take the bullied child by the hand and lead them away, or say, "Stop being mean" to the one causing the problem. Have your child role-play with you to practice these tools.

Sometimes being aware is simply acknowledging the probable outcome of a situation. Every child wishes to do their best and wants to be a positive contributor to the world; they just don't always know how to do so. Being fully awake is knowing that there will be an outcome to your actions, reactions, decisions, choices, etc. right from the start and being able to anticipate results. Helping them to "wake up" and stay awake will aid your child in living a holistic, beautiful life.

Responsibility (Responsible)

From the CwG Bulletin #227:

"This [responsibility] simply means that we take ownership for the part that we have played in life—whatever that part may be. It means that when we do something spectacular that was nice, we don't say, "Oh, it was nothing." It means that when we do something horrible that was not nice, we don't say, "Oh, what does it matter?"

"Responsibility means that we not simply lay claim to our deeds, but agree with ourselves to do something about the outcome of them, if we know in our hearts that something ought to be done. We will know this in our hearts if we are Aware. We will not deny this if we are Honest.

"Responsibility means that we stand ready to fix what we have broken, repair what we have damaged, make right what we have made wrong, put back what we have taken away, correct what we have erred in, compensate where we have caused loss, and mend what we have torn that needs mending. It means that we do not do a "New Age bypass" by claiming that we are not responsible for another person's actions and reactions, but lay claim to Who We Really Are by acknowledging that we are creating it all, and then do something about whatever part of what we have created does not represent the next grandest version of the greatest vision ever we held about Who We Are."

Applying it with your children

Owning your actions can mean acknowledging your active role in anything, from what you say to the behaviors you display.

Children sometimes display anger (a natural emotion) to get an outcome they desire. The question is, what outcome do they want or request?

That is where telling the truth plays a big role. If a child can freely tell the truth and express how they are feeling, they will be more comfortable. They will show fewer instances of aggression because they feel more heard and more secure.

Responsibility means that we not only admit to our deeds but also make an internal commitment to address any adverse outcomes. By being aware and truthful, children can look into their hearts to determine if their actions are in line with who they wish to be.

Have a family venting session once a week. Create a safe space in which everyone can tell the truth about what they have done, and how they felt, without fear of punishment. Make an action plan, together, for each family member about how they want to handle adverse situations in the next week.

For instance:

* If I am working on my short fuse, my action plan might include counting to five with deep breaths before I speak. This will help me to compose my thoughts and not say anything hurtful.

* If I am working on not wanting to clean my room, my action plan might include putting toys away when I am finished with them rather than leaving them out. This will help me see that they are my toys and my responsibility to keep them picked upg.

* If I am working on not taking things personally, my action plan might include a reminder or mantra about being a whole person, not needing the approval of others, and being responsible for my own feelings. This will help me to appreciate myself more, and work towards creating my own reality in a more positive light.

For a child, this can solve many dilemmas of conscience. If they see something negative happening at school, they will feel empowered to be responsible and tell the teacher, tell you, etc. They will have an easier time deciding what is the best thing to do in a situation, and their actions will be less swayed by other people's opinions because they have their own internal compass for their behaviors. They will be less afraid of how others will react to their taking the situation to the teacher because they will feel very secure in their beliefs.

Ask your child to pretend to display a certain action (*within the family as an exercise*) that may get them the outcome they wish for, trying to trick someone into doing what you want (manipulation). Explain that even though you might get what you want, it probably won't feel the same as if you got it through honest means. Discuss ways to be responsible and still ask for what you really want.

* Encourage direct communication. This occurs when we tell people our truth and ask for what we really want without subterfuge.

* Remind your child that being responsible doesn't mean taking on other people's emotions.

You are only responsible for your own actions and making sure they line up with who you wish to be; you cannot control how others take your actions within themselves. As long as you know that you didn't do anything to cause another person harm, on purpose or with the intent to hurt them, you can rest easy that you are acting responsibly.

This doesn't mean that you cannot apologize if that feels right to you. If you do an action that causes another person harm (even unintentionally) it is helpful to apologize and straighten out the situation. Even if this is difficult to do, because it is hard to face people we have hurt, it is another way to show responsibility.

The Feelings Box

Make a feelings box to bring the wonderful ways to be into your daily life.

* Find a box (old shoe box, pretty box, whatever you want to use) and decorate it together as a family.

* Next, make cards with words on them, like:

  * Today I will only say nice things.

  * Today I am honest.

- Today I will take care of my hygiene without
  being prompted.

- Today I am aware of others' feelings.

- Today I will make a new friend.

- Today I will share my real feelings.

- Today I will respond without being asked
  twice.

❋ Have each family member draw a card every morning
  to help them set their intention for the day.

❋ At dinner, discuss how each person lived their card that
  day and any obstacles they encountered.

Lesson 6

IN CONCLUSION, BEING TRUTHFUL, AWARE, AND RESPONSIBLE WILL LEAD YOUR CHILD . . .

. . . to more happiness. It is a wonderful way to bring our mind
and body into perfect alignment with the purpose of the soul.
When the mind is truthful, the body is responsible and the soul
brings awareness, children have the chance to experience oneness with God!

Chapter Seventeen

GOD NEEDS NOTHING FROM YOU

It is impossible in this day and age for children not to have gathered some ideas about God that are different—perhaps vastly different—from what you hold, and what you may have shared with them.

As I noted at the outset of this book, many people talk about God in very definitive terms—and those terms may not coincide at all with your own ideas regarding Deity. So what your child may be hearing on the playground, or in the home of friends, can sound not just very different, but very certain—and once in a while, even very scary.

Then, when your child comes to you for clarity, what will you say? Will you sound as "certain" as your child's friends, and their parents?

Going back to the question we posed very early in this text, suppose your child comes to you and says he heard that he should be "God fearing." Will you say, "Oh, sweetheart, God is our *friend*. There's no need to be afraid of God. God's here to *protect* us and to *help* us."

Or . . . will you say: "Well, honey, I *think* God is our friend. I don't *believe* there's a reason to be afraid of God. My own thought is that God is here to protect us. I *hope* there's no reason to be afraid of him. Let's hope I'm right."

Let's say that your daughter has heard at her friend's house that God punishes us if we don't do what He wants us to do. She's heard that if we are not careful we could wind up going to "hell." Now what will you say? "Sweetheart, that's not true." *Or* . . . "I certainly hope that's not true. Let's cross our fingers."

Yes . . . these questions about how to proceed are not small questions.

What children have learned from simply observing the world around them is that power makes demands. And who has the most power in children's lives? Their parents.

So if parents make demands of their children—and punish their children if their demands are not met—it seems only natural that the children of those parents will assume that God, who they have been told is the most powerful being of all, also makes demands . . . and also punishes if those demands are not met.

And children may hold this as being especially true if God is referred to as God the *father*.

The whole parental image of God means that children will think of God in the way that they think of us, as parents.

There is a way around this imagery trapg. No parents should want their children to be afraid of anything—least of all, of what is supposed to be the Source of All Love.

The way out of the trap, as I see it, involves three steps:

First, differentiate.

Second, cogitate.

Third, imitate.

Shifting your child's reality about God

Step 1

Your child—especially at the youngest age—may assume that God is like you, because after all, you are "like God" to *them*. A huge step in stopping your children from fearing God, then, is to make sure that you stop them from fearing *you*. (See Step 3 here.) But first, it may help them to understand that they have nothing to fear from God because God neither wants nor needs anything from them—for the easy-to-understand reason that God is so powerful, God has anything and everything God could ever want or need.

Make sure you explain to them that while God is all powerful, you are not. Clarify that this is the difference between human beings and God. Maybe use the old-but-effective analogy of a drop of ocean water and the ocean itself. Both are made of the "same stuff," but one is infinitely more powerful than the other. Use this analogy to simply make it clear how much more powerful God is than a human being.

Step 2

Cogitate out loud on the subject of God as part of your discussion with your children in Step 1. "Think about that," you might say after explaining just how powerful God is, using the Ocean vs. Drop of Water analogy. Ask your child what they think that the most powerful being in the universe might need—and why they think God would need it.

Step 3

Make sure that your children are not afraid of *you*. Explain to your children that God has given *you* to them to protect them from harm, and to help them learn what it will be wonderful for them to know in order to live a happy life. So because God has *you* on the job, God can relax and needs nothing from them. It would be helpful to you, on the other hand, if they would promise to listen to you, because your job is to make sure that they have a safe and happy life!

Yet do not make demands on your children, and do not punish them if they fail to listen to you. Exchange consequences for punishments. And allow your children to see that the results of their actions are not coming from you, but from themselves.

Do this by talking to your children in advance of any potential misbehaviors, and getting *them* to create the outcomes that will follow if they fail to listen to you, or if they behave in certain ways that do not work to create a happy life within the family circle.

Ask them first if they can see what things work and do not work within that circle. "Does it 'work' for you to not listen to what Mommy says?" you might ask. *Or . . .* "Do you think it creates a happy family when you talk in a not-nice way to Mommy or Daddy?" *Or . . .* "When you make your sister cry?" . . . *Or . . .* "When you don't do what you were supposed to do . . . like feed the dog . . . or clean your room?"

Helping the kids understand

Explain to your children that all of us have things we "need to do" and that not all of them are fun. Ask them if they can think of things that they see Mommy or Daddy doing that is probably *not* that much fun. Then help them to understand that everybody in the family is included in this Circle of Helping and Doing, in order that things that have to happen actually happen. Like, for instance, Mommy or Daddy has to go to work. Daddy or Mommy has to make dinner. Someone has to do the dishes, keep the house clean, watch after baby sister, feed the dog, etc.

Then help your children make a list of things that they sometimes have to do that may not be that much fun—and of other things that make life easier and help the family out when they do it. (Like listening to Mommy or Daddy, etc.)

Finally, ask your children to help make the decision about what the outcome should be when they do not do "what works" to help keep happiness in the family circle. (Not going to bed when it is bedtime; arguing about what TV shows or DVD's they can watch; talking back or refusing to do what they are asked nicely to do, etc.)

In other words, *let them make up their own consequences.* Write these down and put them in a notebook and let your child draw a picture next to them, or print their name next to them, so that they can see and remember that *they agreed to this;* that this outcome was *their own idea* about what should happen when they behave a certain way.

The purpose of all this? It is so that your children will not think that *you are doing something to them* because of something they have done or not done; that *you* are not *punishing them* for a behavior, but that the consequence or outcome of their behavior is the result of their own decision and choice about it.

In this way they will come to be much less afraid of you (or of what you will say or do) as they move through their day-to-day life, and more aware that the outcomes of certain behaviors are simply consequences that *they themselves have put into place.*

With your children, do not make demands. Simply offer choices. ("Okay, sweetheart, you know what the outcome is that you asked me to write down in our notebook, so now you can make your choice about what you want to do . . .")

This puts the child in a position of power, rather than the traditional place of childhood powerlessness (which produces great anger and resentment in some children). Children traditionally think they *have* no choice when Mommy or Daddy say something or ask them to do or not do something. This technique teaches them that they *do.* It also teaches them that all choices have consequences.

Relate all this to God's needlessness

Explain to your wonderful children that because God has *you* to look after them and care for them, there is nothing that God needs for them to be or do. This is how God made it possible to be sure that billions and billions of children are going to be okay and are going to grow up to be wonderful adults: God created *parents.*

As your children already know (or will know soon), not every child has two parents—and some don't have any. But God always provides *someone* to take care of children, so that they can all grow up to be big someday.

But whether a child has a parent or a grandparent or some other person in the home to take care of them, make it clear that the child in your life is lucky to have you, and you are lucky to have them. Make it a point to tell your children often not only that you love them, but that you are lucky to have them—and why. Tell them what they add to your life.

Children don't want to feel that they are a burden. They want to feel that they are the greatest thing that ever happened to their parents. Seeing and hearing this often helps them remain motivated to continue giving that gift.

Help your children understand that God sees them that way, too. God sees them as the greatest gift, a wonderful joy. And God needs nothing from them because God needs nothing from *anybody.*

Use the television programs and movies that children watch and the stories they read or have read to them to illustrate how the powerful people in those stories sometimes use their power to get *more* power, and they get mad at people who don't do what they say or give them what they want because they want more and more of what their power gives them.

Then explain to them that God does not have to do this, because God already *has* anything and everything that God could ever want or need or desire. Therefore God does not have to use God's power to somehow get "more" of something.

You may wish to use a simple story to help your child understand this. Invite your child to imagine that someone has almost all the candy in the world. However much candy there is, this person has all but maybe ten pieces of it.

Now ask your child what she or he imagines a person who has all the candy in the world except ten pieces needs from one of the people who has one of those ten pieces of candy.

Help your child to easily see—if he or she does not already see—that the Candy Holder needs nothing at all from any of the people who have one of the ten pieces of candy that the Candy Holder does not have. In fact, show them that the Candy Holder would probably *give* some candy *away*, so that more people could have more candy and be as happy as the Candy Holder is.

Tell your child that it is the same way with God.

God has so many good things that God actually gives them away to others, so that all the good things in life may be shared by everyone. But God does not need or require *us* to give *God* good things . . . because God is the person whom all good things came from to begin with!

Through the use of a simple story, your children can come to clearly see and understand this.

Now here, below, are some other ideas and strategies that you might find useful in sharing with your children the idea from *Conversations with God* that . . .

GOD NEEDS NOTHING FROM YOU.

The objective of the following teaching approach is to fill children with a sense of peace that they are not required to do anything to please God or their parents. God, by its nature, is complete and therefore cannot need anything to be "more complete." When we truly understand this, we are free to embrace life with creativity, love, and excitement because we are no longer afraid of failing to please God. By knowing that we do not have to please God, we can also understand that we do not have to please each other either.

Lesson 1

IN TEACHING CHILDREN THIS CONCEPT, YOU MAY WISH TO BEGIN BY . . .

. . . reminding your children about the earlier concepts, "There is no such thing as right and wrong," "There is nothing you must do," "There is no such place as hell," and "Every day you can start over, who do you dream yourself to be today?" Underlying each of those concepts is the all-encompassing truth that God doesn't require anything from us so we are free to create a life as we desire. If we are happy, then God is happy! If we are unhappy, then God hopes we find our own happiness again. How can this be? Because we are God. We are "Godding" through ourselves in every moment.

Lesson 2

SOME QUESTIONS THAT CAN BE USED TO GUIDE THE DISCUSSION ARE . . .

❋ What does God need?

❋ Why do we think God wants something from us?

❋ Why do we think God needs anything?

❋ Why would God ask us to do something for God?

❋ If God could need anything from us, could God still be perfect?

❋ How does it feel to be happy? Does God wish for you
to be happy? Is it a requirement?

❋ What happens if you don't do the things you think God
wants from you?

Lesson 3

WHAT DOES GOD NEED FROM US, ANYWAY?

. . . Nothing! God doesn't want anything *from* us; God only
wants experiences *for and through* us. These aren't edicts and
commandments. They are opportunities. *You are God;* therefore
God only wants you to be who you wish to be. We are each part
of the collective energy of everyone who has ever lived. We are
indivisible parts of the whole, made manifest for this experience,
but in the experience we do not lose our *God-ness.* So when we
speak of God, we are speaking of our single self and the collective consciousness of all of the universe, all at one time! That
collective energy is always with us, helping us create the life we
desire. Even when we can't see or feel the energy, it is there; it
never leaves us "alone." The only thing that can be asked of us is
what we ask of ourselves.

Hopefully, as you have read and used this book, you and
your children have realized that you had embarked upon a journey of the soul, learning who and what God is, your place within
it, and how you can utilize your God-ness to create the life you
want. Most importantly we hope you have removed any vestiges
of the idea that you must please God in order to be fulfilled. God
wants and requires absolutely, positively nothing. Nada. Zilch.

(This is addressed more fully in *What God Wants.*)

Lesson 4

WHEN WE UNDERSTAND THAT GOD NEEDS NOTHING FROM US, WHAT COULD PARENTS BE REQUIRED TO DO?

. . . As a parent, it is an interesting idea that we have no requirements. We find it is most beneficial to parent from love, do our "best," and be kind to ourselves and our beautiful children, being truly loving. God only gives opportunities: God creating God, creating God, who creates God, again and again, time after time. No questions, no demands, no punishment, just love.

Are you having a hard time accepting this? Does your mind take you to all of the "Yes, but(s) . . . ?" Of course it does! Well, breathe and relax . . . see the glory and the absolute truth. You, as a parent, are required to do nothing. Soak that in . . . drink it up! Accept what is.

God is everything and separate from nothing. God is You. No matter what. No matter what! Do you see? If God *is everything*, God can have no lack of anything to be filled, no need for you to accommodate, no demands for you to meet. God is just Perfect.

As parents you will choose, as part of your parenting agreement when you bring children into the world, to fulfill their bodily needs, food, clothing, shelter, etc. But the furnishing of those needs doesn't make you better in God's eyes than if you refused. They are choices you make as part of your human experience.

Lesson 5

TEACH YOUR CHILDREN THAT THEY DON'T HAVE ANY SPIRITUAL REQUIREMENTS!

. . . If God has no requirements of us, how can we have requirements of our children? We, as complete beings, don't have any holes that another person should fill, no spiritual needs that are not being met. We, in our God-ness, are complete beings!

Likewise, children are complete too and have no spiritual needs that aren't being met.

That doesn't mean that we don't have things we wish our children would do. We all want to create a happy, harmonious home. This doesn't have to involve requiring children to act, be, and do things in a certain way. Harmony can come from understanding your family as a partnership of its members. When children learn that in order to have a smoothly running, drama-free house it works best when we all cooperate, they will often willingly do the things you ask. However, it might be helpful to resist getting angry when they do not comply. Part of building their trust in you is staying consistent with your chosen message. If that message is that nothing is required, but you have requests and you would all benefit from a partnership of cooperation, then stay with that! You can revisit Chapter 4 and 5 for ideas about working with children to create a peaceful partnership in which life can be very smooth.

Physical Needs

What about physical needs? Do we have any of them? We are what we say we are; we need what we say we need.

Shelter, clothing, water, and food all seem to be things that we need to survive; and from a physical standpoint, they are very important. These are the things that fuel our physical body (one of the three parts of you—mind, body, and spirit). When we choose to come to physical life (call ourselves humans) we accept certain limitations, one of which is that in order for our body to thrive, we "need" these things, but from a spiritual perspective we need nothing.

When we accept ourselves as God, we can understand that we can call to us everything that we "need." Our children can understand that God is in and all around us, all the time, supplying everything that we could ever need through the divine laws of the universe and through our own creative abilities. That also reminds us since God has everything, and can give us everything, then there is nothing God could need from us.

For instance, we eat when we are hungry; we eat to stay alive and keep our body going. We could never have a bite to eat, water to drink, or a place to sleep, and we would still be who we are, an indivisible piece of divinity. We just may, by foregoing these physical necessities, be choosing to live in the spiritual realm instead of Earth. But if we call ourselves a human, then we will probably want to feed the body. So food becomes a way of expressing Who We Really Are, even though we, in our purest form, do not actually need it.

In that way, by feeding ourselves, our soul is being *that which is everything* in every moment. We don't eat to please God. We eat to satisfy ourselves and to remove the hungry feeling in our stomach, while giving our bodies nutrients. We do it for *ourselves*! There is a connection there; do you see it? Everything we do, we do for ourselves. Everything we do to another, we do to ourselves. In that way, everything we do, we do to and through God, at our own benefit, not out of obligation. We are God creating a holy experience of life, not out of necessity, but out of desire.

Lesson 6

GOD DOES HAVE DESIRES . . .

. . . which stem from *our* desires. But again, these are desires for us to experience life to its fullest; they are not requirements.

Here is what the extraordinary text, *Tomorrow's God,* says about what God does not want:

* "Tomorrow's God does not require anyone to believe in God.

* Tomorrow's God is without gender, size, shape, color, or any of the characteristics of an individual living being.

❋ Tomorrow's God talks with everyone, all the time.

❋ Tomorrow's God is separate from nothing, but is Everywhere Present, the All In All, the Alpha and the Omega, the Beginning and the End, the Sum Total of Everything that ever was, is now, and ever shall be.

❋ Tomorrow's God is not a singular Super Being, but the extraordinary process called life.

❋ Tomorrow's God is ever changing.

❋ Tomorrow's God is needless.

❋ Tomorrow's God does not ask to be served, but is the Servant of all of life.

❋ Tomorrow's God will be unconditionally loving, non-judgmental, non- condemning, and non-punishing."

And here is a very short list of things God desires:

1. *"I desire first to know and experience Myself, in all My glory—to know Who I Am. Before I invented you—and all the worlds of the universe—it was impossible for Me to do so.*

2. *Second, I desire that you shall know and experience Who You Really Are, through the power I have given you to create and experience yourself in whatever way you choose.*

3. *Third, I desire for the whole life process to be an experience of constant joy, continuous creation, never-ending expansion, and total fulfillment in each moment of now.*

I have established a perfect system whereby these desires may be realized. They are being realized now—in this very moment. The only difference between you and Me is that I know this.

In the moment of your total knowing (which moment could come upon you at anytime), you, too, will feel as I do always: totally joyful, loving, accepting, blessing, and grateful." (*Conversations with God, Book 1,* pg. 65)

Lesson 7

WE CAN TEACH CHILDREN TO DISTINGUISH BETWEEN NEEDS AND DESIRES . . .

. . . by first starting with gratitude. Children that feel gratitude for the things and people in their lives can have an understanding that there are very few things that we need to survive.

- ❋ Ask your child to keep a gratitude journal.

- ❋ Have them write or draw at least one statement of gratitude in it every day.

- ❋ They can use magazine cutouts, markers, glitter, whatever will help them say what they are grateful for!

Assist them in knowing that they can desire other things, but that desire does not equate to need, and things do not define who we are.

- ❋ Work with your child to make a list of physical needs and also a list of spiritual desires.

- ❋ Speak with them about how a soul may desire to experience love, but it doesn't *need* to experience it because it *is* pure love. Experiencing it is a pleasurable sensation for the body and mind, but the soul knows nothing except love.

- ❋ Create a dream board to help them visualize manifesting the things on their needs and desires lists. Help them to decide what list each item belongs to. Remember there are no right or wrong answers so if they have a strong feeling about which list an item goes on, allow them to put it there.

☀ Revisit the lists or dream boards periodically to see if the child has changed his mind about what belongs where.

Once a child knows the difference between a need and a desire, it should become very apparent that needs are only used to fulfill deficits or lack of having something. You can bridge this into a discussion about how God cannot lack anything as we described above.

Lesson 8

REST EASY IN THE FULL KNOWLEDGE OF GOD'S PERFECTION AND COMPELETENESS . . .

. . . Remember that God is Love, God has and is everything and therefore cannot need anything from us. Since we are God, we are the same. So that means that all of life is a choice, a playground in which we can be and experience whatever we want without expectation, without fear, and with a knowing that we are always enough!

Chapter Eighteen

YOU DON'T HAVE TO BELIEVE THE LIES ABOUT LIFE

The stories that children are exposed to from their earliest years expose them to a whole string of lies about life—and children come to *believe* them, because they are repeated over and over again.

These lies include the idea that:

* There is "not enough" of what human beings need to be happy, so they have to compete with each other to get what they want.

* Some human beings are better than other human beings.

* Human beings have to fight with each other to resolve their biggest differences, since hurting each other seems to be the only way to get others to "give in."

Thus, children get the very clear impression—from the playground to their own watching of news on cable networks—that Might is Right.

As adults we know that none of this is true, but our children do not understand this because, as I've said, nearly every story they've ever heard—even many stories *written especially for children*—bring them these messages.

Now your job is to help your children separate fact from fiction and to understand that these and many other parts of the Human Story that they have been told are simply not true.

Human beings do *not* have to compete with each other to get what they want, human beings are *not* inherently better because of race, religion, national origin, gender, income, education, political, or sexual orientation, than other human beings, and human beings do *not* have to solve their problems or resolve their differences by hurting each other.

Teaching by inversion

The fastest (and most effective) way to teach your children that these ideas are not true is to *demonstrate* it. And the surest way to get them to believe that these notions *are* true is *likewise* to demonstrate it. And that is what much of the world—including that part of the world around them *in their own home*—is doing now.

Often in our own homes we are saying one thing and doing another.

If, for instance, your children observe that *you* are constantly competing in your world to get what you want, they will embrace as truth the story that humans have to compete with each other to get what they want. Then they will mirror this in their own lives.

If, for instance, your children hear *you* comparing *yourself* (or others of whom you approve) with persons of whom you do not approve, they will embrace as truth the story that some humans are better than other humans. Then they will mirror this in their own lives.

And if, for instance, your children observe that *you* are constantly fighting with *them* to get what you want from them, and exerting your power over them as your means of enforcing your will, they will embrace as truth the story that humans have to fight with each other and overpower each other to get what they want. Then they will mirror this in their own lives.

And if your children watch or hear *you* being verbally aggressive and hurting other people—your employees, perhaps, or a store clerk, or someone at some government agency—in order to fix a problem that you have, they will embrace as truth the story that humans have to fix their problems by hurting others. Then they will mirror this in their own lives.

This is what I call teaching by inversion. You are teaching your children exactly the opposite of what you want them to learn, hoping that your children will do as you say and not as you do.

Yet children will show up in the world exactly as *you* show up in the world. This will happen absolutely, positively, and without question—even as most of *today's* adults are showing up in the world in the way they saw that their parents did. (You have surely seen parts of your parents in yourself. Even some unattractive parts. Yes?)

We observe, then, that in many, many cases it is true that "the sins of the father shall be visited upon the sons, even unto the seventh generation."

Unless they are not. Unless the dysfunctional and non-beneficial behaviors of humanity stops now, with the changing of *our* behaviors, not our children's.

The best way to teach our children and our grandchildren that they don't have to believe any lies about life is to do everything in our power to show them that *we* have stopped believing them.

Then, tell them a new story

A second step that all parents and guardians can take: Tell the truth to your offspring about the mistakes you have made (and may be, in some cases, continuing to make) in your own life, because of your own old beliefs and through your own old (hopefully) behaviors.

Be forthright and transparent in this regard. When children hear their parents say they're sorry for or regret a behavior—either something they may have done to the child, or with another adult in the home—children are deeply impressed. When children hear their parents admit and acknowledge a mistake they have made, children have learned something that no amount of lectures or book learning can teach them.

So be vulnerable with your children. Let them see you not only when you are at your best, but when you acknowledge that you were less than your best. For when you acknowledge in front of your children that you were less than your best, you are at your best.

Then, tell your children a New Story about life and how it works—the story that you wish someone had told *you* when *you* were seven or eight or nine. (Or, for that matter, twenty-seven, or thirty-eight, or forty-nine.)

Start by sharing with them those very first three messages of *Conversations with God:*

* We are all one.

* There's enough.

* There's nothing you have to do.

We, of course, covered these in the earliest chapters of this book. These first three messages form the basis of a New Cultural Story for our species, a New Way to Be Human.

If we are truly all one, then none of us can be superior to any other one of us, because a thing cannot be superior to itself.

If there's enough, then we don't have to compete with each other for what we imagine we need to have in order to be happy.

If there is nothing that we have to do, then we won't be using physically, emotionally, or verbally overpowering tactics to get others to do as we want, because we will live in a world when no one else is ever requiring *us* to do what *they* want. We will be *free*, and we will return the favor to others, allowing them to be free as well.

There are so *many* extraordinary (if not to say revolutionary) concepts in *Conversations with God* that, if taught to children in place of what is now being taught to them, could change our world in a generation.

In *Communion with God* we were given specific suggestions around this. Said that text:

Teach your children that they need nothing exterior to themselves to be happy, neither person, place, nor thing, and that true happiness is found within. Teach them that they are *sufficient unto themselves.*

Teach them this, and you will have taught them grandly.

Teach your children that failure is a fiction, that every trying is a success, and that every effort is what achieves the victory, with the first no less honorable than the last.

Teach them this, and you will have taught them grandly.

Teach your children that they are deeply connected to all of life, that they are one with all people, and that they are never separate from God.

Teach them this, and you will have taught them grandly.

Teach your children that they live in a world of magnificent abundance, that there's enough for everyone, and that it is in *sharing* the most, not in *gathering* the most, that the most is received.

Teach them this, and you will have taught them grandly.

Teach your children that there is nothing that they are required to be or to do to be eligible for a life of dignity and fulfillment, that they need not compete with anyone for anything, and that God's blessings are meant for everyone.

Teach them this, and you will have taught them grandly.

Teach your children that they will never be judged, that they need not worry about always getting it right, and that they do not have to change anything, or "get better," to be seen as Perfect and Beautiful in the eyes of God.

Teach them this, and you will have taught them grandly.

Teach your children that consequences and punishment are not the same thing, that death does not exist, and that God would never condemn anyone.

Teach them this, and you will have taught them grandly.

Teach your children that there are no conditions to love, that they need not worry about ever losing your love, or God's, and that their own love, unconditionally shared, is the greatest gift they can give to the world.

Teach them this, and you will have taught them grandly.

Teach your children that being special does not mean being better, that claiming superiority over someone is not seeing them for who they really are, and that there is great healing in acknowledging, "mine is not a better way, mine is merely another way."

Teach them this, and you will have taught them grandly.

Teach your children that there is nothing that they cannot do, that the illusion of ignorance can be eradicated from the Earth, and that all anyone really needs is to be given back to themselves by being reminded of Who They Really Are.

Teach them this, and you will have taught them grandly.

Teach these things not with your words, but with your actions; not with discussion, but with demonstration. For it is what you do that your children will emulate, and how you are that they will become.

Go now and teach these things not only to your children, but to all people and all nations. For all people are your children, and all nations are your home, when you set out on the journey to mastery.

This is the journey on which you embarked many centuries and many lifetimes ago. It is the journey for which you have long prepared, and which has brought you here, to this time and place.

This is the journey which calls you more urgently now than ever before, on which you feel yourself proceeding with ever increasing speed.

This is the inevitable outcome of the yearning of your soul. It is the speaking of your heart, in the language of your body. It is the expression of Divinity within you, and it calls to you now as it has never called before, because you are hearing it now as it was never heard before.

It is time to share with the world a glorious vision. It is the vision of all minds that have ever truly searched, of all hearts that have ever truly loved, of all souls that have ever truly felt the Oneness of Life.

Once you have felt this, you can never be satisfied with anything less. Once you have experienced it, you will want nothing but to share it with all those whose lives you touch.

Now here, below, are some other ideas and strategies that you might find useful in sharing with your children the idea from *Conversations with God* that . . .

YOU DON'T HAVE TO BELIEVE
THE LIES ABOUT LIFE.

The objective of the following teaching approach is to combine all of the information in the book to assist children in making decisions about how they interact with the world from a place of love and togetherness instead of from fear and ego.

With the understanding that the first two fallacies, or lies, about human life (1. we are separate from each other, and 2. there is not enough for everyone) are untrue, we came to know that "We are all one" and "there's enough." We now know that we can provide enough for everyone.

We can raise children to know that they do not have to fight or compete with each other for the things that they need. They can also know that they don't have to struggle to feel better than others because we are all equal, indivisible parts of God.

The need or desire to see ourselves as better than others, more deserving of comfort, or more of *anything* than others, is purely an illusion brought on by our misunderstanding of Who We Really Are.

We Are Individuated Aspects of Divinity. We Are Each Other. We Are All One. Everything We Do to Another We Do to Ourselves.

Wouldn't it be beautiful for children to fully live as if there's enough love and attention to meet everyone's needs, and to know that when we decide to share, there can be enough food, water, and shelter for everyone?

We can stop harming others as a result of our beliefs, our understanding of the world, or because we feel insecure. We can choose to stop all harmful behaviors towards others through the spirit of love.

We have been creating a reality in which emotions, acceptance, and resources are scarce because we have believed them to be, but the great news is that we can reverse that reality in an instant and find absolute freedom!

Lesson 1

IN TEACHING CHILDREN THIS CONCEPT, YOU MAY WISH TO BEGIN BY . . .

. . . reviewing all of the prior concepts of the book. Ask your child to give you a description of each concept they have learned so far and help them through the ones that feel foggy, adding your own ideas to the discussion to help them gain and retain a fuller understanding.

We ask you to do this because we feel that this chapter is really the culmination of everything you have been teaching your child throughout our time together. We believe a child who embraces the New Spirituality *will not feel slighted* because of what another person has, *will choose to work* for the higher good of all, and *will treat every person they meet* with love, kindness, and equality . . . because to do otherwise will not make sense. These children will build a lovelier, more peaceful world!

Lesson 2

SOME QUESTIONS THAT CAN BE USED TO GUIDE THE DISCUSSION ARE . . .

* Why do people fight? Do they really gain anything from it? Does fighting ever truly solve a problem?

* Do you ever create drama to get what you want?

* Do you ever put someone else "down" to feel better about yourself? Did it work?

* What would happen if you just stopped trying to be "right"?

* Do you know the difference between fear and love? Do you know what it means to make decisions based on your ego instead of love?

* What does "everyone is equal" mean to you? If you accept that no human is better than any other human being, how does that change your view of the world?

* After going through all the activities in this book, do you think there is any chance we really came to Earth to fight with others?

* Who do you consider to be your family? If you understand that you are God, and that everyone else is God as well, how do you want to choose to treat the people around you, from now on?

Lesson 3

FIGHTING WITH OTHERS IS REALLY ABOUT MAKING YOURSELF FEEL BETTER, BUT IT NEVER REALLY WORKS . . .

. . . We fight, struggle, or compete with others, because we think that they have something we need whether it is attention, physical goods, money, or status. The problem is that we nearly never walk away with the "spoils" of the fight that we intended. Not only do we not "get" the things we wanted, but we feel sad, disappointed, and often question whether our actions were worth it. Have you ever had a yucky feeling inside after having an argument with another? In fact, not only do we not feel better than before, but we often feel worse. This is your soul telling you that arguing, fighting and/or harming other people doesn't serve your highest purpose.

Lesson 4

WHY, THEN, DO WE CHOOSE TO FIGHT WITH EACH OTHER FOR THE THINGS WE NEED?

People fight due to fear and insecurity. They think that if they feel they are lacking something, whether it is emotional or physical, they can gain it back by "winning." They also come to believe that in order for them to "succeed," someone else has to "fail."

Anger is a natural emotion, but fighting is not a natural process of life.

Anger is our soul's way of saying "No, thank you, that does not work for me." We do not seek to eradicate or punish our children's anger. We seek to help them find ways to use it constructively to make a change whether in the world or in their own life. We don't say, "You shouldn't be angry." We thank them for expressing that anger and bringing an issue to the forefront. Then while we accept responsibility for our role in bringing about the anger (anger is always a two-way street), we work to help them digest and make decisions based on what the anger teaches them and us.

Parents and children that fight with each other are often struggling to find who is in control.

All of the fighting would dissipate, however, if one of them determined that neither needed the upper hand or to feel a sense of control. We could call this "yielding." When we yield we make ourselves neutral and accepting that each person has their own point of view and reasons for saying, doing, or feeling something. When there is no one to fight against, you cannot have a fight.

Eventually, someone who is angry, upon coming up "against" love and understanding instead of more anger, will use all of their anger constructively and come to a realization about changes that need to occur. Through that process they can use the anger as it is intended and feel complete in a resolution.

Think about what would happen if we all yielded in every situation of disagreement. It would allow the other person to feel heard, recognized and validated. Being heard would diffuse their rage, allowing them to be willing to communicate, listen, and work together to make a change.

* We can help our children to learn how to use their anger constructively by talking through the reasons and the situation that brought up the feelings.

* Giving your child unconditional acceptance, even when they have lashed out, is so important in making sure they know that all feelings are valid.

* If your child is amenable to it at the time, you can offer to hug or hold them while they process through their feelings. Often physical touch will help them to calm down and be able to think.

❋ If, on the other hand, we send them to their rooms or timeout, we could be avoiding our responsibility in the situation, blaming them, and actually cause them to feel more of a separation, instead of knowing that we are there for and with them. At the very least, even if we don't intend that to be what we convey, it might be what they perceive.

❋ If your child is someone who likes to work things through on their own, privately, you can give them a feelings journal; and when they are angry, ask them to write down everything they are feeling and to brainstorm what would make the situation better.

❋ If your child is one that likes to work through things in partnership with you, you can ask probing questions, guiding with your advice, and help them come to their own solutions.

❋ Forcing your agenda on them will not help the situation. It will only make it worse as in order to fully process the anger emotion, they will need to come to their own awakening and decision.

How do we enter into these control dramas? Can they be handled in a positive way?

Think about when a child wants dessert before dinner. This is a common moment of contention in families, and children can throw wonderful tantrums over a piece of cake. The questions we have for you are: Why does it really matter? Can you give an appropriately-sized piece of cake along with the dinner and have them go together? Are you fighting because you are having a power struggle? Does it really matter? Would making the cake a non-issue allow the child to eat both and save a bunch of stress and fighting, thereby getting the child to eat more of their actual dinner than if they ended up on the floor kicking and screaming?

Now there may be situations where you will not want to give in to their requests/demands for safety reasons. We can think of many examples, but let's consider a thirteen-year-old wanting to go to a major league baseball game by him or herself with a friend of the same age. Stadiums have big crowds, rowdy fans, and are not really safe places for a child alone. You can save yourself much arguing by using clear communication.

Tell your child exactly why you do not think it is safe, and help them to understand that you are not restricting them to control them but to protect their best interests. Allow them to see that there are rational, thought-out reasons for your decision. Treating a child with the respect to explain, rather than just saying, "Because I said so," will foster respect in return.

You can even brainstorm, together, to find a compromise where the child gets to go to the game. For instance, you go along but sit a few rows away to accomplish their goal of seeing a game with a friend and your goal of keeping them safe.

Even in the most loving and communicative households, we recognize that you and your child will eventually disagree. We want you to know that disagreeing is not a sign of failure or loss of hope that your child respects and listens to you. It happens to everyone. The most beneficial way to deal with disagreements is:

❋ You, the parent, can change this part of reality in a moment by *stopping*. *Stop* trying to assert your desires over your children's. *Stop* worrying about how their actions will reflect upon you. *Stop* trying to be the one who is "right" or getting in the last word.

❋ You can also teach your children that they do not always have to be "right" or in charge. One way to do this is to foster a feeling of cooperation in your parenting partnershipg. Help your children to understand that you are all truly working for the same goal, that you each have the other's "best" interests at heart, and that you would never intentionally do anything that would harm each other.

- An angry person cannot express rage unless they come up against resistance, so if your child is lashing out, and you make yourself completely neutral, it will diffuse their anger. When we lash back in anger, we actually continue the cycle of anger.

- When we stand down or yield, we allow the other person to express themselves and allow them to process, helping them to come out to the other side!

Children may experience insecurity due to changes in the family (either divorce, birth, death, moving to a new house, etc.) and act out in a way that is uncomfortable for them and for you. You can help them come to terms with their anger or fear in a way that allows them to feel and express the natural emotion and process through it so that they do not get stuck in feelings of rage and/or panic.

If this is happening, you can sit with your child and discuss it, asking if they feel suffering. Let them answer without you interrupting, as they may, first and foremost, need to be heard.

Keep in mind that you want your child to know that you are not judging their feelings and that you believe they are valid. Also, remind them that you do not think you are above criticism for your prior actions, and that you, too, are always trying to dream bigger today about who you are than you did yesterday (in other words you are always trying to recreate yourself anew in the grandest version of the highest vision you ever held about yourself).

Remind your child that you view your family as a partnership and that you are in it together.

You can guide them through their feelings if they are having trouble expressing themselves with questions like:

- Are you angry?

- Who are you angry with?

- Are you ready to work through your anger?

❊ What would help you work through that anger?

❊ What can you accomplish if you channel your anger for positivity?

When they are ready to stop their struggle with you, or whomever, you can give them the space to speak their truth. Hug them or whatever physical thing you do to share love. Try not to fight, blame, or assess guilt or judgment. This exercise can begin to teach your child that everything has "a way out!" No one is working against them, especially God and the universe, but it is all working together to assist in changing the situation.

❊ Allow your child to feel and show their emotions. This trust will break the struggle that once was insurmountable.

❊ This is a good time to remember Chapter 15's notions of being Aware, Truthful, and Responsible. As the parent, when we listen and are aware of all that is being said to us by our child, we can keep our lines of communication open and moving. Be honest with yourself and them about what is going on. Be responsible and accept your part in any of what is going on, communicating that to your child.

We would like to suggest one more consideration in raising children with love and cooperation instead of struggle. Children are being exposed to violence on television, in movies, and through video games earlier and earlier in life.

We encourage you to answer the following questions for yourself. Does media with violence desensitize children to real violence? Does killing someone on a screen make any internal changes in the child's understanding of love and peace? Does objectifying people in movies with violence cause children to see the world as a place in which it is normal to harm others?

What would happen, instead, if you surrounded your child with games and media that encouraged love, cooperation, and creativity? What if your child grew up feeling repulsed by violence, thinking that it was the last thing they could ever imagine participating in? What if they grew up understanding that violence does not serve them as an individual, nor as a species?

What would happen if we had a whole generation of children raised with this belief?

When children choose to look at life as an avenue to Be and Express Divinity, they stop feeling the "me versus you" mentality and instead insist on living in a world of fairness, love, and sharing.

Your children can be pioneers of this in their schools, neighborhoods, or playgrounds. How?

- ❋ By choosing to treat each person they meet with love and respect.

- ❋ By epitomizing the question, "What would love do now?" in every circumstance!

- ❋ By creating anti-bullying campaigns.

- ❋ By starting love campaigns.

- ❋ By making love trinkets or bracelets and handing them out indiscriminately at school to change peoples' days.

- ❋ By including the child that is excluded.

- ❋ By speaking out against unfairness and inequality.

Children around the world are already speaking out for what they believe. Your children can start their own movement of change!

Lesson 5

NO ONE IS BETTER THAN ANYONE ELSE . . .

. . . We are all equal, indivisible parts of the whole. No one part is less important than another.

❋ Remember, you are God, I am God, we All are God!

❋ Another way of saying this is: We are all special. You are special, I am special, we all are special, but no one is more special than another.

❋ It is our individuated specialties that make up the beautiful fabric of life and the Holy Experience.

❋ We all have something to add to this experience. Every *thing, person,* and *object* down to the smallest speck of dust has a purpose.

❋ If we can teach our children to look at each person they meet as themselves, and part of God—struggle, superiority, and a desire to hurt others will disappear.

But we look, sound, and believe different things! Doesn't that separate us? If we could see ourselves from space, would our differences really matter?

No! From space you couldn't even see the things that make us "different" as there would be no characteristics by which to judge each other.

If we all joined hands to become one moving organism, or melted into a big puddle, what would it look like? It would be like the most beautiful rainbow of people, colors, and personalities . . . it would be a picture of the mergence of the whole!

You can demonstrate this idea of mergence to children by taking two cups of water, adding red food coloring to one and leaving the other clear. Point out that at first they are different cups and look different. But when you pour the cups together into a larger cup, it becomes one glass of merged water. The coloring doesn't remain separate and become half-clear and half-red suspended together. The colors blend together to create something new called pink.

Can we see our human family in a similar way? When viewed together, we are each part of the shared *Whole*; but when taken alone, we can look very different. (Keep in mind our physical bodies are made up of 85 percent water; so are we really any different than that cup, anyway?)

Our differences do not have to divide us! When you let go of the final three lies about life, you stop needing to compare yourself to others. You lose the need to judge others to feel better about yourself.

Even if you are already living this truth in your home, we want to challenge you. We want to challenge you to take it even further than just living it and actually discuss and debunk these ideas in case your child encounters judgments and comparisons at school or in public.

Have you spoken directly with your child about prejudice? Have you told them that you would accept them no matter which way their life takes them? Have you made them aware that you do not judge people based on gender, sexual orientation, skin color, nationality, or religion? Have you explained that gender has no bearing on a person's worth or who they are inside? Have you explained that skin color doesn't define a person; it is merely a level of melanin in their cells? Have you explained that love is love, no matter what it looks like? Have you reminded them that there are an infinite number of paths to God and no way to go the wrong way, so no religion or spiritual belief is superior? Have you told them that every country and culture has rich traditions, but that we are all of the same human family so nationality doesn't matter?

We think that when you leave these things unsaid, you leave a void for other peoples' opinions, prejudices, and society's actions to seep in to your child's consciousness and influence their understanding of the world. Do you want to leave that to chance?

Lesson 6

HUMANS DO NOT HAVE TO FIX THEIR PROBLEMS BY HURTING EACH OTHER . . .

. . . We might wonder how this even happens. Humans, as part of the separation theology began to think they were insignificant and vulnerable. They decided that in order to feel safe, they needed to believe in something bigger than themselves for protection. However, once they did, they felt obligated to give reverence to that deity, and also prove or defend those beliefs. This is why we say that the problems facing our world are spiritual rather than political, monetary, or resource-based. If our whole world stopped seeing ourselves as inferior to God and each other, we would stop feeling a need to struggle and fight with each other.

Once children come to understand that *they are God* and that even death is not scary, they can stop needing to hurt others in order to feel okay. At the very base of *all fears is the fear of death*, of moving into un-beingness, of ceasing to exist, and of losing control of ourselves. Children who know that death is the same as birth know that there is *never anything to fear, ever, because when you understand that you even control the time and manner of your death, everything else loses it power.* They stop feeling insecure and vulnerable to the world and other people because they know that they, at a soul level, control the most important transition of all. They can become children, and later adults, who are able to focus their life's work on the only thing that really matters, remembering and experiencing Who They Really Are—and *living* it.

Can you imagine a world where the fear contextual space has lifted and love has flooded in? How could war exist? How could starvation occur? How could unfairness ever be doled out?

The answer is they could not. Those can't co-exist with a species that chooses love, cooperation, and peace in every second of every day and every interaction.

Chapter Nineteen

CONCLUSION

The Children of the New Spirituality, *your children*, will be in a perfect position to start a revolution of love. Because you have been brave enough to consider that the Old Cultural Story didn't have all the answers—you can equip your child to be a light in this sometimes dark world.

In remembering, understanding, embracing, and living their Godness, our children can be the change for which we have waited. They can be the angels on Earth who will set us free from hatred, violence, prejudice, judgment, ostracizing of others, fear, and unfairness.

Their souls are willing and wanted to usher in the golden age of oneness, acceptance, peace, love, and understanding.

Thank you for taking this journey with us. Thank you for your dedication to your children. Thank you for being love and remembering Who You Really Are, so that you can help your children do the same.

Thank you for exhibiting that love is truly All There Is.

. . . And from the depths of our souls and the bottoms of our hearts, we want to thank you for choosing to change your own life, and change the world!

We believe the messages of *Conversations with God* can do just that. And what we know is that the process begins with the Self. The path is the pathway of personal evolution as a means of global change through the evolution of our individual souls, and then of our species.

With us walking the path together, we can carry humanity to where we all know it wants to go, by sharing with our children—our most precious gifts to this world—the New Cultural Story for a New Humanity.

ADDENDA

It is the premise of this book that you have found the concepts, messages, and insights of *Conversations with God* of value in your life, or you would certainly not be interested in sharing them with your children.

With that as a given, we want to strongly recommend that you take the time to read *all* of the books in the nine-text series. You would be mistaken if you imagine that "if you've read one, you've read them all." In fact, each book in this series moves the exposition forward to not-previously-explored areas, carrying its spiritual messages to increasing levels of complexity.

As well, a number of supplementary volumes have been produced that offer expanded articulations of the spiritual and practical applications in daily life of the remarkable thought constructions emerging from the original dialogue.

Taken together, the *CwG* body of work covers several volumes—all the titles of which will be found in a listing at the conclusion of this book.

The supplementary texts extend the original messages into vast areas of human activity, including the specific interests of younger people (*Conversations with God for Teens*); the essence of what it looks and feels like to bring God into one's life (*The Holy Experience*); the common encounter with unexpected and unwanted change (*When Everything Changes, Change Everything*); the ways now open to humanity to manage its seismic political, economic, and social upheaval (*The Storm Before the Calm*); and the one thing in all of this that has true significance in our lives, based on the single desire of the human soul (*The Only Thing That Matters*).

A pinpoint summary of the core concepts in the original 3,000 pages of dialogue can be found in *What God Said*, in which those concepts are reduced to 1,000 words, with chapters following that explain each concept in detail. Then, a highly focused exploration of the misunderstandings of Deity that billions of humans have held for thousands of years is offered in *God's Message to the World: You've Got Me All Wrong*.

And finally, a restatement of the major messages of *CwG*, with our long list of strategies for bringing them to humanity's offspring from post-toddler to pre-adolescent years, is presented here.

Some Additional Activities

Emily Filmore and Laurie Farley, who have created the *CwG* for Parents Home Schooling Kits as part of the total outreach of The School of the New Spirituality, had some additional ideas they wanted to share with all parents, thoughts that did not neatly fall under one of the eighteen concept headings explored above.

We've chosen to present those here, and we know you will find them extremely helpful.

Supplemental Activity #1:

The Actual Truth, You Are Special Just the Way You Are

In this supplemental activity, we will look at the many different ways to love, be loved, and feel love. But most importantly, we hope that some of the ideas and activities here will be of help to you in bringing your child to a place where they can always love themselves and know that they are special just the way they are.

In today's society, we hear the word "love" so often that perhaps the human race has misunderstood the meaning.

As you know . . . ultimately, loving *oneself* is the most important love there is—and may be the most important information about "love" that you could ever share with your child. Yet it is often easier to love others than it is to love ourselves. This activity, below, gives your child the tools to teach themselves to love themselves even though they may not be perfect and to teach others to love themselves for the same reason.

Imagine if we all felt about ourselves the way God feels about us. The world would be a different place. The good news is that it is possible to love oneself that much. It is in the remembering of this, and in the experiencing of it, that a child will blossom into a happy, healthy adult.

Here are some additional activities surrounding the concept of love that you may wish to engage in with your child.

1. You and your child write down as many ways a person may use the word "love." *(Example: I love cake!)*

2. Now have your child say why they think that they, or you, would use the word "love" in each of the ways that you both listed above. *(Example: Because it tastes so good.)*

3. Now, each of you say what you think love is. What is love? What does it feel like? *(Example: Security, or a feeling in my stomach.)*

4. Now use adjectives to describe each other. Take turns, one word at a time. Encourage your child to be honest is using all the words that they can think of that totally describe you. You can do the same. *(Example: You are beautiful. You are helpful. You are sometimes cranky when you first get up in the morning.)*

5. Now ask your child: Do you know that I love you? If they say "yes," ask them, "How do you know that? What makes you feel that?" If they say "no," ask them what you could do to help them know that you love them. *(Example: You could listen to me better, you could spend more time with me.)*

6. In Step 6, you are going to teach your child that love is not perfect. No one in the world is perfect. AND THAT'S PERFECT! This is a wonderful chance to explore what is meant by the word "perfect." Earlier we explored what the word "love" means. Now let's explore what the word "perfect" means. Create a way for your child to see that there is such a thing as perfect love, loving yourself perfectly just the way you are.

a) Ask your child, "Do you think I am perfect? Do you think I am the perfect parent?" They will probably giggle and say, "Uh, noooo . . . " That's great! Ask your child to tell you then how they feel that you are not perfect. Write their answers down. *(Example: You make us clean our rooms. You're grumpy sometimes when you get up in the morning, etc.)*

b) Laugh with your child and admit, "Wow, most of those things are true!" Then ask your child, "If these things are true, does that mean you don't love me?" Listen very carefully to the child's answer. It is here that the child's innate wisdom will show through.

c) Now use this process in reverse. Ask the child, "Do you think that you are perfect?" If they say "no," have your child tell you how they feel they are not perfect. Write their answers down. *Example: I have freckles, I'm not tall enough. (Here they will list the things they do not love about themselves.)* If they say "yes," confirm with them that all of the things that make them different and special are what make them perfect.

d) Now ask them, "If you think you are not perfect, then how can I love you?" Listen very carefully to their answer. After they respond with all the reasons, agree with them that these *are* exactly the reasons you and others love them. If they said that they *were* perfect, ask them: "Is that the reason that I love you and that other people love you? Do they love you because you are perfect?" Listen very carefully to your child's answer. The wisdom of children will astound you. But the trick here is to get your child to *call that wisdom forth;* to let them experience their own wisdom by having them speak it.

e) One possible variation. Does the child have a pet? A dog or a cat? Can the child think of a thing that the dog or cat has ever done "wrong," something that was not "perfect"? Does your child still "love" the dog or cat? Ask the child, "How is this possible? Don't you have to do everything 'right' in order to be loved?" Ask the child to answer the question. The question answers itself . . . and the child will understand the wisdom internally, not simply as something that "my Mommy says."

7. In a final step, you give your child the opportunity to understand that many people think of you what YOU think of you. That's why it's wonderful to love yourself . . . because then, others can feel the same way about you! Of course, God can love you whether you love yourself or NOT! So can Mommy and Daddy, and Grandma and Grandpa! And lots of other people. But you know what? It won't MATTER that they love you because you won't FEEL their love for you if you don't love yourself! You can't feel from anyone else what you can't feel from yourself!

Supplemental Activity #2:

Empowerment

This activity is written to be shared with children of all ages, because it is a very basic starting place from which you can begin to have a discussion about the topic of "empowerment" with your child.

Imagine if your children could hear their souls! Imagine if they were empowered by their own thoughts and choices, at an age-appropriate level!

This is part of a larger process by which children learn how to be creative.

This activity may take a few days to complete. We recommend that you as a parent allow your child the freedom to make choices strictly for themselves—within the normal boundaries that provide for their safety, of course. With smaller children you may want to limit the choices over which they have control to things that you can live with such as clothing, breakfast choices, etc.

We are not advocating giving a three-year-old complete control over the day, as we realize that in most homes, chaos could ensue!! To the extent that you do utilize the empowerment day, however, we believe you will also be empowering yourself, because it teaches your child to rely more and more on his or her own sense and intuition, rather than continually depending upon you.

Definition of Empowerment: to promote the self-actualization or influence of. (From *http://www.merriam-webster.com/dictionary/empowerment.*)

Suggested talking points by day:

Day One

Pick one day a week, or even a month, that allows your child to make their own decisions. Call it Empowerment Day and tell them they can make choices about most everything: from the clothes they wear, to the food they eat, to what they watch on television or computer. Tell them that you trust them to make good choices, and let them do it without your suggestions. You will be surprised how much they will come to you for guidance, but on this one day, do not give them advice. Just say, "You know what? I think you can figure this one out, and I trust you enough to make a choice that is good and that suits you best."

Invite them to keep an Empowerment Diary on this day and write down whatever they have decided. If they are not of writing age yet, invite them to come to you and tell YOU what to write on their Wall Chart or Diary! (This can be a fun activity! But be sure not to make any "faces" or judgments about what they tell you. Just write them in!)

Day Two

The next day, ask them, "What did you like about your choices?" Ask them if there was anything that they didn't like about the choices they made for themselves. Ask them if they could CHANGE any choice, what change they would make.

Day Three:

Have a little talk with your child around the idea of Reality Creation. Refer back to the decisions they made on Empowerment Day. Take out their Diary or Wall Chart and talk about the choices they made. Now ask them:

> *"What reality did you create by making that choice?"*

If they do not quite understand the question, re-phrase it at their level of comprehension. (Ex: "How was that for you?" Or, "How did it feel after you went ahead with that choice?")

Ask them if they can see how their own choice created that "reality." Have a little discussion about this.

Point out to them that there is no "best way" to do anything, there are only "different ways," and that some ways work best at one time, while another may work best a second time. Try to find an example of this that you can offer.

Empowerment Day

Empowerment Day allows your child to feel empowered, which, in turn, enhances in a natural way their intuition and their ability to make healthy, well-thought-out decisions into adulthood.

It may be difficult as a parent for you to release control over to your child (even for one day!). But, remember, it is vital to their spiritual growth for them to have chances to choose for themselves what is the best thing for them in that situation. Eventually, this will empower them to make their own healthy, happy choices when you are not there to direct their choices. After only a few Empowerment Days you will see them begin to make wise and healthy decisions—if they have not done so from the start!

Supplemental Activity #3—Meditation Guide

We refer to meditation throughout the book. Here are some quick tips on how to help your child learn the beginnings of meditation.

Relaxation meditation—breathing

The first few times a child meditates he might have trouble stilling the mind. We recommend you start with a short relaxation meditation. Ask your child to sit or lie comfortably, breathe deeply, guiding the breath with slow, deep inhales and slow, full exhales. Just this act of breathing deeply—with eyes open or closed—is often enough to begin getting in touch with our inner self. Finding peace and quiet in meditation is a perfect experience.

Guided meditation

Once children are able to still their minds in relaxation meditation, you can introduce guided meditation as an invitation to go deeper. Ask your child to close her eyes and breathe deeply, allowing herself to relax and melt, finding her spirit. Through chant (using the sound of *om*), mantras, deep breathing, and guided imagery (one idea: picture yourself rubbing soft, plush, black velvet against your face), many children can find a new, wonderful state of relaxation. You can guide them through muscle tightening and relaxing from their head to their toes.

For example: When Emily guides her daughter through a relaxation process, she instructs her to picture the blackest, darkest, sky she has ever seen, and while breathing deeply, move through her body parts, one at a time to clench and release the muscles in the following order: scalp, forehead, eyes, nose and cheeks, lips, chin, neck, shoulders, chest, upper arms, forearms, fingers, stomach, hips, thighs, knees, calves, ankles, feet, toes, and then clench and release the entire body at one time. Explain that each inhale of breathe brings in sparkling, cleansing light and each exhale breathes out the toxins and negativity she may be holding inside. At the end of this whole process, the parent can remind the child to remain in the relaxed position and listen to, take notice of, and then release any thoughts or feelings. You can talk about any of it together after, if the child chooses, to help explain or even just allow the child to give expression to how the meditation felt.

Questioning Meditation

Children who have practiced relaxation and guided meditation may wish to progress to questioning meditation. We do this by setting an intention prior to starting the above steps to seek answers to a specific question or life choices. They can write a mantra to use: "How can I be happy with this situation?," "How can I know God?," or "What is the meaning of my life?" They can even meditate on the *Conversations with God* concept they are currently working on, seeking deeper understanding, answering questions with their inner voice, etc.

The most important thing about meditation is that we do it. Taking a few contemplative moments to start and end your day can completely change your experience of life.

Additional Reading: extensive passage from *What God Said*

We noted in Chapter Sixteen that *CwG* tells us that the Three Core Concepts of Holistic Living are Honesty, Awareness, and Responsibility. In that chapter we articulated these concepts for children, offering them as guideposts, as specific *ways of being*, that we suggested would make their days happy and their march through life to adulthood peaceful and more complication-free than most lives seem to be.

Yet in order to fully ground parents in the message of *Conversations with God* on this topic, we felt it important to share some of the writing from a previous book in the *CwG* cosmology, titled *What God Said.* This places into context the Core Concepts themselves, and for people who have not read the earlier text, we thought placing this passage with the other Addenda would be useful.

Here, then, is that excerpt:

The search for guideposts begins

I didn't even realize that self-anger was part of my life until I was about halfway through it. Somewhere between my thirty-fifth and fortieth birthday it became apparent to me that I was really not very happy with myself—and that, yes, I was actually *angry* with myself about many things.

Mostly, I was angry with myself for being the person I was showing up as in the world. Not that I was such a terrible, awful, rotten human being, but I sure wasn't experienced by other people in the ways that I thought of myself. In fact, I had a *wholly different idea* internally about who I am from the experience that people around me reported that they were having of me.

"Nobody understands me," I would tell myself and occasionally complain to a few friends. "In fact, I may be the most misunderstood person I know."

Now, none of this may sound familiar to you, or a lot of it may. But I can promise you that what I'm describing about my own experience is not unique. So I began searching for guideposts, for suggestions, for insights into how I could literally pull myself together. And I have to be honest with you, I rejected most of what religions and philosophies and psychology was telling me, because it all felt so simplistic.

Then I encountered the *Conversations with God* experience. And what *it* said, too, felt simplistic. Even, in some cases, unsophisticated and naive. But in this case, I decided to listen, because the experience itself was so remarkable, so spiritually opening.

So I allowed myself to take its messages in, to consider the possibility that there was more here than meets the eye, and that what might appear on the surface to be very simple was, in fact, offering me an opportunity to look at life and to experience myself more deeply, more richly, and with more appreciation of the true complexity of what, on the surface, only *appeared* to be simplistic.

That's particularly true of this Core Message of the *CwG* dialogues. On the surface of it, it seems to be so obvious and so simple, almost embarrassingly naive. *Of course* honesty, awareness, and responsibility are important attributes in anyone's life. That's pretty easy to understand.

But when I looked beneath the apparent simplicity of the message, I saw and found more than I originally imagined was there. Let's look at these three core concepts, one by one.

Honesty

One thing I've discovered in my life is that it's not easy to be honest. I thought it was, but I was wrong. I've also observed that it is apparently challenging for other people to be honest as well.

We have become fractured selves because we have learned to break ourselves apart into little bits and pieces. Some of those pieces are the truth about us in the many areas of our lives, and some of those pieces are the shields that we put up to stop people from knowing the truth. Sometimes, to stop *ourselves* from knowing the truth. (Or having to admit it to ourselves.)

The irony of the human experience is that many parents teach their children to tell the truth, explaining to them that honesty is a very important character trait, all the while modeling lack of honesty—not only in their direct dealings with their children, but in other areas of their life that their children witness.

Children hear their mother lie about a previous social obligation to avoid going to a party she knows will be boring; they hear their father call in sick to work when in fact he's going to a baseball game. Thus, parents teach their children that they should be dishonest in order to avoid disapproval or punishment or doing something they don't want to do. It doesn't take children very long to learn this lesson.

So honesty has become a real challenge for many people, because we've learned that—contrary to what we've been told— honesty doesn't always pay. Too *often* it doesn't pay. Too often it produces exactly the opposite result of that for which we had hoped. So we learn to be dishonest. Hopefully, not about terribly important or really big things. But sometimes, yes, once in a while, even about those.

The plan is not about being honest or dishonest, but about getting through the moment. It's our survival instinct that kicks in, and it is that instinct, sadly, that drives the engine of the human experience. We learn to be honest if and when it helps us to survive, and to be dishonest for precisely the same reason.

So there is more here than meets the eye with regard to this "honesty thing." There is courage involved, and not a little of it. There is determination involved, and not a small amount. There is willingness involved, and not in minute measure. We have to be willing to take the flak that we most assuredly will receive if we decide to be honest about everything with everyone all the time.

We have to be resolved to tell the truth, no matter what. This requires jawsetting determination. We have to have the courage to endure whatever consequences may ensue from our determination and our willingness to be honest at all costs.

If one thinks that this is a simplistic idea, a simple, almost naive instruction, about how to live a holistic life, one is mistaken. It is anything but. So let's just be honest about it: *Honesty ain't for sissies*. It takes a very high level of commitment to one's own emotional and spiritual growth.

Must we be honest … always?

And let's explore *that* for a moment. Is "honesty" really about growth? What does it matter if we are totally honest about everything all the time? Who cares? And if it hurts at least as often as it helps, how can it even be justified in every case? Maybe sometimes dishonesty is the best policy. Could that be true?

If you have questions about all this, as most people do, I want to recommend the wonderful writings of Brad Blanton. He's a brilliant if radical psychologist who wrote a book called *Radical Honesty*. I co-authored a book with him a number of years ago titled *Honest to God*. In it we discuss—"argue back and forth" might be a better description—whether honesty in every single case with every single person was, in fact, the best policy. You might find that dialogue interesting.

I'm not going to get into all that here, because there's a whole book's worth there. But I will let you know that I agree with Dr. Blanton that there are very, very few instances in this life when anything less than total honesty is beneficial.

(Actually, I believe Brad says there are *none*. I don't agree with that rigid assertion, and our disagreement is what served as the foundation of our in-print "debate" in *Honest to God*. What about the soldier captured behind enemy lines who refuses to reveal where the rest of his platoon is hiding? What about the mother who tells the gang leader out to get her son that he's not at home, when she knows that he's hiding in the attic? What about the husband whose wife of fifty years asks on her deathbed if he's ever been unfaithful?

This doesn't mean that I practice total honesty in every single minute with every single person; it means that there are very rare instances when it is not beneficial to do so. Even having said that, I find myself often "protecting myself" by saying less than "the truth, the whole truth, and nothing but the truth, so help me God." I find other people doing it, too. A lot.

So I realize now that to live as whole human beings, to bring an end to the ongoing expression of our fractured selves, we need as a species to work more diligently on what you might think would be a relatively simple task: Just. Tell. The. Truth.

Let me say one more thing about this, if I may. It seems to me that the only way that I could find it easy to tell the truth *always* would be if I imagined that I could not possibly be hurt by any of the consequences of doing so. And it seems to me that the idea that I could not possibly be hurt rests within the larger concept that I have of myself with regard to who I am. If I see myself as an aspect and an individuation of the Divine, I will move through life with a deep *awareness* of both my identity and the implications of that identity. And that brings us to our next exploration.

Awareness

Awareness is a state of being that can become, ultimately, a state of mind. The pathway to awareness contains, as we have previously explored, three stopping points: Hope, Faith, and Knowing.

With regard to the discussion about honesty, my present state of awareness will cause me to either "hope" that my telling the truth will not hurt me, "have faith" that it will not, or "know" that I can't be hurt or damaged in any way.

If I rest in the state of full awareness of who I really am—and for that matter, of who everyone else really is—I will never shrink from being honest. There would be no reason to.

So awareness is surely a bigger key to holistic living than I might have originally thought. Awareness is also used in the context of this discussion as being sensitive to the experience of others, and especially to the experience that I am *creating* in others.

It seems to me that a person who is living holistically is "taking in" the whole of the present moment and of every moment in which that person finds themselves. We listen not only to what people are saying, but to what they are feeling. We watch not only what *we* are saying, but what *we* are feeling. And we become attuned to the fact that if we think we can hide our feelings from others, we are most often wrong about that.

So awareness is about tuning in to the Whole Moment and all that it contains for you and for everyone else experiencing it. This also takes courage, determination, and willingness, because there are many elements and aspects of each of our life's moments that we would rather ignore. They make us uncomfortable, or they reveal too much about us—or they reveal too much about others. "TMI," as we are fond of saying. We don't want Too Much Information about others or about the moment we are presently encountering.

So how do we experience full awareness if full awareness brings us too much information? That becomes a fascinating inquiry. And it lays out in clear terms the challenge faced by most of us as we move through life.

In my own case, I have decided that allowing myself to be open to all the data, all the experience, all the emotion, all the feeling, all of the information that all of the moments of my life hold is the only way to live. Yet, as with honesty, I don't claim to live that way all of the time. But I know that it is the way to go.

And as with honesty, there is much more to "awareness" than meets the eye. Because the more that I know, the more that I am aware of, the more I am responsible for what is going on right here, right now, for how it is occurring, for the role that I am playing in causing it to occur, and for the outcomes that proceed from that.

All of which brings us to the last of these three little words that seemed so simple just a moment ago.

Responsibility

Unless we are willing to take full and complete, absolute and total responsibility for everything in our lives and for the experiences that we have caused in the lives of others, we cannot live a holistic life. We can pretend to, we can act as if we are, but we cannot actually do it. We must accept the fact that we are at cause in the matter of our lives.

I observe that when people learn to take full and complete responsibility for their lives, those lives change. The decisions and choices that people make change. The actions and undertakings they embrace change. Even their thinking changes.

Conversations with God tells us that there are no victims and no villains. The implication of that statement is that we are all responsible for everything that is happening to us, and that has happened *through* us, in our lives.

People's first reaction to this statement when I share it at lectures is to run from it. Folks want to bring up immediately all the instances in their lives when things happened to them for which they were *not* responsible. Yet we are talking here not only physically but metaphysically.

At a metaphysical level, which is the only level from which we can proceed in our lives if we choose to live holistically, we are responsible—and must be, given our true identity—for every event, situation, circumstance, and outcome in our life.

We are co-creating in a giant collaboration with all other souls, but that partnership does not relieve us of responsibility for the role that we have played in every event and condition. Including, at a metaphysical level, the drawing to ourselves of exactly the right people, places, and circumstances that allow us to re-create ourselves anew in the next grandest version of the greatest vision ever we held about who we are.

The most vivid example of this that I can think of would be a person such as Jesus Christ. When we explore his life and his death, we have to ask ourselves, *At what level was he responsible for what he was experiencing?* Was he the victim of his own crucifixion or, at some very high spiritual and metaphysical level, was he at cause in the matter?

If we accept that he was at cause in the matter—that nothing happened *to* him, but everything happened *through* him—then we must ask ourselves: *Have we been at cause in the matter, at a very high spiritual or metaphysical level, regarding every "crucifixion" in our own lives, however big or small?*

If we say that Jesus was responsible for his crucifixion but that we are not responsible for ours, then we are declaring a metaphysical untruth: That we are not all one, that some of us are superior to others of us—and that some of us are, perhaps, Divine, while others of us are "only human."

These statements amount to a denial of Ultimate Reality with regard to your personal identity, and mine. And so we are left with no place to go but to be responsible for everything our life has brought us and has sent *from* us to others.

So it's not all a simple matter

So we see that honesty, awareness, and responsibility may sound simplistic as ingredients for holistic living, yet they are anything but that. Still, they do not have to be experienced as a burden.

The master does not experience these three elements of a holistic life as millstones, but rather as gemstones—wonderful opportunities to move fully into the richness of that expression of life for which all of us came to the Earth.

Indeed, it has been my experience that in the moments when I am honest, when I am just as fully aware as I can be, and when I am willing to experience my own high level of responsibility for everything that ever went on, is now happening, and ever will happen, I feel more free, more joyful, more powerful, and more excited to be alive than I ever have before.

—End of Excerpt—

Teaching our children these concepts may be one of the most important things we will do in our lives. Most parents that I observe seek to teach their children about honesty fairly early. But the concepts of awareness and responsibility were not shared with me in my childhood until much later. In my case, I was by then a young adult.

It was only then that my dad tried to make me more "aware" of how I was affecting other people. Nobody ever taught me to be more "aware" of how other people, and life in general, was affecting me. That is, to pay more attention to what I was feeling, and why I was feeling it.

And it was only when I was a full grown adult, and in counseling with a psychologist, that I was made aware of being *more* aware, so to speak. As was noted earlier, we shouldn't have to wait until our adult years to be given this tool.

Likewise, it was not until I was nearing puberty that I was invited to take responsibility for outcomes in my life in any kind of personal way. I think if a direct line had been drawn for me between my thoughts, my words, and my actions and the exterior circumstances and events that kept presenting themselves in my life, I would have been a bit more circumspect in my decisions and behaviors between 7 and 13.

It's important, however, not to confuse "responsibility" with "fault" in a child's mind. There were plenty of times that I was told that something or other was "your own fault" . . . but that is not at all the same as teaching someone about their metaphysical and spiritual responsibility in the matter of how their lives are being experienced.

Our species needs to tell its offspring that we are collectively and collaboratively creating our own reality. This is not a small matter, nor is it merely an esoteric message. It is the *Instruction Manual for Life.* These are the directions that come with the box—yet most of us have thoughtlessly thrown them away before we give the box to our children and tell them to go out and build a life.

It is our hope that this book has brought you some useful tools in bringing the most important messages of *Conversations with God* to your children or your grandchildren.

You are invited to engage in continuing interaction around this joyful undertaking at *www.cwgforparents.com*.

All titles in the *Conversations with God* series

Conversations with God, Book 1

Conversations with God, Book 2

Conversations with God, Book 3

Friendship with God

Communion with God

The New Revelations

Tomorrow's God

What God Wants

Home with God

Additional Titles:

Bringers of the Light

Recreating Your Self

Questions and Answers on Conversations with God

Conversations with God for Teens

Moments of Grace

Neale Donald Walsch on Relationships

Neale Donald Walsch on Holistic Living

Neale Donald Walsch on Abundance and Right Livelihood

Happier Than God The Holy Experience

The Conversations with God Companion

When Everything Changes, Change Everything

When Everything Changes, Change Everything Workbook & Study Guide

The Storm Before the Calm

The Only Thing That Matters

What God Said

God's Message to the World: You've Got Me All Wrong

Conversations with God for Parents: Sharing the message with children

Children's Book: The Little Soul and the Sun

Children's Book: The Little Soul and the Earth

Children's Book: Santa's God

Supplementary Texts:

Guidebook to Conversations with God
Meditations from Conversations with God
The Wedding Vows from Conversations with God
The Little Book of Life
Conversations with God in a Nutshell

ABOUT THE AUTHORS

NEALE DONALD WALSCH is a modern day spiritual messenger whose work has touched the lives of millions. He has written twenty-nine books on contemporary spirituality in the twenty years since he reported having an experience in which he felt the presence of The Divine, began writing questions to God on a yellow legal pad, and received answers in a process that he describes as exactly like taking dictation. What emerged from that encounter was the nine-part *Conversations with God* series, which has been published in every major language of the world.

Mr. Walsch has told his readers and the media—which has brought global attention to his experience—that everyone is having conversations with God all the time, and that the question is not: To whom does God talk? The question is: Who listens?

He says his whole life has been changed as a result of his own decision to listen. He took notes on the questions in his heart and the answers he was receiving, so that he would always remember his exchanges with Deity. It wasn't until later that he realized he was being invited to place these words into the world, as one of many throughout history who have made their very best effort to hear and to articulate God's messages. He knows that everyone is receiving these messages, and invites all people everywhere to both share them and live them as best they can, for Neale believes the world would change overnight if only a fraction of its people embraced God's most important message of all: *You've got me all wrong.*

LAURIE LANKINS FARLEY is the executive director of the School of the New Spirituality, based upon Neale Donald Walsch's work. She has worked with Neale for over twelve years in multiple areas of his organizations and is dedicated to bringing the messages of *Conversations with*

God to others. She has written a children's book, *The Positive Little Soul: for the children of humanity*. She is a mom and grandma who raised her children with the spiritual concepts of love and oneness, and she enjoys watching them find their own way through the world, sustained by that spirituality. She is an intuitive, and her passion lies in helping parents and children open the lines of communication to strengthen the human spirit for generations to come. She wants children to truly know the gift of Who They Are and Why They Are Here. Laurie can be contacted through the School of the New Spirituality, *www.cwgforparents.com*, or *www.thepureintuitive.com*.

EMILY A. FILMORE is the director of program development for the School of the New Spirituality, based upon Neale Donald Walsch's work. Although Emily holds a BA in Psychology, with a minor in English and a Juris Doctor from St. Louis University School of Law, her career path has been winding and unpredictable due to medical issues. Emily's first priority is to be a centered, loving, and aware mom and wife as she home schools their daughter and writes on the combined topics of spirituality, parenting, and health. She is author and illustrator of the *With My Child Series* of books. Emily is also author of *The Marvelous Transformation: Living Well with Autoimmune Disease* (Central Recovery Press, 2015) in which she details how she made peace with her chronic disease, even celebrating it, grateful for the lessons and blessings it has brought into her life. Her purpose in this life is to help families find their inner strength through humor, kindness, and honesty. She enjoys writing for international publications and is a Reiki practitioner. Emily can be contacted through the School of the New Spirituality, *www.cwgforparents.com*, or *www.emilyfilmore.com*.

Related Titles

If you enjoyed *Conversations with God for Parents*, you may also enjoy other Rainbow Ridge titles. Read more about them at *www.rainbowridgebooks.com*.

God's Message to the World: You've Got Me All Wrong
by Neale Donald Walsch

Dance of the Electric Hummingbird
by Patricia Walker

Coming Full Circle: Ancient Teachings for a Modern World
by Lynn Andrews

Consciousness: Bridging the Gap Between Conventional Science and the New Super Science of Quantum Mechanics
by Eva Herr

Jesusgate: A History of Concealment Unraveled
by Ernie Bringas

Messiah's Handbook: Reminders for the Advanced Soul
by Richard Bach

Blue Sky, White Clouds
by Eliezer Sobel

Inner Vegas: Creating Miracles, Abundance, and Health
by Joe Gallenberger

When the Horses Whisper
by Rosalyn Berne

Channeling Harrison, Book 1
by David Young

Lessons in Courage
by Bonnie Glass-Coffin and don Oscar Miro-Quesada

Dying to Know You: Proof of God in the Near-Death Experience
by pg.M.H. Atwater

The Cosmic Internet: Explanations from the Other Side
by Frank DeMarco

Afterlife Conversations with Hemingway:
A Dialogue on His Life, His Work and the Myth
by Frank DeMarco